IS GOD EVIDENT?

IS GOD EVIDENT?

An Essay
Towards a Natural Theology

by
GERALD HEARD

FABER AND FABER LTD
24 Russell Square
London

First published in mcml
by Faber and Faber Limited
24 Russell Square London W.C.1
Printed in Great Britain by
Latimer Trend & Co Ltd Plymouth

CONTENTS

Chapter One

INTRODUCTION

Natural Theology is a big stiff term. Surely, if it must be used, it should be left to the theologians? And haven't they themselves left it alone for quite a while? It is closer on three than two generations since ranking theologians were writing books with such titles as *God's Plan Shown in Nature*.

Yet all that Natural Theology means is—Can God be seen in nature? Are there any traces of a general plan, of a design true, beautiful, good? Has the universe any discernible meaning? Natural Theology is not dogmatic. It starts with an open mind. It does not begin with a closed canon nor a final revelation. It does not say, You must believe this. All it proposes is that, as we humans find ourselves in a setting, immense and strange, we should look at it and see if it gives any clues. We are more than a little muddled about ourselves. Who are we? What are we? Why do we behave as we do—very often surprisingly, sometimes disconcertingly, not seldom shockingly? What an odd creature! And this capacity to surprise itself and to be surprised at itself—surely that is the oddest of all oddities?

The first thing that anyone asks when he finds himself coming out of shock, confusion, delirium, is, however, 'Where am I?' He does not ask, 'Who am I?' or 'What am I?' till later. And he is right. As we say, the first thing that he has to do is 'to get his bearings'. Then, having got his general balance, he can centre-in. Once he has some broad notion of his situation he can begin to pull himself together.

And, however cocksure, conventional or close-up minded a man may be, this world is undeniably a very odd place. It takes some taking in and the more we know the more we see that that is true. People used to say that Natural Science had banished wonder and cashiered romance. The reverse is, of course, the truth. The dull routine world was the classic world, the ancient world, say, of Marcus Aurelius, the wise and world-weary Emperor who could say in his authoritative *Meditations* that after forty any informed man had seen everything that there was to see.

On the other hand, and equally of course, the wonders that Natural Science has brought to man's attention are often most puzzling, very startling. But wonder is originally a strong word, a very strong word. We say, 'I wonder', when we mean 'I'm not sure'. But when Plato said, 'By wonder are we saved,' he meant something like shock treatment. The phrase conveyed to his first readers the message, 'The shock of a stunning amazement will convert a man'.

And the 'romance' that Natural Science has brought, that too is a rejuvenated romance. It goes back and behind that adolescent sentimentality of Boy meets Girl to the real, first and final adventure of Man meets Nature.

That, then, is the first thing that we can be sure of: this world, the universe, is very strange, as strange as if not stranger than ourselves. And Natural Science is no more and no less than man's effort to make sense of it, to find meaning in it, to catch the drift of it. For we must remember that, though most people now think that science is either just collecting facts or making gadgets, it is, essentially, neither. These are by-products of the wish to understand and the belief that a meaning might be found. At base science is the effort to know where we are—it is an attempt to make meaning and to gauge what we are up against. This is far from easy. No doubt during the nineteenth century many researchers thought that if you collected enough facts then somehow they would turn themselves into Natural Laws. And most people who don't follow research still take their assumptions about science and nature from that century, though its thinking in Natural Philosophy (which was the original and definite term for that activity we call loosely science) is about as far from the

Natural Philosophy of to-day as was the nineteenth's from that of the fourteenth century.

But surely, wasn't it science that destroyed meaning? What about Wordsworth? Didn't that great romantic poet, when science was advancing, denounce the Naturalist because the fellow would 'peep and botanize upon his mother's grave'! And didn't he cry:

> *Great God, I'd rather be*
> *A Pagan, suckled in a Creed outworn,*
> *So might I, standing on this pleasant lea,*
> *Have glimpses that would make me less forlorn.*

Didn't Samuel Butler tell Darwin, 'You have emptied Mind out of the Universe!'

True, in the nineteenth century Natural Science did tend to become dogmatic. It became more interested in disproving and discrediting than in enlarging the small evidences that earlier observation had discovered, and that religion had built into a limited form of meaning. But, as we shall see in a moment, that reaction into denial was mainly in nineteenth-century biology, and because of certain specific nineteenth-century disputes. We must never forget that the advance of Natural Science was not due to its denials, its counter-dogmatic denials of religious dogmatism. True, it won much popular attention and some reputation because it denied, and sometimes refuted, some of the historical, biological and astronomical facts which the small branch of theology we have inherited had put into our world picture. Science's progress was due to its *affirming* a number of new facts and building them into a new and larger picture of meaning. It saw a far vaster universe than had been seen before and it saw the whole of that universe as being due, not to a series of arbitrary acts, but all due to one meaning, one Law. Because we to-day are outgrowing that picture we must not forget that it was an advance on the world picture that went before. Mechanism is no doubt out of date and so has become confining. But it was an advance on anthropomorphism. No doubt there may have been a time when, in turn, anthropomorphism was an advance on a belief that events were completely incoherent, having no connection one with another. Then came the age when men began to believe that events were caused by vast unseen men (a polytheism of gods). Once again that attempt to understand was made larger and truer by saying that what happened was not arbitrary but lawful, orderly, regular 'as clockwork'. Iron law is preferable to anarchy.

So the way to cure mechanism's inadequacies is not to go back to anthropomorphism. We must, and we can, go on, not back. Further, we must realize that we have already done so. For mechanism is a step toward making a still more embracing picture of the meaning of the whole. It does explain fairly well the instrument; it does not deal with the hand or the handler. Mechanism is simply the picture under which we think of perfect regularity, complete Law. Mechanism implies an inventor. To call a process a machine, though that process repairs itself and develops, is to call something by a name which leaves out the specific character of the thing said to be described. It is a greater mistake than to call a man nothing but a quadruped because both man and beast have four main limbs. Secondly, not only does the word 'mechanism' imply an inventor; to-day we have gone on and developed out of that smaller notion of law, which was rigid and narrow, a much larger and growing idea. This includes the conception of a constantly expanding meaning. And it embraces in its scheme the idea that the growing design is a plan which Mind is working out with the aid of Machine. Nothing is clearer than that during the twentieth century Natural Science, which again should call itself Natural Philosophy, has made unprecedented efforts to make all-embracing meaning of all the facts which surround and confront us. And we see that in this effort it has broken out from a great number of those earlier, smaller, narrower generalizations, which the nineteenth century—because it was still so anthropomorphic—loved to call Natural Laws. Man is coming to see himself as one of the partners in lawmaking through his power to perceive and frame creative hypotheses.

The recognized aim of science to-day—one might say ever

since the first Principles of Relativity—is to seek for a comprehensive design and meaning that will take in all the facts, and get rid of any assumptions that stand in the way of such facts, and expand any of the generalizations that have too narrowly confined the evidence.

Now, we must repeat, that is precisely the task of Natural Theology. It has to hold to all the facts, the facts of consciousness just as much as the facts of the apparent movement of a star, and to see that the picture of the whole shall include all. We may indeed say that Natural Theology is the place where man's thinking about Being, Will and Consciousness extends till it joins up with Natural Science, man's thinking about wisdom, thought and consciousness.

We must then ask specifically, Why does theology fear science and science despise theology? As we have already suggested, the nineteenth century is largely to blame, though of course the problem was becoming acute ever since Descartes, at the start of the seventeenth. Both science and theology have one unexpected and overlooked characteristic in common—their structure. And because both of them have neglected to recognize this, their structure, they have quarrelled. They are both triple. Science has three areas or fields in which it can strive to employ its three specific techniques. These techniques are (1) analysis, (2) the tracing of causal relationships, and (3) experiment. The three fields in which these three techniques have been employed are (1) that of physics, the world of the inorganic, non-reproductive, (2) that of Life, the world of the organic, the reproductive, and (3) that of psychology, of consciousness and mental processes. Further it must be noted that whereas, till this century, the threefold technique worked almost flawlessly in physics, this triple method worked less well in biology and ill in psychology. This is an issue to which we must return later. Here we are faced with the fact that only things which don't reproduce themselves can be satisfactorily understood by taking them to pieces, tracking them back to a single line of causes and making them go through defined and confined performances which are planned for them. So the question arises whether analysis and causality are adequate test methods for discovering about the nature of Life, still more of Consciousness. Then we shall have to ask further: If these methods will not serve to help us understand what we are (biology) and who we are (psychology), are there any that will?

Meanwhile it is enough to recognize at this point that science has three separate fields in which it studies and that these fields, though they adjoin, are distinct. The obvious mistake of nineteenth-century science was that because of its success in applying mechanical notions to physics—'dead matter'—it wished to force this method on biology and on psychology as the only method and interpretation. Hence any observations that might point to other than a mechanical explanation—e.g. in biology pointing to connation, teleology and so to enlarging meaning, and in psychology to consciousness being *sui generis*—were suppressed. Researchers found by observation that dead matter always seemed to behave mechanically. Then coming to biology and later to psychology they *assumed* that living matter also always so behaves. And, finally, they made the completely ungrounded assumption that, because living matter was purely mechanical, therefore life itself could only be a by-product of mechanical-chemical processes, an irrelevant steam given off by the machine.

At the same time theology was making a similar mistake. It too has three techniques for finding truth: (1) Reason and argument (apologetics, logic, syllogistics), (2) Tradition (its canon, its corpus of scriptures, whereby it estimates the validity of other findings), and (3) Contemplation (integral thought). And these three techniques have been applied to three fields. The first field is the interpretation of nature (Natural Theology), the second is the interpretation of history (Dogmatic Theology), and the third is the interpretation of the individual soul to itself (Mystical Theology). Theology, just as did science, made the mistake of taking one method which worked well enough in one field and trying to apply that one method to the other two fields. Just as Natural Science tried to make the mechanistic hypothesis into a universal law and then to make it apply to biology and

14

psychology so likewise theology blundered. It forgot that it, too, had three fields, not one, in which it might find valid evidence of God, of supreme meaning. It raised Dogmatic Theology—its particular interpretation of part of history—to a place of autocratic pre-eminence. Dogma was to rule what man should find about God both in outer nature and in human nature. Of anything that man found in nature or in his own mind, he must not ask, Is it true? Does it make sense? Does it yield meaning? No: he must ask, Does the Church's small record of history confirm or deny it? Are these new observations in accord with the casual, unexamined opinions of writers who were, as it happens, concerned with something else, i.e., with searching for evidence not of God in Nature nor even mainly in the human soul but in such part of history as was known to them.

The clash between science and religion came, then, over biology—biology which is the middle term both in man's own nature and in the span of outer nature.

Science no doubt was straining its claims, and gambling on past success in forecasting, when it tried, under the mid-nineteenth century biologists headed by Darwin, to reduce the meaning of Life to the mechanistic laws of physics, 'laws' which themselves were only to rule undisputed in their own field for another fifty years. And at no time had they shown that they could cover the phenomena of Life.[1]

But, equally, we must not forget that religion was overreaching itself and rupturing its authority when it tried, under the command of its dogmatic theologians, to deny the biologists' picture of the size and span and age of Life. Religion could question and counter-challenge the biologists' attempt to show that Life had as little meaning, end, direction as the nineteenth-century physicists thought they had proved matter to have.

They were even more mistaken than their opponents when they fought to prove that Life and the world were created some

[1] Lord Kelvin in his famous formulation of 'The Second Law of Thermodynamics' left the matter open by expressly excluding the operations of 'animate agencies'. But see Chapter V for fuller discussion of this important issue.

four millennia ago. Their attempt, to make their proof of God in History carry the whole weight of demonstrating His existence failed, of course. It was a picture far too brief—a drama that had really completed itself in less than three thousand years. And even more, it was too narrow, confined to the history of a not very spiritually sensitive Semitic branch. The picture it gave of Deity was therefore often morally unworthy.

Hence science won the Pyrrhic victory. It defeated religion on an issue in which religion was afraid of truth. It was clinging to a notion of man that showed his destiny to be brief, abrupt, narrow and unworthily arbitrary. Instead science put in men's minds a design larger but less significant, more vacuous—Life and man meant nothing. Meanwhile religion, defeated in biology, retreated from the whole field of inquiry. The churches became completely escapist. For part of them narrowed into specific 'Fundamentalism', and part fled away from all thinking into social action. They made the utterly unspiritual assumption that man could be improved in his nature by improving his economic conditions.

The moral of this tragic muddle is clear. The two sides, each striving to find meaning, quarrelled over a misapprehension. Hence we must begin again where they fell out. And this time we must take care to begin at the beginning. For the former assumptions made on both sides have failed. On the side of Natural Science the basic assumptions of nineteenth-century physics have been completely reversed. That means, even on nineteenth-century standards, a complete reversal of the nineteenth's case. For physics and its manifestation chemistry, made the 'tortoise' (to use the old Sanskrit simile) on which the less exact sciences of life were supposed to be wholly based and carried. While, in turn, on the 'elephant' of the biological sciences, were reared the shadowy plumes of psychology. If the tortoise becomes spiritualized how much more may the elephant and even more the plumes feel they have a right to soar! The new physics, it has often been remarked, in the last thirty years, is increasingly metaphysical. Indeed it is interesting and amusing to see that materialism and mechanism having been expelled from their old fortress and base are now seeking an insecure and untenable refuge with the biological sciences.

Equally on the side of religion there has had to be abandoned the old narrow picture of human history. The size and consequences of the revolution in physics and indeed in all the natural sciences, have made many people overlook the fact that an equal revolution has been going on in history and in all the sciences whereby we obtain our picture of human nature. Beginning in the thirties of the last century, new technics, and new sources of information on which the new technics could be employed, have altered our picture of mankind as radically as has been altered our picture of his environment. The discovery of the critical methods whereby to estimate documents, the new methods of decipherment of 'dead' tongues, the start of the study of prehistoric man, the exploration of the human mind by such pioneers of the subconscious as Charcot, Elliotson and the Puysegurs, the dawn of respectful studies of other cultures, all this took place when Natural Science was dazzling men's eyes with pictures of power over nature and freedom from superstition.

Hence we disregarded this the greater revolution, the new answers to the agelong problem-question, What is man? Hence to-day religion faces the fact that instead of the Old and New Testaments containing an adequate picture of man and a unique catalogue of the essential events in his story, they compose a collection unique but not supreme. The Old Testament is a short and narrow tale of a provincially minded people who, as is natural with the ignorant, conceived themselves, with little objective evidence to support their prejudice, as being supremely favoured by God. They show themselves as a race more gifted in story-telling than in spirituality. Alongside of them, and before them, we find societies, which not merely paralleled and forestalled insights that Hebrew and Christian thought incomparable, but which went far beyond them in keenness of insight and, as far as the Hebrew is concerned, in purity of devotion.

It is clear, then, that if we are to make a new start we must begin where both science and religion had to begin—with nature. We must first look at that which is around us and in contact with us now. Then, when we have seen what we can find out in this the direct way, we may and should go on to history. For history is a close-up and vast magnification of Natural History. Then, thirdly, we shall rightly come to individual man, the separate consciousness. He, in turn, is a vast close-up and magnification of human history, of mankind as a whole.

But surely if we are to start once more at the beginning examining nature, if we are to see whether the new facts about it which have come to light show meaning, that is an immense task! Indeed it is. The new information is both extensive and heterogeneous. It is often overlooked that one of the motives for trying to reduce all nature to physics and all physics to mechanism was the great convenience of so simplifying one's thought. Facts can be handled far more conveniently if they are considered as being purely quantitative and unchanging units. For example, once allow that the phenomena observed in biology may not be fixed actualities but shifting potentialities, then the difficulty of ordering them, still more of understanding them, is immensely increased. Further, it is quite clear that this is what has actually happened. And this problem has arisen not only in biology. In physics the doctrine of the 'Field'—of atoms interacting with interdependence through extensive areas—has come to stay, to grow and to disturb the old definitions and certainties. While in psychology even the 'half-breed' psychophysiologists—who unlike all other half-breeds have succeeded for long in dominating the society on which they intruded—even they have to own that *Gestalt* can ask them more questions than they can answer by their atomistic faith.

The problem of arranging the new evidence, and seeing whether thereby we may find meaning in nature, is therefore obviously for an authority. But that raises the further requirement, the finding of an authority. He is still to seek. Experts there are in plenty. But experts will not do. Indeed they are increasingly incompetent. That is recognized and they are the first to recognize that. Specialization continues unabated, indeed accelerated. And specialization means that the more competent the specialist becomes in his closing corner the less adequate he must become in any field beyond it. Specialists to-day are picked ever earlier and are confined for life in their more engrossing, more exhaustive, more exclusive study. Patrick Geddes was an outstanding botanist. He told a friend of the writer that he left his special science and plunged into the undeveloped but human studies of sociology because botany even then was divided into over forty sciences in all but one or two of which the knowledge of any one botanist was certainly inexpert.[1]

There are, then, no authorities. Nor will specialists ever become such. On the contrary, specialists must become increasingly unauthoritative on any life-size issue or question. Nor will Time wait. If you find yourself on a sinking ship and the captain (the original Natural Philosopher, the original name for the original scientist) has dissolved into his feet that can feel about inside his boots, his hands that are fingering the bridge rail, and his tongue which is carefully exploring his lips, you yourself will have to see about lowering the boat or plugging the leak, whether such initiative was or was not approved by the captain the last time he was *compos mentis*. If you find yourself in a new country, of course it is best if you can find an 'Information Please' officer. But really new countries generally lack such. Pioneers have to make maps, not to buy them. Those who follow can often have such helps. We are all pioneers to-day, marooned

[1] This immensely important but still disregarded fact has lately been stressed by Dr. C. D. Darlington, F.R.S., in a brilliant review entitled 'The Fragmentation of Science', in *Nature*, April 1945. In reviewing Professor Schrader's intense study of 'Mitosis' Dr. Darlington quotes, agreeing with the author's expressed sense of frustration through specialization and the failure to arrive at any comprehensive meaning or explanation: 'The lesson in specialization in techniques and in material is necessary. Specialization in theory is arbitrary and restriction of data is a contradiction in itself.' Dr. Darlington concludes: 'In planning scientific theories we must have a point of view of our own, a theory of our own.' This is, of course, to say that facts can't make theories, only men's minds can do that. *Theoria* in Greek, we need to remember, means contemplation—the integral thought that surveys as a totality the whole field. Analysis and criticism are helpful, essential, but only after, to bring to clearer focus a part, found by the full-range view of the whole.

on a new shore. The frontiers of the mind keep on rising on every hand. Not only is there the profoundly new physics. The new biology is just as startling. The new psychology—not the outworn attempt to explain away consciousness, but the real wish to study it—is no doubt the most startling of the three. Beside that we have a new picture of history.

Nor should we despise early maps because they are crude and tentative. They cannot be otherwise. No country is new when it is adequately mapped. A crude sketch may be more valuable than the most perfect map of an overrun spot, if the sketch points to tracks and routes that lead to really virgin land. We have so often said that the good is the worst enemy of the best that we often overlook the converse truth of the proposition— the best is the worst enemy of the good. Waiting for authoritative perfection and finality, we lose all. Time is of the essence of our condition.

The collection of possible correlates that follows is, then, certainly no thesis on Natural Theology. It is, in the original sense in which Montaigne coined the word, an essay—an attempt, a sally to see whether one can track out what one has glimpsed. And as Francis Bacon did with his *Essays*—taking the essay form from Montaigne—these findings, jottings, soundings and data are the bearings that a man makes—that every man must make —as he tries to be true to two things: the new fact which presents itself to him and his reaction to it. Here is a datum—if you will a 'sensum'—And now what does it mean, what can I do about it?

Everyone to-day has to ask himself, as we are rushed ahead and see ahead of us unsuspected involvements and responsibilities, is anything opening out? Can we guide our speeding selves along any opening?

That in brief is the writer's apology for attempting this essay. He believes that the new data are aligning themselves. To him it seems that the new data in physics, biology and psychology, data which everyone may review, are building up a new large picture of meaning. He is sure that the data that he has come across in the current periodicals of research can be greatly amplified by others. He offers these few findings in the hope that when such tentative essays have shown that a case for Natural Theology does exist, others, far more competent in ordering the material, and possessed of far fuller information, will produce what might rightly claim to be a true thesis.

Chapter Two

WHY NATURAL THEOLOGY IS NEEDED

Two provisos are necessary when we would start again in building up the basic structure known as Natural Theology. Natural Theology is necessary. In this chapter it is hoped to show that without it the other Theologies—Dogmatic and Mystical, the Theologies of History and of Personal Experience— really have no base. They cannot for long hold man's allegiance or yield him their great profits. But Natural Theology itself must observe its limits. It is the first of the Theologies and has a right of precedence. But that also means that it is preliminary. It begins, and without it there is no sound beginning of religious faith and life. But it is but a beginning. It is not conclusive. It is in itself essentially partial, preliminary, and so cannot be conclusive.

That is understood by many and for that reason many put it aside. Even if the evidence that it can bring forward is considerably better than that adduced during the nineteenth century, still many people feel it hardly matters. The traditional Churches say they have the tradition, the witness of history, or their history, and the Protestant Churches which have been 'modernized' claim they have experience, the actual working fact that in the individual life religion works, if you will use it.

And this argument must not only be met, it must be allowed. The first and finest proof is the life that religion can make a man live. And back of that is the historic organization which preserves the rules and the training whereby the man who lives the deeply spiritual life has learned to live it. Natural Theology, beside these two, is surely such a 'poor third' that even if its 'running' were greatly improved could it really matter?

The pragmatic test seems to hold the field: A religion is true if it produces religious lives, and that Church is truest, however odd its forms may seem, if through these forms, these technics, it can train men to high religious living. And though we may call this proof pragmatic and associate it with William James it is strongly held by those who have spoken from and for the great Church of Authority, the Church of Rome.

> *For Forms of Faith let graceless Zealots fight*
> *He can't be wrong whose life is in the Right*

was said by Alexander Pope who remained a Catholic when being a Catholic in Britain was far from a popular thing. More remarkable, a generation later the reigning Pope held and promulgated the same view—that that Church is truest—and is proved truest—by the saints it can produce. Pope Benedict XIV was a remarkable man. He has a triple claim to be remembered. In that amazing record of human personality, the roll of the Papacy, he holds a high place. Not only unspoiled by supreme power, he adorned a throne on which had sat men both so noble as to make imitation difficult and so base as to excuse—at least by the powerful suggestion of precedent—any weakness. He was not only a capable administrator, a just ruler, a wise sovereign, but, in the position of a priest-king, he wielded powers which his subjects had to consider semidivine. He was not only gentle and humane, but, with all the grandeur of his office and the cares of state he preserved, to an outstanding degree, that cheerfulness of humour and happiness of spirit which are the clearest proofs and fruits of real humility and truly sane detachment.

His third achievement no doubt sprang from this second gift. Not content with the heavy task of steering the great conservative-authoritative Church in the changed weather of the Century of Rationalism, he found time to research into the bases of his religion's authority. He worked to give Catholicism a case with which it might answer the criticisms of the Age of Reason. With care he spent much time in revising—what he saw to be central in the Church's apologia—the Roll of Canonized Saints. From this work he then drew what he felt to be the decisive answer to the Church's critics. He asks, Is there any other Church, religion or philosophy which can produce lives of such superhuman and ultrasocial character and value? He declares that he can find no such records of equal achievement among Protestants or Secularists. Of the other religions, he knew only of exoteric Judaism and Islam (e.g., he does not seem to have had any knowledge either of the Chasidim or of the Sufis). Therefore, on the grounds of his argument, he is free to draw his conclusion: That though the methods and disciplines of Catholicism might seem strange and inexplicable to an age which asked for visible proofs of everything before permitting any process to be employed, nevertheless these processes worked. And we must remember that this for long remained the only proof of any diet's adequacy. Before vitamins could be extracted their presence was demonstrated by the effect such 'accessory food-factors' had upon those who were fed them.

The pragmatic, the practical proof of religion's power, therefore, could hold the field. Nor could any progress in economic technics or abstract and applied physics dislodge or discredit it. Secularism could only make two partial and negative replies. First, it could say and did say that religion did not produce saints—'whole men', men of superintegration—but only fiction characters or neurotics. When a psychology was invented to support materialism and disprove consciousness naturally it urged this solution of the problem. It could allow no other. But as that attack was pressed to discredit sanctity, the defence strengthened. Historical study cleared away many sham reputations but it made it harder than ever to dismiss the fact that religion had, time and again, produced authentic saints. Religion could claim among its numbers men of a moral energy and height of selflessness which secularism could not equal or indeed approach.[1]

The second negative reply then alone remained: Saints were

[1] Lately vivid confirmation has been given of this fact. When inquirie were made as to which type of prisoner in the concentration camps endured with least psychological damage the frightful ordeal, time and again it was discovered that it was the religious.

24

not worth having for two sufficient reasons. In the first place, all social problems were really economic and economic plenty would solve them. In the second, the saint himself was an extravagant answer of outraged life to intolerable social conditions. The extreme self-sacrifice that he practised was unnecessary either for himself or for others in a scientifically run state.

This argument has however itself proved unsound. The major problems of industrialized man are not—we have discovered—productive nor indeed economic, but psychological. The conquest of inanimate nature is not our grave issue. It is conflict in ourselves and between ourselves that we have to solve and which otherwise will destroy us. We certainly stand in immediate and pressing need of men who can save us from ourselves and who can show that they can do so by evidencing that they have been saved from their divided selves.

The Church of Rome repeats: We and we alone have produced saints and we alone can and do. As the first part of that claim has been substantiated as far as the West is concerned we must examine the second. Granted that the Catholic Church has in the past produced supermen of unique social value we must ask further, Is it doing so to-day? And secondly, can it say, now that we know the world better than Benedict XIV could know it, that nowhere in the whole world—not merely in a West that had to choose Catholicism or Protestantism—have saints been produced? To take the historical question first, when we ask it we discover a fact of vital importance.

When we trace the history of sanctity in the Catholic Church we can and must observe two facts. The first we have noted and allowed. That Church has produced saints. Further it is clear that that Church is still producing characters of such intensity that they are canonized and have vast numbers of devotees who have—they claim—received benefits from these their patrons and would model their own lives on these patterns. But the same justice that allows, and willingly, that the Catholic Church produces saints has also to note that a change has come over the quality of the holiness that has been produced. Up to the end of the seventeenth century saints were produced who were in every sense of the word, whole men, supermen. Thereafter—perhaps due to the Quietist controversy—the saints are no longer as intellectually powerful as they are morally lofty. A Bernard, a Thomas, a Bonaventura, or, in the later centuries, a Neri, a Xavier, a Bellarmine—thinkers and practical geniuses of this sort may still abound in Catholicism but they do not attain to a similar height in sheer goodness as did these earlier psychological giants. The men and women canonized to-day and through the last two centuries are as intense but they are narrow. They are one-pointed but they lack breadth. Their intelligence quotient is generally low. The span of their minds is not at all equal to the depth of their hearts. They have much heat but nothing like the same light. Hence they can, like the two of the more popular saints of to-day—the Curé d'Ars and Thérèse of Lisieux —appeal strongly to their own Church but they have little appeal outside. They are simply and inflexibly Fundamentalists. It is worth noting that the last specifically Catholic thinker, who adds to the growth of European philosophy, is the philosopher Malebranche of the French Oratory—the French Oratory which at that moment was beginning to produce under Eudes that intensely emotional and anti-intellectualist devotionalism culminating in St. Margaret Mary's immensely popular cult of the Sacred Heart. Janet Stuart, the Superior General of the Society of the Sacred Heart who died in 1914, remarked in one of her letters from Rome that it was clear now that the Church was tending to make saints of children and of very childlike persons. A further reference of importance is given by the fact that that very Pope, Benedict XIV whose pragmatic judgment of the authenticity of a Church has been quoted (its power to produce saints) and who himself did so much to order and define what the Church considers a saint to be (see his *De Servorum Dei Beat: et Canon:*) showed in what direction his Church was going by a ruling of great importance. Petitioned by the Gallic Church to permit a special devotion to God the Father, he refused to allow it on careful theological grounds. As the special 'devotions' have proved a fairly close guide to where the new dogmas and definitions of the Church will arise, it is clear from this ruling—and the years that have passed have certainly confirmed it—that the worship of the God of Nature, God the Creator Father, was felt by the Curia by the middle of the eighteenth century to be something from which the heart averted itself. Only through the Avatar and the co-Avatar, the heavenly mother, could approach be felt to be at all possible to the God of Nature. Again to quote that Catholic poet Alexander Pope:

> *. . . presume not God to scan.*
> *The proper Study of Mankind is Man!*

Yes, even when we are studying or aspiring to God we must never go beyond a God Man. The very Pope who uses the pragmatic proof as evidence of the historic claims of his Church, warns off from the attempt to adore the God of Natural History. We must then keep two facts in mind: the first is that the Church is producing saints, the second, that they are childish in their minds. This is not to say that the Church does not contain in it —and still further attract to it—minds of great acuity and ability. The point at issue is, Do these converts or these great 'birthright' executives of the Church become saints? They do not. About the intellectual honesty of their conviction no careful or unbiased observer has a doubt. Among the many debts we owe to psychology, and perhaps also to anthropology, is the fact that we are past that time when it seemed that the dilemma offered in such cases could only be met by the alternative fraud or fool and when, as in the sad case of Charles Kingsley and J. H. Newman, it was impossible for the first to call the second a fool but had to say that the 'pervert' was a fraud, dishonest. But we also have to allow that the Catholic phrase that 'a convert believes, but hardly ever further down than the neck' is itself a psychological judgment of penetration and based upon careful observation. And we have to advance it further. We have to add that no Catholic that has had a fully modern education, that has lived conversant with the climate of modern critical studies and whose mind has been alight with the modern outlook, but has found a certain limit to his faith and its power of total conviction. Baron von Hügel is a brilliant example of this. He was a man of singular devotion, warm and deep, as his studies on prayer have shown, and as all who knew him bore witness. Yet his whole religious life was stressed and striated with conflicts which arose from acute intellectual difficulties in receiving the dogmas of the Church in the way that the Church said they must be accepted and in the way, we must add, they must be accepted if they are to produce that intensity of life and conviction that produces sanctity. Sanctity, that immediate proof that a religion works to the full height of its claims and is therefore for all practical purposes true, can only be produced by those whose convictions have not only no reservations but whose faith is so deep and simple that it is incapable of any subrational inhibitions. It must seem to such believers as absurd to doubt God as it seemed to a nineteenth-century rationalist to doubt the existence, presence and constant activity of 'Natural Law'. Further, the Church is right when it says, 'These our saints were saints because they believed what Dogma teaches. It is the Tradition and their unquestioning, enthusiastic faith in the Tradition, that made it possible for them to become saints. They claimed that it was so, and we can prove it by the fact that only these beliefs produce that result.'

There is an answer to this claim. It runs as follows and is popular to-day because it claims to be psychological. It maintains that it is true that saints to-day are still appearing in the Catholic Church but it denies that they are made possible through its dogmas. Saints are made—and the lowness of their intelligence is a further proof of the fact—because they are people peculiarly liable to 'suggestion'; suggestion, that convenient word which has relieved modern psychologists from the formidable problem of answering the question, What is Faith? We are often told by such critics that provided the mind is simple enough and the method sufficiently impressive then anything can be believed and acted upon; its rationality or its absurdity in no wise affect this capacity.

But if the appeal is to psychology, to psychology we must go and as in this case it is to a particular aspect of psychology—the study of 'suggestion' or as it had better be called, hypnosis—we must see what actually hypnosis tells us about human intellectual capacity and mental power of acceptance. It seems to be true that simple people do yield to suggestion more easily than complex and critical characters. But it does not seem to be true that any suggestion, even when given with the full force of hypnotic aid—i.e., when the surface mind has been put out of action by hypnotic trance—will be accepted by the deep mind. The facts are complex but from the time of Charcot and Janet and through such researchers as Milne Bramwell and Wingfield certain conclusions seem to be fairly clear: Any suggestion that would outrage modesty or fundamental morals seems to be resisted by the deep mind. It is true that in some cases it would seem possible that even this resistance might be worn down. But in these cases there seems to have been at first an assent to such a surrender. In short, only a weakly bad person—or one who only shrank from evil because he might be punished—could be made to commit, by suggestion, evil acts through the hypnotic power of a strongly bad person.

It is clear that the Catholic saints do not come under this category. Secondly, there seems a clear understanding in the deep mind that the marvellously acted consent which it gives to the suggestion—e.g., that the turnip it is given to eat is 'really' a peach—is an act. A number of careful experiments show that it is aware that the turnip is a turnip to which by a creative act of imagination it gives all the gustatory and other responses that would be awakened by the sensation of peach-eating. Thirdly, and perhaps most important, this power of creative belief has a clear correlation with objective fact. This is proved by evidence that shows that the belief is only maintained for a certain time— generally not beyond a fortnight—when if the facts of outward experience continue to deny the inner conviction, the conviction begins to fail and finally vanishes. It is an assumption of those who have not followed hypnotic work with care that anything can be believed and for ever. The saints' belief grew as the years went on—that it broadened in clarity is a proof of its validity, not a proof against. Had their faith been due to nothing but a blind hypnotic suggestion then it would not have begun by being good, steadily have been sustained and become better, and finally been unwavering and often all-embracing.

We cannot then say that the Catholic saint is one whose character and to some extent consciousness has undergone changes solely because of a certain method and technique of mind-training, a method which bears only a chance relationship with the dogmas from which the Church claims that it is derived. The saints became saints not because they took to a method which they thought would prove a convenient and efficacious therapy. They became saints first and foremost because they believed with complete conviction (because assured that it was reasonable) every positive thing that the Church taught. Had they not been able to do that they would not have been able to alter their characters and their consciousness to the extent that they did. We have proof of this counter-proposition in the fact that those whose education has made it possible for them only to believe because it would be therapeutic for them so to have faith, those who know 'the facts of nature' are against their 'reasons of the heart', who believe in spite of knowing that they can give no proof, indeed in a defiance, *quia impossibile*, because they must have a private comfort, these never have a calm and deep faith that really alters them. Querulous, defensive, 'always trying to out-sneer the sneer they fear' and, if given power, bitterly persecuting, that is all they gain by their sad effort. It is little use to them and less than none to their religion for it is one of the most telling arguments against its truth.

We can and must allow then that though the saint is the final proof, the last word about the truth of a religion, he is not the first. Further, we can say that this final proof will never be arrived at, this last and closing word never be spoken unless and until quite a number of preliminary words and proofs have been taken and tried, allowed and agreed. So we have allowed—and we have seen modern psychology in the specific research of hypnosis confirms this—that a saint cannot produce himself unless he first believes—and probably for quite a long preliminary time—that what he is about to do has about it no shadow of self-deception. For a considerable stage of his life he must have had no doubt as to the nature of the universe. He must have either accepted from the start and never departed from the conviction of the spiritual actuality of the cosmos, or he must have come back to that belief, not because it might prove helpful to his character but because his thinking brought him inevitably to such a conclusion. Then, as a necessary deduction from those discoveries resulting in that finding, he sees that he must act in accordance with the nature of things and not in accord with the current illusion and mistaken notion. He attempts sanctity not as a splendid defiance of the hard facts of life but—and this of course is very hard—as a steady and quiet correction by sane action of the insane habits and conventions of those around him. It is doubly hard; for it is not only unpleasant to our animal nature, it seems pretentious to our social nature. But, however hard it may be, this course is possible because he sees there is none other open to him. If you have accepted the Copernican hypothesis then, though it may not be popular with a Ptolemaic world, your outlook and your course of action must be heliocentric. As the saints have said, there was nothing else to do, if one was to remain sane.

But when we have allowed that the saints could not have produced their praxis, their psychological methods, exercises and results, had they not believed that what they were doing was simply to live in accord with the true nature of things; when we see and recognize that their whole life was the ethic and behaviour pattern deducible from the cosmology they were certain was true; then we have to ask, How was it that they were able to accept that Tradition with its views of the universe and of the ethic those views indicate? We have seen an increasing number of people cannot accept that Tradition. In fact, we can in this respect divide humanity as it now is into three groups. The first is the largest—at least in the West to-day. It includes all those who have let the Tradition go and so of course the chance of becoming saints, because they could not believe the Tradition in its cosmological dogmas to be true. The second is that still large class who under the severe psychological need, because they find that they go mad or bad if they accept a mechanist view of the world, *on that ground*, 'swallow'—but never really can digest—the Tradition. As a number of Catholic converts have said, 'For the sake of the Mass I'd accept any dogma and yield any scientific finding'. These we see gain an uneasy relief but they never attain to 'wholeness', sanctity. Conflict between heart and mind disturbs their peace and too often embitters their relationships with others, and what their actual casualty rate, their collapse into neurosis and psychosis, may be, must be sadly surmised. We know that a suggestion given steadily and strongly to a level of the mind, that is unable either to defend itself from this summons or to give an honest and wholehearted assent, does produce some of the most serious of mental strains and ruptures. Indeed as all know who followed with care the development of psychoanalysis, it was because of the deep and dangerous resistance that was found to follow many hypnotic treatments that analysis was proposed as a way of questioning the deeps of the mind as to the reason of their resistance to proposals that were obviously therapeutic. And to-day psychoanalysis is having to confess that one of the requirements that the deep mind must make before it can accept and build into the character the new recommendation, is that this recommendation must not only be convenient, it must be true. It must not only be a way of easing the self but of facing the nature of the universe. The peace must be a consequence of having found Reality and known Truth.

The third class is then that small and till now diminishing group of those so simple that their native hue of resolution was never 'sicklied o'er with the pale cast of thought', whose deep mind was never troubled with the thought that perhaps they were accepting something *Als Ob*, just because they would not dare face what Life actually was. One thing is clear: escapists may make converts, they will never make saints.

The conclusion from these results, results which are of course commonplaces with all those psychologists who study and advance sociology, is that religion will give out. It will gradually use up this last remaining base-layer of simple minds. The capacity of believing, right through, that what you practise is literally true, will have been used up, worked out. Such students of mankind are accustomed to tell us, for example, that no one who has gone beyond a certain grade in college ever becomes a Jehovah's Witness. This of course is not to say whether or no that type of Witnessing is true or false. But if the correlation is true it would establish the fact that, should education continue, dogmatic conviction would decline. That again would not mean that churches would disappear. It would mean that they would have lost the power to produce their final proof and chief use—men of absolute and 'supernatural' authenticity.

This deduction is true if one more step can be established, a step which the psycho-sociologists—because they are specialists—take for granted. But because we are not specialists we must look at that too. It may be inevitable—but again it may not. We can examine it by putting our inquiry in the form of a simple question. What makes the simple saint of to-day who unquestioningly accepts his Tradition—and so can become a saint—what makes him accept the Tradition? We have seen that the answer, popular among psychologists twenty years ago, has not stood up to experiment. It is not true that the human mind will accept any suggestion, however wild, build that into its structure of reactions and become a fuller and more creative person in consequence of this blind belief. The fact is that the simple person, however simple, is not blindly irrational. He, or she, accepts what the Tradition teaches about the nature of the universe because, and this is the final and vital step, that teaching seems to him and her rational. Tradition, Authority, may after that first step become one's guide. But it cannot do so, before that. If every fact of one's actual, intense, immediate experience denied those dogmas then one could not accept them, or only in so perfunctory a manner that one's life would remain unaffected. The dogmas are accepted because they seem to complete and fulfil propositions which observations of nature suggested and partly outlined.

This is the ground which the Catholic Church, indeed far the greater part of all Western religion and nearly all Eastern religion, have taken. Dogma is not contrary to reason. It does not

c   33

deny the deductions that any sane mind must make from an open-minded study of its environment. Dogma and all theology are simply a completion of what began by Natural Philosophy, the desire to make sense of one's surroundings and to understand one's situation in them.

But before drawing the conclusions to which such findings would point for religion as a whole, we have to ask: 'If, as we saw at the beginning of this chapter, the Church of Rome can claim that it produced full saints—super-whole men—because they believed wholly and fully, and, further, that the saints which it produces to-day are full and whole only to that point to which they can believe fully (they have to be of very simple intelligence so as not to know of post-anthropomorphic cosmology) is Benedict XIV right about geography as he was about history? Does no other religion produce saints? Certainly Asia has done so and does. Leaving aside the Sufi saints of Islam, Brahmanism (Vedanta) and Mahayana Buddhism—to mention but two—have never ceased to produce the highest holiness, the most complete and most selfless goodness. Here is spirituality showing its full fruits; freedom from physical craving, from economic possessiveness, from social desire for recognition, and that triple freedom removing all fear. We find such saints in full peace and joy because constantly aware of the Presence of the Eternal and constantly devoted to all creatures because filled with that compassion which the Eternal they know has for all His creation. Nor is that all. Religion in Asia yields goodness as intense as that of Catholicism, and, added to that, the sanctity reared in Vedanta, Mahayana or Taoism is not intellectually arrested. It is fully mature mentally. The only possible conclusion that can be drawn from this is simple but very profound and very hopeful: Cosmology does give rise to ethic: what you believe to be true about the nature of things that you will and must attempt to act out in your life. The Catholic picture of things, its cosmology, was sufficiently true not to be contradicted by the information possessed by medieval scholars. It is not true enough to-day. The Vedanta-Mahayana-Taoist picture is far vaster, and, far from being contradicted, is being increasingly confirmed by modern science. And final and most hopeful fact: this Sanskrit cosmology (the Taoist is more gnomic and inferential) not only gets rid of the intellectual difficulties—such as the crude Hebrew geology and astronomy fossilized in the Christian dogmas—difficulties which have turned modern informed minds from religion—but it gets rid likewise of those even more serious moral difficulties—such as eternal damnation, predestination, and that this life is man's only chance—difficulties which have proved even more serious stumbling blocks to those who would give their lives to loving God wholly.

This then is the explanation of why the Roman Catholic saints are now tending increasingly to be child saints, also why adult sanctity can and does exist where the cosmology is of full intellectual stature and, finally, why saints can be produced to-day if, but only if, we have a Natural Theology.

We have then come to the first of our basic conclusions. We may sum it up in three terms: It is true that the life lived is the conclusive proof of the truth of a religion. But it is conclusive, final: it is not the first step. And as it is not the first step, we cannot leap on to it. So, secondly, we find that those who have attained to this station of absolute conviction for themselves and absolute authenticity of witness for others, did so because they were able to base themselves on the step that led to being able to live the life—the honest conviction that the life lived and the practices followed were not lived and practised as a convenience, as a convenient self-deceit. We have seen, had that been so then, not only would such lives not have rung true to us, they would not have rung true to the practisers themselves—they might have been honest converts, they would never have been saints. And, thirdly, and conclusively, we have seen that they who became saints were able to attain to step two—the acceptance of the tradition and the praxis—because they first took the first step: they had been able to see in nature the outline of a plan and purpose. They believed that they saw a preliminary outline that made sense of experience—both of its beauty and its struggle its joy and its pain. Then they looked round and they found a tradition, *which starting with these natural universal facts* (of pain and pleasure, of beauty and ugliness, or purpose and pointlessness) went on, and never denying them, completed them and showed how (1) by adding a further hypothesis and (2) enlarging by praxis one's own actual experience, one might come to complete acceptance of the scheme of things and completely expressive and constant creative reaction with that scheme.

Chapter Three

WHAT NATURAL THEOLOGY CAN PROVE

We have now seen the necessity of a Natural Theology. Religion can be a therapy—no doubt it is the best, the only lasting one. But there would seem to be a Therapeutic Paradox similar to that famous Hedonistic Paradox on which Professor Henry Sidgwick, the authority on ethics, so often and so wisely dwelt. For, as the only way to be sure of attaining happiness is not to pursue it but to pursue meaning, when happiness appears as a by-product, so too with therapy. There, also, if we seek first Meaning and Truth we shall find, and alone shall find, that, as we seek truthfully to understand, to face and include all the facts, we ourselves are healed. And not merely are we healed; we go from strength to strength; we pass from a light that shines more and more until we emerge into the perfect day. Not only does our own path become clear, we begin to see at last the landscape as a whole.

Religion's power to act therapeutically depends, then, on our knowing it to be true, whether it would or would not serve the betterment of our health. Of course there are some people who still will say, 'What does it matter if the saints to-day are all simple-minded and incapable of understanding that the anthropomorphic world is ended. Reason is failing. We shall all come back at last to sit at their feet. The saint doesn't need to be sensible.'

But, as a matter of fact, he does. As a matter of fact Fundamentalists are not pure intuitionists and affirmationists. They do argue, because they do honestly and rightly believe that their power of belief rests on their rational conviction, and that on that was built the further experience brought to them by their holy life of prayer and contemplation. And, as they argue, and as they are unintellectual, they actually help unbuild and un-convince those they would edify and win. Were a Fundamental-ist a pure intuitionist probably everyone might be edified by him. But such do not seem to exist. We are pretty certainly ask-ing for something that cannot take place—for as we have seen that kind of deep conviction must spring from a mind that be-lieves that its faith is based on a reasonable outlook. Even such a simple and open soul as Ramakrishna was continually arguing and demonstrating, sometimes very poorly. As Bernard Shaw said once to the present writer, 'As long as a man says to me, "This thing I surely know," I am impressed. But as soon—and that is generally in the next breath—as he says, "Because," well then I turn away'. The tragedy of childish sanctity is shown pre-cisely here: Because it argues, has to argue, and because of its lack of intellectual maturity must argue badly, it can only in-fluence those in its own Church or sect who already agree with it. It cannot face and overcome any real intellectual problems.

We have seen that the *Pons Fidei*, the bridge of faith, of that faith which is 'the choice of the nobler hypothesis', the most meaningful picture of things, is a bridge of three piers. To get to the third, where we touch the shore of firm, rocklike certainty, we must get on to the second, a tradition, a system of beliefs and practices which allow us to pass out on to the third. And, again, to reach that central pier we have to get on to the first, the pier which abuts right on our present actual everyday experience, the viewpoint which we can take up without having to commit ourselves to any practice, join any system or organization, still less attempt a steady and sustained alteration of character cul-minating in new and wider understandings and apprehensions.

And now that we have traced our trouble back to this point, we see that the breakdown is just here. Natural Theology must come back, it is pier one, it is foundational, it is the tortoise on which the others have to ride. Otherwise the two further piers are sundered from us, out in the tide of the uncrossable river.

WHAT NATURAL THEOLOGY CAN PROVE

But it is one thing to say Natural Theology must come back. It is quite another to bring it back.

However desirable it might be that He should be proved, *can* God be proved? There can be no doubt that most people would now say No. The layman in the street certainly believes 'science has disproved God'. The layman in the pew believes that God can and must be believed in, and therefore needn't, can't and must not be proved. Faith is believing something which Truth denies and Revelation is the exclusive alternative to experiment and discovery. This point of view has been put with force, authority and learning by Dr. Karl Barth, the leader of Neo-Orthodoxy and also is given support by Dr. Emil Brunner in his book just translated as *Revelation and Reason*.[1] The scientists who, we have seen, are becoming yearly less authoritative in any but narrowing fields, such specialists on the whole incline to assume that some other science than their own has disproved God. The minister, generally having had a student's course in metaphysics and often being better read than most in philosophy, history and psychology, feels that proofs of God are best left alone. Ministers' reason for so feeling is generally due to two conclusions to which their studies have led them. There is the historical evidence of the defeats which the Church suffered owing to its attempt to force conviction with syllogisms and ill-sustained arguments. There is the psychological evidence of the little effect that such proofs, even when accepted as logically satisfying, appear to have upon conduct.

So the vast majority of what we call modern people, people who feel that they are up to date, have undoubtedly settled down to believe that there is no proof of God. If you can accept a specific Revelation then you can believe. If you can't you

[1] 'Brunner is convinced that a theology which permits itself to be drawn into producing proofs to support its view of revelation has already "thrown up the sponge". . . . Hence Brunner sets the antithesis: either faith or proof—you cannot have both.' See essay on Brunner by Professor J. McCreary in *Christendom*, vol. xii, No. 2, Spring 1947. Dr. Karl Barth's position is even more compromising. According to him man is wholly depraved and so fallen that he is incapable of grasping Truth and by that truth coming to any knowledge of God.

don't. It is all a matter of The Will to Believe and Reason has nothing, and can have nothing, to do with it. But if people reject Reason they must be consistent. To publish an argued polemic against reason is to show that the principles of logic have not been grasped. And yet such an authority, for instance, as Dr. Emil Brunner argues with forensic skill in his attack upon views which he wishes to discredit. Indeed it is impossible for him to reject, as he does reject utterly, Natural Theology, unless he can argue that it is false and he is quite willing to do so. This is not, of course, to say that such minds are not capable of accurate thought. But it is to say that a wish to discredit reason is so powerful emotionally as to lead all the dogmatists (whether traditionalists such as Barth and Brunner or mechanists such as Freud) to make fundamental errors in their thinking.

What is clear beyond dispute, and with this we can start, is that the phrases of dismissal, e.g., 'science has disproved God', 'God can't be proved', are certainly too vague. To take first the term which appears in both of these 'blanket' propositions, the key word, the verb 'prove'. What do we mean by proof? Let us take it in the first proposition. There we come up against one of the primal limitations of proof—'You cannot establish a universal negative.' That leads to consideration of positive proof. The only proofs which can claim to be complete, invariable, are proofs from abstract logic and mathematics. And they are so only because, from the original propositions, there has been abstracted everything that might be variable. One and one make two because first of all we have decided that one is always equal to one. Directly we add to the abstract notion of one the quality of some one *thing*, then one thing added to another thing does not necessarily result in something exactly double. Quality has come into the proposition.

To say that science has disproved God would be to say that God is a proposition of mathematics. He is then an abstraction whose elemental nature we have defined. So, and so only, can we establish by logic whether such a quantity is present or absent in the formula we are examining.

But mathematicians—though they have sometimes claimed

with some force of argument that they alone are true scientists, because they alone deal with definable propositions—are not usually men who argue much about God for, again, they would say that they only work with material which they have constructed for their own uses. They are not interested in raw facts, happenings, phenomena, but in the way, with the simplest abstractions, the mind may play its game of accuracy, and out of symbols construct patterns.

Indeed we may say that not until we come to the sciences that call themselves the sciences of Life does the issue of Theodicy arise—the task of 'justifying the ways of God to Man'. True it might, and sometimes may, have arisen when discussing physics, the principles that govern the movements of inorganic, non-reproductive bodies. But even in astronomy and geology the issue is not acute. True, from the nineteenth century time-scale and space-span, the universe seemed to have taken a long time to reproduce anything on which either a moral or perhaps an aesthetic judgment could be passed. Further, it was considered to have used up a great deal of room in getting ready the stage for the human drama. But even from the time of such simple apologists whose thought was so plain that it fitted quite conveniently the polished rhyming of Pope, it was clear that if there was a God, though His intentions might have been highly honourable and generous towards man, that did not compel Him to make a universe that should be either wholly comprehensible by man or—even less—wholly colonizable. As long as man himself lives in a 'decent bound' and his moral sense is not outraged by what he can perceive going on in that bound (and as far outside as he can see) he has obviously no right to criticize the scheme because it seems too ample in size, too vast in time. After all, if you are supposed to be contemplating the work of an Infinite Power it would surely be surprising if things were otherwise and we found, instead of a fabulously vast universe, one that was obviously constructed with a cheeseparing economy.

The Sciences of Life do raise the question of good and bad, of suffering and joy, of success and failure. No one can say that a star which is turning into a cinder or evaporating into an ever thinner gas, or exploding, is a failure, a tragedy or a moral problem. To use such terms about the inorganic—though we do sometimes—is always to employ that anthropomorphism, that 'pathetic fallacy' which is one of the worst sentimentalities. As we shall see later when we come to the Sciences of Life, this is a danger which we have to guard against even when trying to evaluate the meaning and destiny of other living creatures than ourselves. But at least when we are dealing with other forms of life we are dealing with something that is analogous to ourselves. As long as we see no sign of life, no evidence of sensation or choice, the scene of moral issues may be in course of construction, but the actors have not come on the stage, still less the first lines of the play been spoken.

We have then reached the point when we can say that whereas about issues over which there can be no moral dispute (e.g., as to whether 7 is 'better' than 9 or 4 more 'perfect' than 3—issues which we must note in passing *did* concern and disturb thinkers still tied to anthropomorphism) we can have something like a closed and complete proof; about other things, living issues, this is not possible. In short, the nearer we reach those problems that really concern us as moral questions of right and wrong and the choices so involved, the less we can have an absolute proof. Because of this, then, many people, too often moralists, rush to the other extreme. Mathematical proof not being obtainable we then decide to be tragic and say there is no proof whatever to be obtained. We have an outbreak of slogans which are all of them emotional from 'Faith alone', 'Believe because it is impossible', right across to 'It is only on the foundation of an unyielding despair that the soul's habitation can be built'. These phrases are rhetoric, they are not argument; nor would they carry any conviction did we not every now and then like to be relieved from the patient work of sifting proofs and finding truth, and give way to histrionic gestures.

For though it is not possible to have absolute proof about anything into which quality enters, and in dealing with Life one is not dealing with simple abstractions of quantity, it is possible to have a working proof, one that leads to results. All the proofs that deal with phenomena—with the data of our experience of the outer world—are proofs which depend on the Balance of Probability. This is an obvious fact. Yet we have largely lost sight of it because we have forgotten that the natural sciences, in their search for invariable principles, tended to speak of those hypotheses which had stood up for a considerable time without needing drastic re-scaling, and with few large exceptions to their working, no longer as hypotheses but as Natural Laws. We have claimed that we have discovered an iron invariability in an outer nature, a blind indifferent repetition.

This dogma was first stated about the stars. In the eighteenth century gravitation was taken by those whose information was more general than particular (e.g., Voltaire) as the explanation of all astronomy. By the intellectual dominating class during the nineteenth century the same simple idea of Blind Law was much more rashly extended to the Sciences of Life. During the first quarter of the twentieth century, and still more rashly, less demonstrably, mechanism was asserted as an explanation of consciousness itself.

So when we say that science has disproved God or that God can't be proved, what we are claiming, if the words are being used with any accuracy, is that a certain hypothesis which is working so perfectly in the study not only of the inorganic but of the Sciences of Life that it is overwhelmingly probable, shows that God is not to be found in anything that we can perceive. Mechanism does explain everything and mechanism rules out Mind of any sort, all the more any sort of Good Mind. If 'God can't be proved' is an accurate term, it means that the balance of probability shows when we study nature that there is no plan or purpose visible or at least no plan or purpose of which we can approve. The sentence has to run so because that is the actual way in which people argue when dismissing Natural Theology. We shall have to develop this issue more fully in the following chapters, on our Physical Setting and our Biological Inheritance. Here it must be enough to point out that we must take this objection in its two divisions. The first question is: Can any plan be seen, or are we confronted with incoherence? Tennyson stated that fear in the well-known line about Despair,

'The stars', she whispers, 'blindly run.'

Like all poetic language it is both telling and tantalizingly uninformative. No doubt the stars have not got eyes. But 'running blind' introduces the notion that you are always colliding with your fellows in a series of accidents that happen because you and they have no paths or rules, courses or processes. Now that is not true of stars. Orbit, path, balance, these seem to compose the almost monotonous rule of the interstellar road. Indeed such authorities on sidereal order and development as Sir Arthur Eddington and Sir James Jeans were both agreed that it looked as though the relationship of space to star was a matter of most exact balance, and certainly the former was of the opinion that the number of electrons in the universe not only controlled the very size of the universe but also the distribution of the nexus and nodes of atom-clusterings which result in star formation. [1]

There is then a plan, a very obvious order. We may say it is too large and dauntingly inhuman. We may choose with that writer of an almost too neatly needleworked style R. L. Stevenson, to say that the mind 'freezes at the thought' of the scale on which the astronomic picture has been drawn. But we cannot say that it is not a picture. Further, as the human mind is generally impressed by size—as we can see from our words of praise being nearly always words of magnitude—we cannot say that the picture is not one of considerable magnificence. It may perhaps lack variety. But then, if it is a background, stateliness rather than detail is demanded even by our aesthetic standards. Nor should we object if the aesthetic standards of a Mind which shaped the universe might, because they are vaster, be grander even than ours. Further again, as astronomic exploration advances, we have discovered that the outer universe is not nearly

[1] Indeed the theory of the origin of stars and in particular of the solar system which now appears to find most favour with astronomers is the coagulation of all giant bodies out of meteoric dust. See 'Earth Model and Meteorites' in *Nature*, 10th June 1944, p. 718.

so lacking in variety as the nineteenth century imagined. Then there seemed nothing but a horribly limpid Space lit at fabulous distances by points of fire, intense but almost as featureless as the Void. But modern astronomy enriches itself every year with hitherto unsuspected qualities. It now presents a cosmic sky one quarter of which has in it clouds of various dusts. In the clear spaces we glimpse exploding suns, suns such as Lyra Beta, in shape like dumbbells, suns in waltzing couples and even ballets of half a dozen partners, suns like corkscrews, suns like the white dwarfs so heavy that a square inch of their matter would bore into our hardest ground like shot dropping through soup, suns like the black dwarfs of which Sir Spencer Jones, the Astronomer Royal, has written that they are so dense that not only can no light get away from the intensity of their gravitational field but Time itself goes slow as it passes such clots of density, such masses of massivity. Surely such an astronomy cannot be accused of lacking variety.[1]

There is, then, a plan as far as we can see, and, at night, there seems no doubt we can see very far. And, further, that plan is one of great stateliness, does no one any harm, and shows a fascinating number of peculiarly strange qualities and developments. It is both deeply impressive and highly intriguing. Indeed its intrinsic interest is so great that we know that the finest minds in every generation have given up all their time just to study this tremendous spectacle. And, what is further to our point, though we are apt to raise the cry of 'Escapist' over any who would spend too long in equipping themselves to help others, against the astronomers this accusation, so often brought against the saints, has never been uttered. We have known for centuries that these stargazers did not expect any personal improvement. Still less could we hope that they would bring back

[1] The Story of a Star once thought to be so simple: a glow, a glare, a glimmer and a gloom every month grows more elaborate. Pulsing stars—our sun is one—may blow up at any time. The wreck may be a white dwarf. But some white dwarfs pulse after collapse and each giant red star has a white dwarf at its core. These are some additional variations to star history reported by Dr. P. L. Bhatnagar, *Nature*, May 1946.

anything which might be of use to us. Their instruments are so costly that they are the only scientific apparatus that can compare in cost with those other ultra-expensive instruments with which we kill one another. Yet neither this cost nor this withdrawal of brains that might plan for us better weapons, have aroused protest.

In short, 'The stars' don't 'blindly run', they run according to a plan of some immense proportion. And the puzzle of that design has been so delightful that to know more of it many of our best intellects have felt they could not better spend their lives. And, though our civilization, never overcharged with intelligence and needing increasingly a higher quota of high technicians, has always had, since the discovery of astronomy, to suffer this Draft, there has been no organized protest on our part, rather a certain envious approval. These pure and apparently pointless researchers we regard apparently as our aristocrats. We are proud to work that they may enjoy their refined sport. Whether such lives have in any wise been to our benefit we cannot say. Perhaps, like the exploration of the infinitely small—which resulted in atomic power—we may find the study of the infinitely great will put an equal giant-power into our hands. What is clear is that the contemplation of that outermost plan and purpose has not frozen the minds that looked out on it nor turned them into despairing dwarfs. They have found it exhilarating. The suicide rate among astronomers is very low. The expectation of life respectably high.

A plan can be seen. That then must be allowed. The next question or challenge is, of course, Is that plan good? As we have said Good is really only an issue when choice is brought into the discussion. In physics, where, as far as we can see, there is not present the kind of consciousness we know—if consciousness at all—Choice, and Right and Wrong and Joy and Suffering do not enter. Yet in another sense, even at the vast distance that the inorganic lies beyond our direct consciousness, and the stars lie outside our immediate experience, we can say there is not lacking a Good and indeed a high Good. The synonym of Beauty is Loveliness, and Love and Goodness are as close to each other as Loveliness and Beauty. Kant did not know much about astronomy and the astronomy that he knew was rudimentary to ours (he actually gave it as a dictum that one of the things which must always be unknown was the chemical nature of the stars' substances! And this within a generation or less of the discovery of the spectroscope. A warning against ever asserting what cannot be found and may never be known!) Yet he owned that the spectacle of the night sky was to him equal in shared supreme magnificence to that which he did admire and far more closely understood, The Moral Law Within. And ever since his time we can say that astronomers have not been inclined to disagree with his appreciative judgment of the heavenly spectacle. Ignatius Loyola, in many ways a character that does not call before the mind's eye one in love either with Loveliness or Beauty, he too used to be moved to tears by this one spectacle of all natural phenomena—the night sky. Astronomers to-day may not have Ignatius's view of the kind of Mind that orders this vast manifestation but they have seen in the lit Abyss something that is both of great beauty and also of some strangely touching appeal. After all, it is odd that a creature of this size on that scale should be able to follow so much of that cosmic dance with the appreciation of an enthusiast for the ballet. It is even stranger that the stupendous splendour of the major stars, some of which could embrace—it is thought—the greater part of the solar system in the span of their mass, should come to have any meaning for him, or, indeed any appreciation of their size, because the ocean of their radiance is mirrored for a moment in the minute and distorting mirror of a human retina.

The plan then, as far as we study it in its largest frame, is also good in its way. It is an aesthetic success, as far as it goes; and it goes far; as far as it is taken to go—that is as far as we can trace 'Extension and Mass'—as far as we are dealing with lines, planes and volumes. Moreover, it intrigues and stimulates the human mind, and the problems it sets find their solutions in very strange and profound directions. This last point, of this too we must postpone discussion till the next chapter. All we may say here is that up to this point, God has held His own. He cannot yet be dismissed on charges of brutality or mismanagement. True, what we are seeing works, as far as we can see, by strict law but that does no one any harm. Further, we must remember that to say that something is run by law and rule does not rule out that it is run by intelligence. That intelligence is not necessarily less so because it happens to find law and rule convenient and indeed comely ways of producing certain effects, a happy device for employing a certain beautiful economy and engaging all the mustered material in the ultimate result. Indeed, as students of the history of ideas have pointed out, the notion of mechanism, of the universe being a vast, orderly and tidy instrument working according to rational law, was one that was brought to its present pre-eminence in the popular mind by the eighteenth-century Deists. These were strong, if still only partly informed, believers in Natural Theology, who from the fact that the universe worked so well, at least outside the complex behaviours of life, came to the conclusion that it was the work and manifestation of a superbly rational and inspired Mind. The Cosmos was a proof and exhibition not only of Power, but of Wisdom, a Wisdom equal to the Power, of the display of which there could be no doubt. Such, there is no manner of doubt, was the clear conviction of minds such as Kepler's and Newton's, Halley's and Leibnitz's. Indeed, not until the problem of evil and issues involved with Life began to seep in from their field of this world into the field of the stars, did people begin to think that because the universe was large it could have no Maker that could care for quality, and because it worked with great and manifest order it was impossible that it demonstrated anything but a blind and indifferent Force. The Mind behind the universe, the first astronomers held when they sketched out the methods of His working from the findings of their telescopes, was clearly so powerful that He might be omnipotent, and as clearly so competent in making vast and orderly patterns that He might also be omniscient. They had discovered nothing to suggest that He was neither of these things and much that would propose such conclusions. To a world as ordered as it was to eighteenth-century thinkers, the fact that it was highly probable that the Maker and Minder of the universe was Eminently Wise and Powerful, had to suggest that it was almost as necessary to think of such a Being as Good. Surely one so Rational and so possessed of Power to make actual what His Wisdom approved and planned would not be backward in dealing well and justly with all His creatures? 'Shall not the Judge of all the earth do Right?' So, *a fortiori*, shall not the Maker of so much order see that all parts have justice and order and a fitting beauty given to them?[1]

Such a Being would then care for values, for if He cares for Truth and Order and the Beauty which accompanies such spacious and creative Economy, He certainly cares for Goodness.

We must repeat that it is only as the eighteenth century wears on and approaches its last quarter that the ideas which till then had seemed to give it a classic content, and assurance of an ultimate optimism, begin to wither and that doubts arise. It is profoundly interesting to note that at least since the eleventh century when each of these centuries reaches its seventies, a new power of expansion—and so of necessity, of disintegration in its canon of understanding—begins to be apparent. With Adam Smith's thought and even more with Townsend's there are raised questions that will lead men to doubt that Life is an ordered process. A shadow falls on the bright rationalism of the Deists.

It was right that the simple optimism based on astronomy should have to face up to the more complex problems that were about to be presented by biology. For roughly speaking the science of the eighteenth century was at its best in astronomy.

---

[1] Sir Edmund Whittaker in the 1946 Donnellan Lectures (Trinity College, Dublin) has indicated that, of Aquinas's Five Proofs of the Existence of God, the Proof from Order has lately obtained confirmation beyond what Aquinas himself hoped. For Thomas says that the starting of the ordered Cosmos, creation, could only be established by revelation. But as present-day scientific cosmogony studies show that the universe cannot have existed from an infinite past, at least if the present laws of nature were in play, then there must have been a time when the whole process was initiated. Also the all-over validity of common mathematical principles for the whole Cosmos would show that a single Mind patterns the entire layout.

There it found its distinctive triumphs. The nineteenth was to see its interests, its achievements in observation and, it must be owned, its extensions of dogmatism chiefly in biology. The mistake would seem to lie not in studying biology, and therefore in raising the problems of Life and suffering to which the answer given by 'the fair, inhuman heavens' was all too wide and unspecific. This closer inspection was bound to come. That a thinker as wise, subtle and kindhearted as Bishop Berkeley could dismiss the problem of evil (with the easy argument that as it was so necessary for man to learn by Law therefore he would have to suffer till he understood how not to violate it) shows a mind so delighted with discovered order that it was willing to pay any price if only that order and its goodness be not questioned. We who have so often submitted to human tyranny when the choice seemed for us between order and disorder have no right to blame the Bishop. The real mistake was one which we shall study at the beginning of the next chapter, the mistake of thinking that there is only one 'science' and that therefore it is possible and right to transfer the criteria, say, of astronomy to those of biology. If the outer universe, which is non-reproductive and non-sensory, moves by simple laws, then these, too, explain living processes, and living processes are therefore moved with as little volition by themselves as stars or comets. The movements of the stars we have seen involve no moral issue because they have neither free will, connation nor sensation. But living creatures certainly seem to show they have the last two. And the type of living creature with whom we are most concerned, man, certainly possesses the last two in far higher degree than any other animal and he always acts as though he had the first. Had biologists studied Life without the presuppositions which they had taken over from astronomy, had they been true empiricists —they would no doubt have uncovered the problem of evil. But that would not have made them, off-hand, assume that God could not exist. There would have been a problem, not a conclusion. But, having decided that the nature of the universe could be fully understood by astronomy, that mechanic physics was the basic explanation of all movements, and then having found that living things move and run into accidents and pain and ruin and death, then these good observers, but far from clear thinkers, assumed that there could not be a God. It was *possible* that there was a God as long as He was moving the heavens on a vast and orderly plan. For it was clear that the stars did not suffer, as clear as that man did suffer and all animals, being like man, must suffer too.

We must also remember that the age of the dawn of the Sciences of Life is also the age of what called itself Sensibility and we call emotionalism. Men were emotionally tired of Reason and wished to be romantic. They had reason for their reaction—for Reason, though it had made sense of the outer world and was promising control over that world, had not explained man's inner world nor given him control over himself. They were then full of protest. And one of the commonest ways in which Romanticism expresses its protest is by sympathizing with the 'wrongs' and sufferings of everybody and everything. It not only 'dies of a rose in aromatic pain', it sobs that flowers can fade, gushes over mice and kittens—though the relation of the two is anything but a sentimental one—and even wishes to lavish sympathy upon the evening star—a splendid exhibition of illuminated carbon dioxide—or the sunset. It does so because it feels Reason has failed it. And indeed Reason had failed to induce man to be as rational as the universe which Reason revealed. A sentimental age when it romanticizes is really an age relapsing from an attempt at self-order into a passionate individualism. And, as one determined to assert the ultimate and indeed exclusive value of the individual, it has a horror of death and indeed of anything, education, discipline, growth or judgment, that might change its precious self into something else. Individualism is the final value and therefore things which are not individualized must be made so and kept so. Hence it is always extrapolating and projecting itself into all around it and commiserating with everything that must change—looking on change as a horror and clinging to the past, longing to restore what has already become something else, wishing to put chicks back into shells, children into their cradles, adults into youth.

And with the dread of death goes also the dread of pain. Sensibility always ends by becoming pure sensationalism. Feeling is everything, Sense is not worth bothering over. At the end this results in pure sensualism, and often in great cruelty.

Hence what could happen when these two things came together: (1) the emotional wish to sympathize with everything, to treat Life as a tragedy and order as a tyrant, to despise the idea of law and believe that freedom meant the right and duty to follow every impulse and be 'natural', and with this (2) the new interest in the Sciences of Life, which new interest nevertheless intellectually took over the canons of the physics made to fit the facts of astronomy? There was bound to be confusion.

We may say then that the point we have reached in our argument allows us to say this: If we are to know whether there is meaning in nature, we have to discover two things about the universe. First, when we look at this universe we have to ask: Is it *impossible* that it could be a manifestation of a Mind Wise and Good? We have seen that it is not impossible. There is evidence of order, pattern, design and process. The greater part of the universe seems to be background, as far as we can see; and beyond that we must take care, at this point, not to go, or we cease to be empiricists. In the part that we are directly up against—the planet we live on—there seems much Beauty, perhaps more than in outer space and among the stars. There is also more wonderful ingenuity of processes, for reproduction is certainly more wonderful than fission, explosion or expansion. And no one can deny that there is manifest, as nowhere else as far as we can see, an intensity of Goodness, the presence of selfless devotion. This is a quality which in our age, still heavily weighted with sentiment against sense, we often rate higher than meaning or understanding. Yet of course in our world all these things are met by their opposites. True, the more we study Beauty the harder it is to be sure whether there is anything which is not beautiful if only the eye is sufficiently trained to see it. And as to Truth, again we see that the very complexity of the problem may mask its richness rather than expose its chaos. Truth is usually defined as 'correspondence'. If we could rise to the height of the great argument, then, as musicians are inclined to say there may be no discords if you had the power to listen with real power to resolve, so, too, Truth may be everywhere. Truth delighting the mind with the fitness of things as does Beauty with their seemliness. Everything may be 'fitting' because nothing may, ultimately, be inapposite. But about Goodness, there we find the true tug of war. And it is there undoubtedly the issue must be fought out. When people speak of badness they do not primarily mean ugliness or error. Though these things may lead to badness, badness itself *per se* is the desire to damage. It is malice, hatred of good, the love of seeing others unhappy and frustrated. It is before that power, if power it be (and not a lack that somehow appears as positive malignancy), that we find our courage quailing and our faith failing. It is when we see the apparently innocent enduring torture, worst of all when it is inflicted by another conscious creature but adequately daunting when by disease the victim is helplessly consumed, it is then that we begin to say there cannot be a God. The beauty of the world, the majesty of the heavens, the order of the stars, the power of the human mind, the skill of its works, the ingenuity of the forms of life, shake like a mirage, and behind we dare not look, fearing to see some awful revelation of heartless indifference or, worse, contemptuous amusement.

It is then at this point that we have to decide our next question. Granted that, till we came to study Life and sensate creatures, we could say by studying the outer 'dead' universe that God was certainly not an impossibility—is that enough? Can we not, and must we not, go further and have to ask, Is He an improbability? As long as we looked at the stars we could say, they themselves are a wonderful machine, so wonderful that we feel that there must be a Mind behind them and working them. But when we look at Life and think of the Machine Minder and see the kind of muddle that goes on in Life, then, though we may allow He exists, we have to say that though He may be wise what is the evidence that He is good? We have seen that there is one point that most people who stage such discussions leave out: They have assumed that God directly drives and orders all the world (and indeed all Life) by the same laws that He runs the stars, and, because these other things have no freedom, so must it be with man. There is no wrong done stars or rocks, because they are not conscious. But man is conscious and so a wrong is done him. The point left out is that as he is conscious, so, too, he may not be tied as are the stars. His suffering might be due to his freedom. It is possible that when you are tied, really tied, you are unconscious: and, conversely, when you are conscious, really conscious, you are really free.

This is a big and nodal issue and belongs to the next two chapters. Here it has to come in, in this form, because it bears on what this chapter has to define—the nature of proof. We have seen that when we view Life (and being living we cannot leave it out and be content with stargazing) we cannot be content with saying that it is possible there is a God, no, not even with saying that it is probable, from the order and beauty of things, that there is a good God. Our probability must be of a certain height. It must not be content to rule in physics and there to establish truth and a kind of beauty. It must also be more than a bare likelihood in the Sciences of Life and the study of consciousness. We must prove that there is not only more order than chaos, more beauty than ugliness and more goodness than evil, more joy and creativity than pointless pain, we must show that there is more meaning than non-meaning, more positive love than either wickedness or indifference in the scheme as a whole.

But when that is allowed then we must turn to the other side. More than this no critic has a right to ask and for two reasons. The first is of the nature of proof and though it has been the motto of this chapter it must be repeated again because it is so often overlooked in argument. Complete proof, hundred-percent demonstration, the power to explain every possible exception, has never existed in the establishment of any Natural Law. They are all probabilities; they all have exceptions; they all can only claim that they have worked more or less so far. But we are right in trusting them so long as we keep an open mind. If the facts which are considered anomalous are gaining, then the

'Law' must be modified. If the exceptional facts gain a majority and hold it, then the Law must go and a new one take power— as in modern physics when it demoded classic physics. Further, and this has not been mentioned yet but will order our inquiry from this point, the facts about physics—in spite of the revolution in the Laws during the last generation—attain to a very considerable height of probability. It is true, as Eddington illustrates, that once in so many, many quadrillions of times a brick instead of falling to the earth might fly up from the ground. You can take no action for breach of contract with the universe if you happen to be present when one of the principles fails to work, or works backwards. You were never guaranteed that it wouldn't. You were only told you could back your luck pretty heavily that the sun would rise to-morrow—though of course one day it pretty certainly will not. But when we come to the facts of the Sciences of Life then the height of invariability, the probability about which we can prophesy, is much lower and less. As an observational fact we have to own—whether we can make use of the information or not—that with Life something of the indeterminate and unforeseeable is far more in evidence. This element, hated by mechanists, is now recognized we all know as far down, right down, into the bases of physics.[1] But there it is so slight that on any life-size scale—on any scale that it makes an obvious difference to us (provided we don't go monkeying with the atom and such invisibles) we can leave it out of account. But when we come to Life which matters to us so much more than matter, and our own living beings as men— then the element of invariability and so the chance of discovering Iron Law, is far less. And, finally, when we come to the third great division of scientific study—the knowledge of mind—there the variabilities, for all we know, may be so great that the hope of making psychology a science in the way we have made physics, may be based upon a completely false analogy. We do not know—and we must then wait. But meanwhile we can say that

[1] Heisenberg's Principle of Indeterminacy runs: 'The more accurately we determine the position of a stream of electrons, the less can we determine the momentum and vice versa.'

the nearer we get to where the shoe really pinches[1]—to that suffering and that frustration and that outrage of values—from all of which only man at his height of sensibility and mind can suffer—the less we find evidence that he is tied by Iron Law to whirl like an Ixion on a wheel of endless torture or helpless, like the good Titan Prometheus, to hang waiting for the eagle of a vindictive Zeus to tear his liver.

We have then a balance of probabilities, high in what least concerns us and where we most value order, less in where our physical bodies and our minds meet in biology, and least where we feel we need freedom most—and where as a matter of fact we all feel, whatever our theory, that we have it most.

That is what we have. We have a right to ask that we should not have to prove more than what has always been taken to be proof. What is required of us, and no more can be required, is that we should meet the common standard of demonstration required of and by both sides: by those who sought to show there was meaning and those who sought to deny it. Biology has never been able to be really mechanistic, for it always allowed that there was a striving. Even the doctrine of Natural Selection grants that there is striving, the struggle to survive, through which, however blindly and brutally, something wrought and won and became. That is the undeniable fact, however much we may try to explain it away—the lowest slime has ended in man. Only religions of extreme 'Idealism', the philosophy most repugnant to science, have ever taught the view that man is an utterly degraded creature, that Life is now a phantasm of evil and that once in the beginning the earth was walked by gods while to-day even in our highest type we are base, we have in 'Aristotle only a ruined Adam'.

If, then, this life is a struggle and a striving—to attain perfection beyond what man is—to restore him to his pre-fallen estate as the old religions say—then we should expect that no more proof would be available—'would be provided', glosses religion —than would bring out from man the effort to know more and to become more. Here we are on common pragmatic ground.

[1] This point is developed further at the close of Chapter Five.

We know in order that we may live and we are let teach ourselves that we may grow. Therefore it must be a partial knowledge that we have—or are provided with. The first step it is
true is given to us. We are given tools and we are shown a way
and then we must open it up ourselves to the top of the moun-
tain of vision. He who says, 'I will not move till I'm shown the
final vision', will have taken away from him even the sketch
map he was given and the tools. Life clearly shows that—the
fossils are the Lot's wives of those in whom striving, physiological faith, failed. Faith, then, is the choice of the Nobler Hypothesis because it does not outrage the facts, nor, when it is true faith,
suppress them, as narrow science and narrow theology do. But,
putting them all before it in order, it makes choice of that pattern
and plan which may be the more costly but is the more meaningful, the most inclusive, the largest, grandest pattern of meaning. Belief, too, proves to be an illuminating word. As Faith
turns out to be creative Hypothesis (as Faith is the question—
challenge: 'What meaning do you put on the facts? The larger
or the smaller? The less grand or the nobler? The one that takes
in Life and Consciousness or the one that would pull them down
and dismiss them as aberrants of material movement?'), so it is
with Belief. The word means 'choice', 'lief' being the Saxon
word for 'choice' or 'love'. 'I would rather have it so,' says the
soul, and so, out of two possible meanings, chooses one. So thus
we see choice, the power to throw one's weight, always comes in.
One decides. From the facts as they stand visible from our common standpoint, there is just a balance in favour of a larger
meaning. True, from this low standpoint it is a narrow one and
one you can dismiss if you wish to be content with a smaller,
meaner, more self-regarding meaning. Meaning of some sort you
will have to elect for. Mechanism or materialism or any other
theory are not to be found out in nature. There only were facts,
data, in a wild plenitude of apparent incoherence. So whether I
say: There is a great and complete design, or say, There is none,
because the whole thing is a machine, I have made a choice, I
have, out of the facts, selected and chosen a picture which I then
fill in to establish my case. But the choice was a choice. One or

the other picture of things was not forced on me. And further, it seems demonstrable that the evidence—even when one does nothing about it, doesn't stir a finger to turn a stone or turn one's head enough to see another star—the evidence even at this ground point does show a slight balance in favour of sense against nonsense and in favour of showing more sense if we would trouble to move to a slightly more favourable point for observation.

If then we are in a world of striving, where Life grows to greater apprehension by struggle, then we should expect that we should find just such a set-up. All science has advanced, we have seen, by using the Law of Probabilities. All the spectacular results of science have been based on nothing more than that. And further and deeper, all the triumphs of Life, without which there could have been no triumphs of science, have also been based on striving from a lesser knowledge to a fuller, and, through that striving, not only gaining new knowledge but also new faculty, and not merely new faculties but also new being, new life, new consciousness.

We have now seen the two reasons why the Balance of Probability is what we should expect as enough, and, rightly enough, for us to start with, in our search for a comprehensive meaning. Any other information, either less or more, would frustrate the process of living in which we find ourselves and in which we see ourselves as part of the picture of that pilgrimage which we see stretching behind us in the record of Life.

Having then established that what is needed for intellectual discovery and also for moral progress would be a knowledge of Life and its setting which would make it more likely than not that a God exists, we have now the frame of our inquiry and can turn to see whether the evidence gives us this.

Chapter Four

THE WORLD OF LAWFUL FREEDOM

We have now seen two things. In the first place, it has become clear that what we have to establish is that there is a probability that this experience, in which we find ourselves, is, on the whole, one that makes sense, has purpose, expresses values, and, further, we have *not* to establish more than this and ought not. Secondly, we have found that this probability has to be established in three fields or areas and that it need not and should not be of equal height in each of them. For the experience we are undergoing, it is clear, is threefold and in three layers. There is first the outermost layer, the environment, outer nature which seems to be orderly, repetitive, unconscious, inorganic and, as crystallographers (those scientists whose specialty is to study the structural pattern on which solids tend to compose) say periodic, working in a closed circle. There is then the second layer, that of the living body and bodies—a link between what those bodies contain (or make an anchor for) the soul, and the physical environment. The specific characters of a living body are its power of growth, of repair and, essentially, its capacity to reproduce, whereby, when it has reached the full range of growth and must decline, it displays its third and more remarkable power of defying death. The third layer is consciousness itself. This is so intimate with us, it lies so close to our being that indeed we can hardly regard it as a layer at all. We take it as the core, as ourselves. This is the reason why it has proved so difficult to study analytically.

It is necessary to draw attention to this fact of the triple nature, the tri-concentric plan of our actual experience, for it is commonly disregarded. And it is most often overlooked when dealing with the question as to whether there is discernible meaning in our experience and if so whether that meaning is 'Good'. Because of this disregard, this oversight in analysing our actual situation and recognizing with what we find ourselves presented, we have tended—unconsciously—to carry over the *deductions*, made from the data of the outermost circle, as rules and criteria ruling what data may be found in the two inner circles. Further, we must note that in the selection of data to be studied there may be and nearly always is a canon of selection, an *a priori* conception as to what shall be thought worth while studying and what shall be treated—and dismissed—as insignificant. This, of course, is to introduce at the very start, and to use as a powerful censor, a standard, not of observability—the only standard that true empiricism can admit—but a principle of value. This may be necessary; it probably is. If it is, it tells strongly in favour of purpose, meaning and value being of the nature of things. But if it is, then we must examine far more carefully than did nineteenth-century scientists the relation between observer and data, between objective and subjective. And certainly we must not say that we are interested only in facts, and that making any collection of facts is pure scientific research when as a matter of fact we do not act on such a rule.

Psychology has now shown that man is a pattern-making animal. Further, it has shown that by the way men make their patterns they may be divided into two main classes. Thirdly, it has been found that these two classes give us a very useful distinction whereby we can estimate two fundamentally different forms of character and indeed of vitality. There is the 'expansive' type, the acceptor, and there is its polar opposite, the 'compressive', the selector, the critic. The expansive is the hypothecator. Out of a random pattern, such as a blot, this type makes a picture which includes every part of the blot's contour, but *adds some further detail* to complete its 'eidetic' picture. On the other hand, the compressive type is the abstractor. Given a blot in which to see the outline of a scene, this type makes his picture also. But having made it, he says, Part of the blot's contours *have to be left out,* because they are not needed to make the design. The one type is then creative and the other critical. This is not to say that one can be used without the other. As far as we can see they are necessary for each other and in a really balanced nature they would be found combined and used, if not simultaneously, at least alternately. But we may add that the expansive type should have the initiative.[1] Without it there can be no advance. For though conservation and compression and stabilization are needed, if they are treated as the whole of the process they finally exhaust the power even to persist. To-day thought is so much dominated by the processes of physical science and that science is so much dominated by that critical analysis that can divide but not combine, that we see in consequence a world whose thought is largely arrested, whose hope is much like despair and whose faith has been so long treated as credulity that it can only function if it shrinks from any knowledge of its processes or any attempt to understand its source.

We start this chapter then with two findings. The first is that we ourselves who find, find by a double process—first by an act of integral thought, of insight whereby we glimpse a meaning which, starting from a basis of what we see, extends with a power of invention, creation, design or hypothesis—any of these terms serve here—to cover prophetically what will, might or should be found. Then comes in the second, and complementary, part of the process whereby the critical faculty is set to examine these extensions. What sight has glimpsed actual touch is made to investigate and to reduce to 'manageable' proportions—or to dismiss as misapprehensions. It should be noted, however, here

[1] Whitehead has rightly called the first century of organized scientific research the seventeenth century, par excellence the Century of Discovery because the basic insights were so profound. And he, and all other students of the history of science, have also noted that these insights, these fundamental hypotheses, were made on what later analysis-dominated generations could and would have maintained were totally inadequate evidences. Indeed it is clear that had the standard of censorious criticism (or critical censorship) been as high in the seventeenth as in the nineteenth century the great basic insights would never have been made. For they had to be made by the insight of integral thought and not through critical analysis.

that there should never be by the truly critical mind—the mind of deep judgment—a total dismissal of evidence. The interpretations put on that evidence by the finder of it may well be wrong. The problem then arises why did he so misapprehend and what was the actual nature of the thing that he did so mistake? When science has taken this attitude toward finds, often it has discovered in the fact reported something far more startling in its ultimate meaning than the finder himself imagined. Unfortunately, as has been proved by the history of the study of meteorites and ball lightning—not to mention sorer subjects—scientific thinkers have seldom tried to re-interpret what their informants told them. Once they were certain that the theory was wrong they dismissed with contempt the observation which had suggested the theory of the layman.[1]

The second finding is that this double process of insight and criticism has to work in three conjoined but different fields, that of the inorganic or material, the organic or living and the conscious or psychological.

This distinction of all natural science studies into these three great fields is so important that the rest of this book will be divided into three chapters. In them successively will be distributed the evidence that would suggest that the world we live in, the life that flows in us, and the consciousness which we experience, all show signs that we are environed, vitalized and made aware by and for a purpose greater than ourselves but one in which we can find interest, deliverance, delight and indeed consummation. That this threefold distinction is not one made by an amateur, to establish a conclusion helpful to a theory,

---

[1] Lavoisier and his great confrères, indeed all the scientific academies well into the nineteenth century, refused to allow that any stone could fall out of the sky. Their reason was so obvious—to them—that any evidence, they felt, must be dismissed without examination. For those who reported these anomalies saying they had seen them, clearly thought that such objects were fragments detached from the sky's solid blue vault. Had, however, these scientists of six generations ago accepted and investigated the *fact* they would have been started on the way to a number of unsuspected discoveries about the minor planets, the state of the upper atmosphere, the structure of the earth and the possible fate of the whole planetary system.

pleasing to the moral fancy, may be shown by the fact that it has for a number of years been recognized and emphasized by the students of that latest of the philosophies, the Philosophy of Science. Dr. Herbert Dingle, who has lately taken the chair of the Philosophy and History of Science at London University, has throughout his studies in this important subject made these three divisions basic in his interpretation of the process and development of scientific thought. We shall give the rest of this chapter therefore to the environment, the inorganic frame in which all life and all the consciousness we know, find themselves enclosed and indeed encapsuled.

We can best and most succinctly consider this if we start from where we are. It is always most objective not to take up some position which as a matter of fact, we do not occupy, such for example as the rim of the universe or the nucleus of the atom, but where we find ourselves. When we do that we note a fact which may be of great importance but is seldom commented on. Man seems to be in a middle position. Often we are told that the earth's position is arbitrary and unimportant to the point of insignificance, when we compare it with that of the giant planets even—such as Jupiter—let alone the mass of the sun itself, let even more alone the size of the solar system, the size of the Galaxy and the size of the Space-Time universe. Hence, runs the rhetoric—it is not argument—what must one think of a creature to whom even this submicroscopic grain, the earth, appears to be a majestic globe?

But that kind of peroration was more suited to the age of sensibility than to one of accurate and actual observation. For the size of the universe bears, according to cosmogonists, some intimate relation to its structure—it is not vaguely vast but is as big as it can and has to be. As has been noted earlier, such a thinker as Eddington (of whom, when he died, his astronomer peers said that his mind perhaps more than any other contemporary's held in fruitful balance the observational knowledge of astronomy with the power of mathematical insight and interpretation of the observation), spent the final and most fruitful years of his life in laying the foundations for the argument that the size of the universe bears an exact relationship to the number of electrons. How this discussion will end not even the cosmogonists seem yet to be sure. But one thing seems to be agreed: that only by our understanding the ultimate charge out of which the universe is composed may we understand the proportions of that ultimate structure. This is, of course, only to find fulfilled the prophecy made by that remarkable thinker already referred to —Malebranche—who when shown the first microscope said wisely, 'This is an end of Size'.

In his first popularization of the mathematical thought which was building up the new physics[1] Eddington naturally drew attention to this fact and pointed out that man could consider himself very vast or very small according to the direction in which he chose to look. If he looked 'up' at the stars and hunted about he could find vast masses of faint flame—so faint that they would make a good vacuum if compared with the dense air we breathe—the giant stars, the largest known 'objects' in the universe. Against such oceans of ultradiluted gas man may consider himself as quantitatively utterly insignificant. But if he looked 'down' at the electron, then man's body becomes a vast universe over which he broods like a creative demiurge. Eddington suggested that the hippopotamus would neatly ride the beam between an electron at the one end and at the other end the giant red star Betelgeuse. But now that Betelgeuse has had to yield the place to still larger if vaguer stars and no one knows whether the electron may not lose pride of smallest place to the neutron (as it has no electric charge and so could be less than an electron) maybe man is the middle term of all things even in this material matter of mass—leaving aside that he alone seems to have the mind in which neutron and giant star have any real distinction.[2]

Once we have recognized that even physically we are in a very central place we can look out from our point of cosmic vantage and see what else we may discover as to our bearings.

[1] *Stars and Atoms*, by Arthur Stanley Eddington.
[2] Some stars are apparently much bigger than we see them as their outer layers are a non-luminous but fairly transparent gas.

The next thing is not less remarkable. It is a further confirmation of our centrality. We discover that from where we stand there go 'up' (or in one direction) wave-lengths of vibrating energy—waves that grow larger and larger until we already know of such that are miles across from crest to crest. We know these waves from radio work on them and for us in twenty years they have come to be commonplaces. While at the other end, 'down' from us we find the short-waves, smaller and smaller, more and more penetrating. And with them we have an ever longer utilitarian familiarity—for they have been known to us since Röntgen's work at the end of the last century. Yet these waves carried us into a new cosmos. We learned that out of such invisible but intense rhythms the whole of the universe was composed, that space was full of them, that light, without which our whole science would go blind, was but a small selection, a fine snippet in that inexhaustible tapestry weaving itself ceaselessly, with the visible universe embroidered like a fine stitching of gold thread on its fathomless black velvet.

So once again we saw ourselves central and this time our centrality suggested a further possibility. We found that our animal senses were such—were 'electro-magnetic detectors'[1]—that out of that middle and minute section of the wave abyss to which they responded, they composed the light, coloured, warm and sounding world. Again to quote from Eddington, he pointed out that we take for granted air, water and earth as things of such almost monotonous frequency in our experience, matter of such common sense, that even the Greek mind took them to be elements. Nevertheless, this is a very provincial assumption. As far as we may learn from our power of scanning the universe, in which our world is a sub-speck, air, water and earth are perhaps as rare as our earth is small. Our spot, if we use common sense, in the accurate sense in which that word was coined by the late medieval thinkers (as the consensus of the senses), is a very peculiar spot, of peculiarly rich variation of loveliness, and, as we shall see in a moment, of peculiarly strange provision as a protected observation post.

[1] See next chapter for elucidation of this phase.

Even from the planetary position this becomes clear. For our earth we find holding a middle position not only in size but in orbit. On the giant planets not only might the atmosphere prove too dense, asphyxiatingly dense, for an oxygen-fired creature to function. The gravitation-field of such masses might not only hold down gases dangerous to us—Jupiter and Saturn it seems clear from spectro-analysis are wrapped in dense frozen fogs of methane gas—but bodies of such weight would have such a gravitation pull on any creature that it is hard to see how any animal could ever raise itself off the ground and become upright. Of the importance of the upright position there will be more to say in the next chapter. Smaller planets—of which we know numbers now—cannot hold an atmosphere because their mass being so light they cannot prevent the finer gases such as oxygen leaving them naked. Such seems the state of the moon, a body equal to a number of the smaller planets and one on which no atmosphere has been detected, save possibly in the sheltered corners of some of the giant ravines and craters.

When, then, we look out up and down the plane of our orbit and the orbits of our companion satellites we find ourselves in between the two possible competitors to optimum place; on the outer side Mars and on the inner, Venus. Mars we now know has a temperature of some 60 degrees Fahrenheit on the equator—the thermocouple has shown that. The snow caps on the poles are water frozen—not frozen carbon dioxide. That has been shown by spectro-analysis. They melt as the North and South Poles turn, seasonally, to the sun. And in the hemisphere being exposed to the sun the generally reddish tinge of the planet becomes blotted with a greenish hue. This might be vegetation producing foliage. The trouble about that argument was the thermocouple's accuracy as a heat detector. For it showed that the heat over such temporarily green areas was lower than on the red—presumably desert areas. Now, however, a Soviet botanist has shown by careful measurements that with the most northerly—the Arctic firs—such as the Sitka spruce—the leaf has been so modified—or is of such primitive form—that it acts in the opposite way from the leaf of trees in temperate or tropic zones. Instead of cooling the air around it, it actually gives out its own sheath of warmth and so prevents the tree from being destroyed by the intense cold to which it is exposed. As the winters in Mars must be far more severe than any we can at any point on this globe experience—because the distance from the sun is so much greater and the atmosphere is so much thinner and its power of retaining heat so much less—we should expect to find that kind of foliage and tree-form. So we should not be surprised to find these green areas warmer than the red. All observers are agreed that the planet looks red because it is actually rusted—nearly all the oxygen has been taken up and is held in the rocks.

Mars, therefore, the planet that lies next outside us, is a planet at the very end of its life. There may be supermen on it or super-insects. We do not know. The Palomar 200-inch telescope opened in 1948, Dr. E. P. Hubble said, will be able to settle the speculation as to whether there are or are not canals driven down the planet to carry from the poles the water that thaws there each summer. But if man is there, or a creature of intelligence, his story is nearly over. As we shall see later, there may be super-superfine creatures there, of an energy and economy we could never produce here—at least until the parallel advance of climatic austerity and constitutional vital reaction has turned us into creatures of a metabolic efficiency as much above what we are now as we have surpassed the sluggish dinosaurs. But that is in the fabulously far and problematical future and has nothing to do with to-day.[1]

On the other side of us lies Venus—a middling planet in size —both Mars and Venus being somewhat smaller than the earth. And as Mars is becoming unfitted for life as we know it so Venus it seems is not yet ready—its dazzling appearance being due to a cloud which spectro-analysis has shown is made of carbon dioxide. Under that gleaming blanket there may well be going on the kind of preparations which accumulated that mass of water and vegetation, that vast forcing house in which, as far as we can find from our own desiccated record, was the lush

[1] This issue is followed up in the next chapter.

beginning, the basic capital with which we were endowed on this planet before specific animal life appeared.

These are commonplaces of the A B C of planetary astronomy. Still even they are sometimes overlooked when we are taking our bearings. They do suggest that our place is 'oddly central' if, in the old Greek phrase of Aristophanes sneering at the atheists: 'Blind Whirl is King.'

We may then note one more thing before we leave our solar system position. The giant planets seem a pure waste. Granted that Mars was once the favoured station and that Venus might well be the heir apparent, or the throne preparing—why such masses as Jupiter and Saturn? Of course we cannot say for sure. But when such facts are used to point out the clumsy and obvious uselessness of the scheme of things in which we find ourselves, we have a right to use any information that may show that it need not be simply a fool's oversight or a vast demiurgic indifference to any of our values, that made such a frame of things. Granted always that if there is a Mind, His thoughts are not our thoughts nor His ways our ways, nevertheless, if there is any possibility of kinship between us and Him—and if there is not why try to find meaning at all—then, though many of His purposes would be outside our comprehension, those which concern us we should be able faintly to understand. So it may be relevant to our argument to mention here that twenty years ago astronomic observation had apparently established a correlation between the sunspots and the position and pull of the giant planets on the photosphere of the sun.[1] For long before that

[1] The information drawn from special papers on the present state of our knowledge regarding sunspots and the planets was summarized in *Sky and Telescope*, September 1944. It is now agreed (1) that the giant planets exert a 'trigger-action' on the spots, (2) that conversely there are noticeable the following planetary changes at sunspot maxima (*a*) Jupiter's albedo—reflected light—increases, (*b*) Mars' solar caps shrink, (*c*) earth temperature is not increased (see later, in this chapter, on the upper atmosphere as a comprehensive thermostat) but Nile river maximum flood is at sunspot maximum while the Temperate Zone rivers (e.g., the Parana) are at such times at minimum flow.

Further, Dr. C. G. Abbott of the Smithsonian Institute reports from daily

it was known that the sunspots are giant gun-ports through which burst out charges and broadsides of short-wave radiation and that these upset radio, make giant magnetic storms in our atmosphere, and pretty certainly, because such short-wave intensities can touch the genes in the chromosomes in the reproductive cells, can affect the forms of life that can appear. This is a theme which was almost the last extension of science to appeal to that immensely popularizing mind, H. G. Wells, in his final scientific romance *Star-begotten*.

But this again properly belongs to our next chapter. Yet, before leaving it, we must note one more fact that would seem to suggest that our idea of size even in the inorganic may not be the decisive factor as to what can take place in the vast universe of planets. Observations made at Meudon on the sunspots, at the same time as the effect of the giant planets was being studied, seemed to show that even the minute mass of the earth might affect these fabulous whirlpools. For there seemed some evidence that when the earth came fully abreast of these abysses, some of which are so big that twenty earths in line could be sunk in

readings made at a Spanish Cordoba observatory of the spreading of calcium clouds on the sun's surface, that the expansion of these heralds three days in advance noticeable weather changes on the earth and that these changes persist for seventeen days after. We are then it would seem at least headed toward a true Astrology, a real science of the Stars that can begin to link them up with our lives, instead of having to remain contented with a mere numbering or cataloguing of them—Astronomy. How this may develop, how the entire area of outer space may yield us findings invaluable in helping us to understand our health and the future of our race has been suggested by a number of correlations between stars and cells, from, e.g., Dr. W. F. Peterson's (College of Medicine, University of Illinois) correlation of sudden increases in male births with sunspot maxima to the correlation of cancer incidence with exposure to cosmic radiation (Dr. F. H. Figge, University of Maryland Medical School. Cosmic Rays, he shows, increase cancer in mice injected with methylcolanthrine). The increase of male births may be due to the fact that the male sex being the less stable of the two and the additional short-wave radiation making for chromosome upset, more males result, just as atom bomb radiation will go a step further and produce increasing numbers of physiological 'monsters'. Peterson thought social disturbance (war, etc.) increases at such maxima because the nervous system is then also under increasing strain.

them, they seemed to change shape as though it might be possible that even our minute pull did affect them.

A final factor in optimal planet size and position may be suggested by the fact that a planetary mass and its position from the sun has been discovered to be, apparently, a far more delicate balance than the astronomers of even the nineteenth century suspected. The tidal stresses set up inside the liquid or gaseous cores of planets by the pull of the sun against the centrifugal draw evidently can disrupt the whole body. Outside Mars there lies the Asteroid Belt. Twenty-five years ago Ludblad of Stockholm estimated that this must be the wrack of wreckage left by a planet, or planets, that exploded. Now (see Nature, 31 August 1946) Dr. Barnothy of the Institute of Experimental Physics of Budapest has also calculated that the asteroids were once a single mass which he calls Asteroida which blew up when it had contracted to a body about the size of Mars.

We may, then, be in a much more balanced, delicate and central-beam-riding position than the first casual Copernican glance made us think.

When we come to our actual situation, when we climb down from the stars and begin to look about at our actual lodging, that feeling is greatly strengthened.

After all, do the stars really matter? We are fond of talking about their size and so getting a kind of thrill, as the French would say a *frisson*. It is the faint and cultured form, the 'china-tea' flavour, of the shudder we feel at real horror. The 'raw whisky' palate, the rank and popular taste responds in the same way by getting its thrill from reading of someone else's murder. We like to think of ourselves as gallant waifs and castaways, drifting through the more than Arctic night to our Doom! We must never forget—it is a commonplace now of any careful study of Tragedy—that man when he finds it too hard—or too costly—to find meaning, falls back on feeling himself the misused gallant; the tragic fellow defying the stars; the one sublime being of sense being crushed by senseless mass! 'Comedy' as we see from the last world masterpiece in that genre, means not farce and fun but that in the end Meaning triumphs. So Dante saw his great Trilogy. It is certainly no joke with one-third given up to Hell. But he holds, and his age held with him, that even if one-third is terrible the supreme meaning of the rest redeems the whole from squalour and frustration. His meaning of redemption was no doubt too narrow, far too narrow. With that there will be an attempt to deal before this essay closes. But that Meaning is the thing that matters and not pleasure, nor pain, nor the clever joke that tries to laugh everything off; that is the fact that we have to keep in mind if we are to remain sane and have the surplus energy that can help others.

Copernicanism, we must then remember, really took the stars off men's minds. And undoubtedly they had managed to get the stars terribly on their minds. Astrology may be nonsense but it is no joke. Were it true, the harshest science could not be more severe. With alchemy you may trick the elements; with demonology you may enslave your ghostly enemy—at least for the time being—but with astrology you can only know, and if the stars are against you, you must bow. For, though they are far beyond your reach you are not beyond theirs and they have you tied to their blazing apron strings. No, it was not a nice picture, however much you might pay the court astrologer to rig your horoscope. Beside it, the rather theatrical sigh with which the high-school mind looks out at 'a vast, mainly empty, emphatically indifferent universe' has about it 50 per cent of affectation and 50 per cent of relief—we can do as we like, the stars don't care a damn and they are the proof there's nothing beyond.

We must then as realists allow that the universe and its stars are in point of fact very small, as a sensuous matter they are insignificant. Venus, our small white neighbour, is 240 times brighter than any other star and, at its best, it just succeeds in being seen as a faintest white fleck in the sky at daytime and at night in casting a faint shadow. The odd and striking thing is that men ever attended to such tiny glow-points that did nothing to them.

So let us turn to our actual lodging. Then at once we find a number of increasingly odd factors about it and the more we

study the invisible the odder our station and coign of vantage
begins to appear. For we must remember that astronomy often
behaves and speaks as though we were really some sort of super-
genie stretched out among the galaxies looking them over and
remarking on their curious lack of variety, their boring tendency to go in for number rather than variety. That point of
view, as we have already noted in the previous chapter, is
somewhat modified with the discovery of more and more odd
stars and stars of matter never known on earth. Still it remains
in the mind of the ordinary man and some of those ordinary
men we must repeat are in some extraordinarily small field quite
often astronomic experts. Astronomy—and we laymen nearly
always assume it as a fact—often speaks as though it were a full
science, able to employ the three methods of science, strict linear
causality, analysis and experiment and that it was able to live
up to T. H. Huxley's definition of the science of his day,
'Organized Common Sense'. It is certainly not that. For as we
have seen, common sense is the consensus of the senses. We look,
then we listen, next we try and get a whiff of the thing—this is
certainly useful with such animals as the skunk—fourthly, if we
are as daringly empirical as a small boy, we try to touch, and
finally, if we are as rash as a baby, giving all in order to know—
we try and taste. Now few of us, when we come to years of dis-
cretion, remain as searching as that. And whether we do or no,
no one has ever been able to apply common sense, the real
thing, not that bundle of prejudices we try to pass off as the
authentic test method, to the stars. Indeed, we are so placed
that we cannot even hear them, much less bring them nearer
home to ourselves by touch, taste or smell. And if we did hear
them they would deafen us. We can see them, but even with
that the first, and, as our proverbs found out thousands of years
ago, not the least treacherous of our senses, we cannot be sure
that we do see them as they actually are. It is a primary commonplace of astronomy that you must always 'calculate for
displacement', that is, the star is never where it appears to be.
Nor can we suppose offhand that its shape is as it appears to
us. For not only do we see it through a lens which we have made,

the telescope, and not only is that instrument so limited that according to present astronomic knowledge it will never be able to show us the disk of any star, but we see the stars always through another lens. Their shape is not known by observation but by deduction; but further, we cannot really be sure what their colour is. For the main lens and filter through which we view them is the atmosphere and the more we study that, the less can we regard it as a clear and true medium. The atmosphere is now known to be a most complex and selective lens only admitting those radiations which are not harmful to Life. This—as far as giving objective knowledge of anything the other side of it—is like saying that the stories told by a cautious nurse to a two-year-old child are realistic reports of what adults say and do. She is telling it what at its stage of gentle growth would help it to grow—not what actually goes on. Still further, as we saw a little earlier, our eyes are such that much that makes up actual stars would probably remain invisible to us even were we able to look at them from the other side of our curtain atmosphere.

Finally, we cannot say that our approach to the stars, our astronomy, is a real and full science because it breaks down so badly on the three tests as to what a science should be if it is to establish its claim to objective knowledge. For, firstly, we cannot experiment with stars. Emphatically they are clean out of our reach. They go as they go and not as we choose. And, secondly, we cannot trace their behaviour by causal deduction. As already noted, we cannot watch a star grow old. Sometimes we suddenly see one burst, but what led to the outbreak we do not know. Some stars we say are old and some young, but the biography of no one star has been written or ever will. For we cannot live long enough, we who live too short a time even to witness one year of the planet Neptune. The one nebula which can be seen with the naked eye, the central 'star' in the 'sword belt' of Orion, shows on large telescope photographs as a tempest of flame. Spectroscope analysis seems to show that this is, as it looks, an explosion of fire, and that each of these tongues in this typhoon is lashing through space. But though this picture has been studied for more than eighty years—for the first fine drawings were made by observers with the Ross telescope—we have never seen the slightest displacement of the finest edges of one of these fringes of flame. To us they are as still, as to the sub-second blink of the quickest photographic plate appears the beat of the mosquito's wing. The stars are moving, but our life moves too fast for them to be to us other than fixed. The third method, that makes a process 'scientific', analysis, we do attempt to apply to the stars by the brilliant and fertile analogies of spectroscopy. And it is highly probable that if metals burned in a flame in an earthly laboratory give a certain spectrum band, and the light of a star thrown through a telescope and then passed through a prism gives the same spectrum band, then in that star those metals are burning. Of course it is not direct observation even here, but deduction. Here then is the point at which astronomy approaches most nearly to being a truly empirical science.

We have now looked up through the sky-light roof of our lodging and have discovered it is made of an odd glass. It will be worth while to examine it a little further. For here we begin to come across what up to that point was only faintly suggested —that our position may be so suitable, so neatly adjusted to permit growth, that there may be something about it that we have to call by Henderson's[1] well-known title—*The Fitness of the Environment*. We have noted that the atmosphere does prevent

[1] Dr. Henderson's *The Fitness of the Environment—An Enquiry into the Biological Significance of the Properties of Matter* (1927). In any essay of this size attempting to survey in brief outline the whole field of Natural Theology, Matter, Life, and Consciousness, the Inorganic, the Organic and the Psychological, it is impossible to enter with any fullness into the evidence for the strange chemical aptitude of our material surroundings, their odd suitability for Life and its development. Dr. Henderson as a geochemist has compiled a book which is so condensed in its information that if part of his argument is quoted the whole must be cited. The book's profound originality consists not in the fact that any of the information was not commonly known to geochemists, but because, not being biologists, they had not considered whether or no this world was peculiarly devised for Life. No one who was adequate to answer the question had till then thought to ask: If Life fits the Environment and the Environment was there first, does it fit Life?

us having a clear view of the stars, even when it seems to show them most clearly. But when, to go back to the simile, the nurse tells the child only partly what adults actually do, she does try to tell him all that it is safe for him to know. What is screened out is that which might hurt. So with the air above us. We do not know that the sun and the stars do send out radiations inimical to life as well as those essential to life. We have only just begun to list those which can damage us. It begins, however, to look as though we are strangely intolerant creatures—in fact only able to take what we are in these conditions given. At this range, we can take the sun—out on the orbit of the Asteroids we should freeze, on that of Venus we should have to be under continual cloud, on Mercury's we should combust. But even at this the nicely-chosen range round our stove, we have to have a transparent blanket so as to give us just what we can stand—light but very little ultra-violet, heat but very little infra-red. Further, the structure of this blanket is of a very unsuspected elaboration of weave. As Sir George Simpson, head of the British Meteorological Service, said to the writer, it looks as though it is a very complex and efficient thermostat. This seems necessary because as the sun has been found to be a Cepheid—a variable, a pulsing star—its output of heat therefore varies. As we cannot shift out or in to another orbit as the heat rises or falls we have to have a screen—as our tolerance of heat and cold is so slight. It seems that the upper atmosphere supplies that screen. For when the heat increases this draws aqueous vapour from the sea and stores it as a haze-screen high up and when the sun's heat decreases the aqueous vapour falls down to the sea, the sky is clear and more heat comes in. There may also be a method of storing carbon dioxide as it pours out from vol-

As Dr. Henderson sums up, and many of his fellow experts have come to agree, there is proof that 'beneath adaptations peculiar and unsuspected relationships exist between matter and Life'. He adds that the cosmic process is linked with the living organism, and the evolution of the universe and Life are one. Together, the inorganic and the organic, dead matter and living matter are a single development the results of which, if brought about by a living creature, we would call designed. His last word is that we are compelled now to look upon the universe as 'in its very essence . . . biocentric'.

canoes and vegetation, and as this gas helps retain heat so the earth has another possible layer to its blanket. The screens for keeping out deadly short-wave radiations, more deadly than cold, are however more remarkable. And, without these, life could never have started. For though low germs such as fungus spores can bear interstellar cold the cold of liquid helium— and the heat of boiling water and above, a few flashes of the right short-wave length and they are done for.

It is only twenty years ago that meteorologists became certain of a fact that seemed to contradict one of the clearest assumptions of common sense—that the higher you went the colder it would be, until, without break in your fall in heat as you rose in height, you would find yourself out in the cold of space. Then came the stratosphere where the cold, though terrific, did not increase as it should have. Next came the discovery that in the outer layers of all there was a belt, perhaps not more than some miles thick, perhaps the Ionosphere, where the heat must be by our standards, positive. If the deductions from the way meteors burn, as they hit that hot torpedo net, are to be relied on, then there must be a belt above us, in which the temperature is no less than that of boiling water. In going to the moon we shall have to remember, then, not only to guard against being refrigerated but also against being quick-boiled. And it may not be extravagant to call this upper veil a torpedo net for we have to be screened from short-wave radiations but also from more obvious missiles. As we have seen, astronomy little more than a century ago was outraged at the thought that there could be meteorites. The sky had no roof and those who claimed that chunks of it had fallen on the earth were obviously self-convicted superstitious liars. We know that such a fine researcher as Lavoisier so expressed himself. But astronomy to-day suspects that perhaps a billion fragments of meteoric refuse do fall on the earth in the twenty-four hours. The snows of the upper glaciers have been found full of that nickel iron dust which makes the substance of the metallic meteor. What is the effect of being hit by a fair-sized falling star we can judge from the Arizona pit and the much more certain scar left by the Siberian monster that fell in 1908.[1] It is surely odd that, as the sky has evidently to be full of these deadly derelicts rushing about, and we have to drive along these infested traffic lanes, we should have been wrapped in a veil of air and that that part of it, too thin to fly in or to breathe in, nevertheless proves to be an amazingly efficient protector, a protector so unobtrusive that it allows us such a clear look through that only in this generation did we suspect that it was as strong as it was invisible.

In short, we may say that we are a kind of egg-creature, a pupa, which must have, for this stage of its growth, warmth and a gentle light. The egg lets the chick have warmth but not the light, which at that stage would sterilize the germ. Likewise in the vegetable kingdom, that strange succulent from South Africa makes itself, in the burning desert, an eye to let light but not the parching heat down to its centre where its seed cannot form unless it has light but little heat. So we too are similarly situated. If we shrink from praise as being anthropomorphic, we must call our situation one of odd happiness, a one-in-a-billion luck.

We turn from looking up at our roof and look down at our station—and here again we find ourselves in that curiously middle position. Above we have this curious atmosphere to screen us; below we have as curious a lithosphere, a raft of rock, to support us; yes, and to insulate us also—this time against the strange inner heat of our own seat and base, the mother earth. The new notions of geodesy are certainly as odd as those of astronomy. Once we thought of a massive firm earth, a wearily dull uniform lump on which we crawled. All variety was in the film in which we lived. That picture has gone. The world itself has become almost a sprightly object, delicate and sensitive and changeable and as full of unpredictables as an April day. It seems a commonplace now of geology that we are floating on a subsea of fire—a notion surely as unsettling as the Copernican

[1] The moon is probably hit very frequently and Mr. H. H. Nininger, the well-known observer of meteorites, believes that the stones called tektites are chips from the moon, splinters flung off with such violence that some of them have rebounded till they fell into the earth's field and so were captured by us. This gives us some idea of the force of the impact.

shock that the whole bubble floated in the void. The lithosphere, the crust of rock, the raft on which we huddle, floats on the magma. Whether the continents drift or no seems still to be too hot a geological controversy for a layman to venture on.[1] But both sides seem certain that the crust of the earth is extremely flexible. As a summarizing article on vulcanology in the well-known scientific weekly *Nature* said the other day, the basic problems of the nature and meaning of a volcano remain unsolved. A further odd fact may be mentioned: that in many volcanoes the heat of the lava increases as it comes to the surface. These are certainly not 'vents of the infernal fires'. A suggestion made in the discussion over which Dr. E. C. Bullard, F.R.S. presided may throw light on this apparent anomaly. The central heat seems sufficiently insulated never to melt any rocks we know. But when geosyncline conditions thicken the rock then it may melt. Hence the thicker the insulation the greater possibility of volcanoes. Vice versa, the thinner the rock layer the less danger of being fused. Earthquake records would seem to show that the earth is composed of a series of fairly sharply divided layers,[2] and at the centre is the 'nickel-iron core', that central mass—which the moon lacks and maybe some of the planets— that mass which may have something to do with that mystery of the earth, its magnetic field, that field which may have something to do with the nature and powers of life. Indeed it is possible that geodesy is on the brink of a revolution in its science as great as that in physics and indeed started by it. In the *Royal Astronomical Journal* for 23rd March 1945 a discussion was led by Dr. Bullard on 'The Thermal History of the Earth'. The first remarkable fact is that we are so insulated by the lithosphere that only 20 per cent of the observed heat-flow we can measure on the surface can be accounted for by cooling of the central

[1] See latest summary of findings in favour of vast drifts. These findings are based on separation of flora between South and North America and linkage of flora between North America and Eurasia, so they would point to continental movements late in the history of Life. *Nature*, 10th June 1944, pp. 717–18.

[2] In the next chapter when referring to the co-operation of the atmosphere with Life's evolution a newly traced and strange connection between one of the earth's iron layers and our mammalian advance will be noted.

'melt'. The second fact is that the surface heat-flow is mainly to be accounted for by the radioactivity of the crust, the lithosphere itself. Some ten to twenty kilometres depth of granite produces enough heat to account for our surface warmth. Granite is faintly radioactive. Below the granite there may be no radioactive rocks. The continents ride on granite rafts, cups or castors. The oceans are held in basins of basalt—a harder but less radioactive rock. So the heat under the oceans is less. No granite seems to be under the ocean beds. Have we here then once more a thermostat, one complementary to that in the sky, so that our basic heat-flow is kept constant? Later on we shall be considering the relationship of sea to land in the balance necessary to Life and its advances. The ocean kept in basalt coolers, the land mounted on granite warmers may be another balance in this amazing adjustment. Certainly our strange base limits our actual prying into our foundation as much as our skylight prevents us from having anything but a safe, carefully screened view of space and stars. The deepest boring made only goes 15,000 feet down vertically. Compare this with the height of Everest and even more the great deep off Borneo where echo-soundings seem to record a depth of eight to nine miles. It looks as though we shall never bore deeper. The shaft closes in, the air piped down discharges its moisture in the changed pressure, the floor of the shaft rises up. We are pushed back to our place by invisible pressures. Again we see ourselves as creatures of a middle stance, of a curious balance, between an air-screen keeping from us a blasting invisible intangible dark-light and a rock-screen—of perhaps not more than ten miles thickness—keeping us from being incinerated by our own heat and yet supplying a particular warmth. And in that film we wander, and run and finally rush about with such a sense of security and proprietorship and being on our own, by ourselves and for ourselves, that free of all other care and scruple, bored with our security, indifferent to the wonder of it all, contemptuous of the thought that we may have been provided for and, maybe, are being watched, we make gadgets and set about trying to get rid of one another in wholesale numbers.

Such in very briefest seems to be the purview of our station. If this is all chance—that a creature that can think finds itself in such a delicately balanced and yet favourable position, where it can grow and see and yet not act irrevocably: is kept from flinging itself into the void; held back from upsetting things too quickly to learn what it is up to—if this be blind fortune, well, surely words have to be stretched somewhat to meet old prejudices, old prejudices that have decided that the universe cannot contain any Purposer other than man.

Yet with that phrase, 'Where he can see and yet not act irrevocably' we do enter the most vital part of our inquiry, indeed the point where the controversy between those who hold to the large and noble meaning and those to the less and the mean meaning are at issue. For the old Natural Science of the nineteenth century could allow that the scene in which man found himself was ready to let him alone. The previous cataclysmic world picture, for example, in geology, had gone in favour of Uniformitarianism. The world would stay put for as long as the species would last: man had an indefinite lease. The sun giving out was the one concern, and Kelvin had to own—as he did not know that it was radioactive—that it was a puzzle that it managed to be so economical with its fuel. In the end, millions of years ahead, there would be a quiet heat-death and meanwhile man could tidy up his earth, uninhibited by taboos, enlightened by reason, informed by science. That was the not very penetrating foundation on which Humanism has raised its rather ambitious—and up-to-date ill-substantiated claims.

The men who actually thought, however, found a darker cast permeating their minds as they reflected on 'nature's ways'. To leave aside till the next chapter the problem of the Life process, of the ways and methods whereby living creatures sustain themselves, enjoy themselves, increase and change, and man appears and advances, we have here to see the beginning of this problem. For it begins to appear in the environment itself. Granted that man is oddly placed, is he not fixed, 'framed', as the slang os violence says? In this strange scene in which he finds himself if he more than on a scaffold, given no doubt a fine view of the crowd, the cart he came in, even the houses and the hills around and incidentally of the gallows too? But what does that serve the poor victim? He is there to be—in the hangman's phrase of the eighteenth century—'turned off'! For if the laws of nature are uniform and man is simply a resultant of these and if they have ground along for millions of years, why then he is here for a moment and in that moment he can only look on. He has neither freedom nor the time, were it granted him, to make that freedom in any wise effective. The glaciers will again grind to the finest silt for the ocean floors the highest towers he can build, the finest agricultures and manufactures that he can plan.

So first we must glance at the Time problem. And it is here that the most startling addition has been made to our knowledge. For some twenty years it was known that the problem of Time had been puzzling increasingly all astronomic thinking. We had just learned to reply to 'What is the universe?' 'A Space-Time continuum.' When back they came at us with 'Which Time?' and 'How many?' Then we were told that such experts as Professor E. A. Milne, F.R.S., were of the opinion that there were needed six forms of Time with which to handle astronomic experience—and there might also be physiological time to be added to the six. Clock time to which we had trusted as something objective all the experts seemed to regard as a pretty enough artificiality and useful in its way for boiling eggs and such minutiae. Then in the last decade, culminating with the present acute controversy—always a sign that something big is coming to birth—the new notion of Time began to show what difference it would make. As far as seems to be agreed there would now be only two times, T. and Tau time. Into the intricacies of these only the mathematician can go. But critics and enthusiastic appreciators both agree that if this new theory is accepted then we shall have to have quite another view of the universe, of the time it takes and of our place in it.[1] We used

[1] See the communication made in *Nature*, 25th May 1946, by Professor Arthur Holmes, F.R.S., Grant Institute of Geology, Edinburgh University, by a 'new method of Earth's age estimation based on Nier's isotopic analyses of lead samples from Galena and other lead minerals of known geological age'.

to think that the stellar universe was practically eternal, the human span insignificant and in between was the geological record. The latest readings through the use of the radioactive evidence of rocks indicates that the first rocks formed 3350 million years ago—that seems the radium-clock recording. Man of course lives seventy years, how old his species is there is now lively controversy, but still most authorities would give it little more than a million years and some not that. All the mammals may not be more than sixty or seventy million years in age. Life in its simplest forms is thought to be traceable back perhaps two thousand million years. There seemed some fair measure of agreement among experts about such scales. And this time-table was stretched across a picture of a sun that somehow spent part of the previous time in distributing planets (about that there has never been agreement since the nebular hypothesis—the simple picture of a sea of fire, curdling into little specks of denser flame —lost expert support). The planets which had, of course, been bits of hardly cooler sun, being smaller, soon cooled. Hence, among other things two conveniences: (1) the small spot on which we and all life can find foothold being already solidified, and (2) the sun, not yet having become so. In short we live and can only live between two events: (1) this piece of the primal sun-stuff having become cool enough to hold us and (2) the large central piece of the sun stuff in turn becoming cool enough to be stood on, when of course we shall freeze. That picture took most of its elements and convincingness from the kind of events that we knew, e.g., that the fires we saw in space were like our fires—and so went out after a certain calculable time. We have seen Kelvin's surprise at the fact that the sun wasn't yet as cool as it ought to be. Now we know that the sun is radioactive and for all we know may, like a gigantic concertina, swell in and out forever. It is a Cepheid—a pulsing star. It is also an orange dwarf. Orange dwarf Cepheids, some experts in star explosions think, are more likely to burst than any other species of star. So the old Stoic notion that the universe we see, the solar system at least, if not the whole Cosmos, may end in a flame flash and not in a heat death, is coming back.

82

But not only may the solar system be far more cataclysmic than astronomy thought possible in the nineteenth century, our whole notion of Time and of the Cosmos in which our system is a speck may be too like that little local method of recording, clockwork. For not only do the problems, How did the earth and the other planets take up their positions? And how does the sun keep going? bother the astronomer. He has far vaster worries. The main one of these is the largest. That is the spectral shift. Briefly, most experts seem certain that a shift toward the red shown in the spectra of far-out galaxies shows that they are all rushing away from us. Of course, we are used to the fixed stars really being rapidly moving bodies. But as with the flames of the nebula in Orion, we thought that the movement was on so vast a scale that it could never matter to us or even to our minute solar system. For all practical purposes, for all matter even of geology we might still take the so-called fixed stars as fixed as ever. But when the deduced speed of the furthest observable galaxies was calculated, a very awkward fact emerged. It began to look as though at the time that the earth was more or less a formed body the universe must have been quite intolerably congested. For, if these rushing away galaxies were going at a constant speed, then at a certain date they must have all been piled up one on the other in a dense mass. And that certain date was dangerously near the time when we need a nice open, cool space for the earth and the other planets to spread out and harden. Here then is the point at issue. According to the latest cosmological theory there are two points that stand out and startle a layman as much as an astronomer—and mean as much for him as for the expert. The first is that the time that the earth is said by the 'radium clock' estimate to have taken in forming to its present state is about the same as the time that the galaxies are estimated to have taken to go from the centre to the rim of the Space-Time continuum. That would seem to mean that the vast difference that we thought must exist between sidereal age —the time the whole universe had lasted—and the geological record, the time there has been an earth, does not exist. It has taken just as long for the tiny planet we live on to form as it has taken for the universe to expand. So, of course, the next question is, Expand from what? And here we are prodded out of our complacency by the second point. If the universe has expanded to its present size, then at the time that it began—at the time the earth began—earth, sun and the whole company of galaxies was contracted to atomic proportions. Professor J. B. S. Haldane—an enthusiastic supporter of Milne—indeed suggests we can get over the problem of how the sun ejected or formed planets—a small, but to us quite an interesting riddle—by saying that when the whole primal sun-stuff, the nucleus of the solar system to be, was submicroscopic then a single photon of energy would have been enough to eject a series of what one may call atom-seed planets.

This matter of cosmogony has been dealt with at some length here—though of course hardly even in vaguest outline—because of its great importance to our understanding our basic position. It is the final break-through of the new cosmology. The old cosmology of the classical physics always held this threat over man: You are little to insignificance and your lasting power is equally ridiculous—now run away and play with thoughts of a God that cares and of work worth doing for your fellows and for love of Him! And now we see that picture of the universe turning over before our eyes. This fabulous size is actually able to become an equally fabulous smallness. The Universe, as Sanskrit thought declared some three millennia ago, swells and shrinks, a cosmic tide, the 'breathing out' and 'breathing in' of that awful consciousness called *Deus Manifestans* and *Deus Abscondidus*, the temporal aspect of the Eternal, the unending interchange of Prakriti and Purusha, matter and force, inertia and spirit. Nor can we say that though the universe may yet contract to 'manageable proportions' yet time is still against us—it will last too long for us, anyhow. For Time and Space are aspects of the same thing. The earth, as it hatched Life, took a certain span, the span, according to this theory, that the whole universe takes to go from its seed to its full-blown flower stage. And so at the time that man appears and is full grown, at that moment the universe, too, is at full tide. Can this mean that when a self-conscious being appears the universe has at last formed its seed, within its vast fruit and now is ready to collapse? Such thoughts cannot but occur as the alternative cosmology now that the old cosmic picture is gone—the picture of a universe utterly disregardful of man because of its utter irrelevance to him through its size and its age.[1]

[1] The whole of this Milne controversy can be followed in the various numbers of the leading British scientific magazine *Nature*. There it will be seen in the papers that Milne has submitted for the last few years, in the criticisms of such authors as Dingle and in the supporting arguments and deductions of such appreciators as Haldane the vast and at the same time practical issues that are at stake. This is a dispute as important as that on the Origin of Species or the Copernican hypothesis and no doubt will awake as strong feeling. Milne incidentally seems to think that the present mathematics using the present data suggest that the universe—under the aspects of its two forms of time—is both continually coming to an end (at its 'rim', where stars tend to blow up) and continually beginning over again. Seen therefore from all-over Time it continually renews—and the Second Law of Thermodynamics does not apply to it. As the Sankya philosophy says, Purusha—consciousness-energy—and Prakriti—mass-space are eternal and continually interplay, causing expansion and contraction. Seen from the point that we or anyone may be occupying, the universe does come to an end—the Second Law is true. Thus it looks as though we are right at the end: The geological record, ending in man, is seconded by the cosmic record ending—with utmost expansion—in the phase of manifestation and so turning back into the phase of pure potentiality.

See particularly Professor Milne's communication to *Nature*, 3rd February 1945, where he gives a brief précis of his work since 1936. Here are some of his *obiter dicta* (from 'Proceedings of Royal Society' A.165.354.1938): 'It is not a fanciful speculation to see in the interplay of radiation keeping t-time with matter obeying the classical laws of mechanics on the tau-scale a phenomenon giving rise to the possibility of change in the universe *in time* and so an origin for the action of evolution in both the organic and the inorganic universes.' 'I have long been aware that all theories of the solar system require drastic reconsideration in the light of the fact that when the solar system was born dynamical and optical conditions were very different.'

Milne then answers the objection that if the universe is expanding then in the past there must have been constant collisions (if not a total jam); that when the universe was at its primal collectivity the size of each actual object was proportionately lessened. Both space and matter were equally contracted and so, on submicroscopic scale, you had the same design and proportion of universe which now is dilated at or near the maximum of its macrocosmic expansion.

IS GOD EVIDENT?

Perhaps it is unwise to use such material at present. At the same time we must at least claim that if the results of the new cosmology are not yet ready to rule our new datum lines at least we must and can insist on being relieved of the old limits made by the old and disproved cosmogony. The argument so often

Next he proposes that on that microcosmic scale a single light photon could disrupt our then microcosmic sun, and so distribute microcosmic planets. He adds that light photons at that time were of far higher energy than now. He suggests the immense force of this may be still shown to some degree unspent in the cosmic radiation. This leads to a further and very serious change in our basic assumptions. The Speed of Light was taken till lately as the basic constant. Milne suggests and some experimental work in France has seemed to support the idea that Light may 'age' and tire, going more slowly.

Haldane had already suggested that a single photon had disrupted the sun, a queerly modern rendering of the Fiat Lux. Earlier (*Nature*, 6th May 1944) he had drawn the following most illuminating conclusions from his work on Milne's mathematics. Pointing out the consequences of the theory for geology and biology he shows that on the common-sense time-scale, the day and year are now much longer than in early geological ages and actually now a saurian's fossil remains have become considerably bigger than they were when the animal was alive! He adds that the geological years (rated by radio-activity) are not the years of the star systems. Further, he points out that the amount of energy needed to break down the acids for any muscular work has not always been what it is now so metabolism couldn't release the force it now releases: so, go back far enough, and the force needed for a cell to divide, could not have been summoned and, for a very long time, no life-form could muster energy enough to move. Therefore 'almost all eternity on the tau-scale (time scale of universe) was past' before life could begin and even in the pre-Cambrian six hundred, ninety million years ago, the energy available for all animals must have been only half what it is now. Conversely looking to the future even if the universe should go toward a heat-death 'the mechanical efficiency of chemical processes may so increase that life is still possible'.

This final conclusion certainly seems to support the hypothesis, illustrated in the succeeding chapter, that Life itself may be holding its own and even winning against death by defying the Second Law of Thermodynamics. Ice age conditions and extreme cold of an intensity fatal to us as we now are, may be just the prophetic perfection of future climate for the man of the energy that will then be, a creature of such vitality that he would find our present temperate world as suffocatingly enervating and stuffily fume-ridden as we would find the carboniferous atmosphere that delighted the dinosaurs.

86

used by the mechanist astronomers and physicists that they could show that man couldn't count, by their power to demonstrate a time span quite irrelevant to life and a space that made any notion of life's importance ridiculous, that argument has fallen and must be definitely cleared out of the way.

But once we have seen that the new frame of reference in which we find ourselves is not the vastly indifferent thing we thought, once we have seen that the time needed to bring life to flower and fruit in a self-conscious being is the time that the universe takes to unfold, we still have the main issue to settle. The real weight of the secularist attack against the view that man really mattered, that he had objective value in the universe, was not in the picture of the universe. The attack on man's values, by showing that he was physically very small in a universe of such size, and that he lasted not a split second in comparison with a universe of such age, was of course not an argument, but an appeal to the emotions. The point of the attack, as far as it was rational, was in the attempt to prove—and to many the attempt seemed as good as settled—that in a universe that worked by mechanical law, whether man had appeared or no, whether he thought he could think and imagined he could will, it was clear that these notions must be chimerical. Of course neither is this really an argument, for if you argue that man cannot think with any rational and objective force but only deludes himself that he is doing so, you, being a man, must be deluding yourself and your argument falls. Reason cannot be used to disprove reason. Still the appearance of Iron Law did seem very impressive and we must remember that it was not physicists who from the start had made such play with this idea, but theologians from Augustine down to Calvin. Therefore we must pay attention to one further point in the new theories of the new physics. We have already noted Heisenberg's Principle of Indeterminacy. And about this there is now no controversy among experts. Nor do those thinkers such as Earl Russell, who combine philosophic knowledge with high mathematic ability, deny the importance of this principle for our metaphysics, and so for our ethics. As Bavink has pointed out in his *Anatomy of*

Modern Science it means that mechanism has been disproved where it was held most certain that it would be established. Inorganic matter has shown itself to be unpredictable and if that is so then of course that is true of the organic and of the consciousness that rises above it. Free will is not an illusion of the mind filled with *folie de grandeur*. Science till now—as was noted earlier in this book—has advanced through using the law of probability. It was mere prophecy that in the end there would be found strict causality—a prophecy which as we now see with the Principle of Indeterminacy will never be fulfilled. [1]

There is not space in this book to indicate how man fell into the mistaken fancy that blind necessity rules all. The mistake seems to be due to the fact that when in his thinking man became capable of noticing connected series of events—*post hoc, propter hoc*; because this comes after that, that caused this—at first he had naturally to simplify his method. Therefore he could only notice what we may call 'linear causality'. He confined himself to one series of events. So at one time he thought the mother gave all to the child, fatherhood was merely a protective device and contributed nothing to the child's real being. Hence heredity was traced only through her—matriarchy. And then later it was held that the mother simply made a home for the man-seed and so heredity was traced only through the father—patriarchy. Gradually people began to see that causality was a much more complex matter and that in fact Life and all processes were part of a woven field in which effective threads of sequences crossed over and combined with each other, lay latent and then emerged. Hence the enormous and still growing complexity of modern genetics with its recessive and dominant characteristics, its linked inherited factors and the ever fresh devices with which attempts are made to preserve some notion of caus-

[1] The whole of this issue was raised with some thoroughness in *Nature* in 1944 under the title of 'The Collapse of Determinism'. (See particularly *Nature*, 22nd July 1944 and 10th March 1945.) Professor H. T. H. Piaggio, summing up the present views and findings, quotes Von Neumann's judgment that 'the results of Quantum Theory cannot be obtained by averaging any exact causal Laws', and himself concludes, 'The balance of present evidence is rather against complete causality'.

ality. To this problem we must return in the next chapter. We must close this one by seeing what is the dynamic with which the study of our environment leaves us to-day. We have seen that man has been put back into the very centre and balance of the universe and neither space nor time denies him a critical situation and perhaps a decisive position. But can he do anything about it, or is he just the pawn with which the great master closes the end-game with a single incomparably apt move? The significance of the Principle of Indeterminacy cannot be overrated for when we examine it we find that it indicates that our will is of a nature precisely to correspond with the kind of universe with which it is confronted. The great complex lock is matched by a perfectly cut key. For the fact of indeterminacy runs right through the three great divisions of science, as Bavink has pointed out. It is present in the study of human consciousness, in the study of living matter and now we see it is present also in the study of 'dead' matter also. No one can say what an individual will do, must do. No prophecy foretelling each man's fate will be able to say, Iron Law rules mankind and God has predestined all men to their fate. But, said the physicists of the 'classic' phase, the soul is only steam of the body and we know what the body will do. How? Because it is merely a chemical mixture. And how do you know how molecules behave? Because molecules are made of nothing but atoms and atoms of electrons and electrons are little 'billiard balls' obeying blind force with perfect mechanic regularity and we shall soon observe them. Observation has shown that this is not so; calculation, that it will never be so. The tower which was to be founded on rock has been bored down to base—and there has been found not bare-faced fact but a mystery of amazing strangeness. What has been found is disconcertingly strange if one thought the universe must in the end be stupidly dull, futile, frustrant. But, though it loses none of its strangeness, its mystery, it becomes something about which one can do something, about which one can do all that is in one, if one does not assume that the universe is senseless.

What if the universe was meant to co-operate with man, what

if it was and is his frame, what if he is the central point, the superfine pivot on which it turns, what if he is the photon, the super-seed of force which it has produced and by which it is fulfilled? We have seen that we must rid our minds of the anthropomorphic notions of size that man couldn't count in such bigness because of his physical smallness. So here is the actual Law that can be perceived in the inorganic, the organic, and the realm of consciousness. It is the Law of High Numbers and its co-operative complement is the Freedom of Low Numbers. The Law of High Numbers is the Law of Statistical Probability. When you are dealing with great masses then you can predict how they will behave. And this Law runs right through the three fields of science study: With millions of atoms in play you can tell how masses of inorganic material will behave with a high degree of certainty—so high as to be practically invariable. With millions of living cells in play, with masses of protoplasm, again you can detect certain high degrees of probability—though not as high as with the so-called 'dead' or non-reproductive forms of matter. With millions of living people again census statistical methods can make such forecasts that it might almost be said there were population laws and vital and mortality certainties. The forecasts of birth increase, death rates, yes, even suicide rates per thousand are curiously accurate and reliable. But no one can point to any specific individual and say he will die this current year, still less that he will commit suicide. Nor with the amoeba can anyone say just here and now will it put out a pseudopod. And finally, with the atom no one can say, now and here will the electron be shot off, or vanish from this orbit to appear on another. So we see the Liberty of Low Numbers running alongside with the Law of the High.

The practical result of this is the actual but amazingly apt world in which in point of fact we find ourselves. We are used to it, but when we analyse it, it certainly is strange enough for people to wonder at. And, if they feel at any cost they must explain away either design or our power to co-operate with design, people may say that this strange principle will be found to prove the ultimate senselessness of the universe. But this is faith and prophecy, not factual observation. The facts refuse to be further denied. The old Calvinism, the later mechanism, both appealed to hard facts. They have appealed to Caesar and they must stand by the appeal. The Law is so framed as to leave freedom, the freedom so granted as to preserve law. The two extremes of arbitrary anarchy and servile tyranny are both avoided. Law is there, but not as a blind denier or oppressor, an impossible standard; it is there as a teacher. It is a path through the jungle of events, it makes sense of things and when you break it, it does not break you but pushes you back on the path. You sow ill and reap ill, but you learn from the ill reaping to sow better. Freedom is there but not as blind caprice. It is there that you may co-operate with law until with that which is given you and handed you, you may compose perfectly. And that composition is a chord, threefold: Through the composition that man may make in art by studying beauty, rhythmic design: Through the correspondence and congruence and fitness that man may make in science by studying truth, objectivity: Through the interest-affection that man may feel by the study and sympathy with his fellow creatures, through goodness and loving-kindness.

In short we find ourselves not in a world of an indifferent law, about which we can do nothing and care nothing, but in a world of Lawful Freedom. That is the fact and so acting on it man has risen both to power and insight. Everyone who has made anything of his life has acted on this assumption—that they were free to keep a living and creative law. And so living they came to ever fuller freedom of creativity as their insight into the richness of the Law steadily deepened. But few of those who have so lived have thought what such a fact actually indicated. It is a very strange balance to find. And it has results that are none the less strange because they are both sane and beautiful. This is not the world we should have expected to find. Though we have to own that taking the world in any other way and trying to make it work by any more practical selection of the facts, not only means that we must suppress some of the known facts, but that the lives we try and live in this smaller

and wrongfully deprived picture of things, become mean, frustrant, futile and tragic. We felt it was too good to be true that
the world could sanction sense, could be meant and made to
yield us sense and meaning. But so the facts prove it to be and
when we live by those facts such are the actual results we get.

Only one conclusion can be made from this—this world has
been arranged so that we could so live—if we wished. We are
not forced so to live, we are not compelled not to suppress the
facts if we wish to have a narrow and mean picture either because we cherish the selfish hope to enjoy ourselves better on our
own, or if we wish to shut other people out from happiness and
be alone 'God's Elect'. But the actual picture is that He is no
one's property but the Father of all and as He is the Father of
all He would that all should live and find their happiness in
working for all in a common creativeness.

That is the frame we are in. The first great question has
yielded this amazing answer. Where are we? We are in a world
of Lawful Freedom. Yes, it is odd, strange and very good. But
goodness does not prevent a thing being true—that to assert so
is mere pessimism. Its truth must be based on factual evidence.
There it is, and if it proves to be pleasant, well, we must accept
it. It is pleasant—but that does not mean that it is not costly.
Cost and enjoyment—these two are no more mutually exclusive
than goodness and truth.

Now, having dealt with the first of the studies in which observation can be employed, we can go on to the second. In this
frame, this world of Lawful Freedom, what are we? In this universe that works by Lawful Freedom what are the powers, the
capacities and the rules of the life which has formed us and
sustains us? What force drives us? Can we accept this great opportunity of position? Are we free to act freely and creatively
toward our setting and in the frame of this great opportunity?

Chapter Five

LIFE AS CREATIVE CHOICE

This world is a place in which it would be possible to be creative and free. But are we? That is the point to which our inquiry has come. We have seen the first great obstacle is out of the way. The vast frame in which we are placed puts no obstacle in our path if we could act creatively. Indeed it seems to suggest that if we chose to do so we might add something of incomparable value and aptness to the immense composition. Our smallness does not prevent or hinder our significance.

We have then arrived at Life. What are its laws, how does it run, what force moves within us, by what current are we charged, run, carried? That we are in a world of Lawful Freedom would serve us greatly, if we are ourselves free. To know that you are not in a prison, that the door is unlocked and you may walk out as you please—that is good—provided that you are not a paralytic or a convulsive spastic. Without his concert grand a pianist cannot show his power but a grand piano is of no use to a giant panda.

This was the position of most men who tried to take stock of the sciences in the nineteenth century. During the eighteenth most thinking people had realized that the mechanic universe evidently did not care much what they did. So within that large and slow-moving frame they were free to play out their play for their day. Even when the Age of Reason and the belief that all men could easily be rational, had begun to fade, still men thought they were free to follow their emotions and, on the whole, their emotions were fine. Rousseau had been against Hobbes's earlier estimate of what primitive, unrational man had been like. But in the mid-nineteenth century Hobbes came back with a vengeance. Biology was held to have proved that by nature Man's life was nasty, short, brutish. Nor had this unpleasant nature been changed because the creature wore clothes, ran machines and poured out words. Man was a creature of instinct and instinct was the same blind law that ran the stars, running this scrap of more complex but still blind matter. 'Just look at Nature and listen to Darwin', said informed people, 'and you'll soon be cured of any notion that you are nice or that you could make anyone, including yourself, better.'

But before we turn to study what was supposed to be the history of Life, we must first study the thing itself as we see it before us now. Science is not history and though history is very important, it is even more important to keep science from getting unconsciously mixed up with history. The nineteenth-century biologists were not nearly as careful about that as they needed to be. Hence the source of many of our muddles and some of our tragedies. Evolution—the theory that out of simpler forms all the higher are derived—may be true and has a considerable degree of probability about it, indeed we may say it is the most probable of all speculations, if it is called not 'evolution', which means a simple unfolding, but 'epigenesis'—Professor James Ward's word—which means the emergence of something which is actually very different from its root. Yet we must never forget that all theories of how the higher types appeared is theory, deduction, not observation. In that sense it is not true science at all. We cannot experiment with the hypothesis, for we cannot run time back like a film or try other combinations. We cannot analyse our problem: viz., take the creature from its environment and try how would it do if we gave it three legs instead of four or three hands instead of two. We cannot even be sure we have a clear sequence of cause and effects. For our record is so badly broken that we can never be sure where fresh lines of causes may not intrude and blend with the line we wish to trace and believe to be the *causa causans*.

If then we are ever to consider the history of Life and try from that to define what Life is, we must first study those forms presented to us now, and especially that most powerful form—and that which most concerns us—man.

What is this creature, if we try to take stock of him before assuming that he is either beast or god? Men have fluctuated between these two estimates. But they have seldom been able to pause on the centre of the beam. We then need to ask, may not man be man, neither beast nor god but a unique creature? We have seen that his place is unique and very central. He seems to be in an 'optimum' place, may he not then be of optimum size, an optimum creature, exactly suited for his station between beast and some being freed from physical limitation? That, we must repeat, is the kind of notion that would naturally occur to anyone who found man's place, the situation in which *Homo sapiens* functions, to be the curiously apt place which we see modern findings have discovered that it is.

And when we come to study with the same modern means the body of this creature we certainly find that it is a wonderful balance. When it was first explored by anatomists they hoped in their materialistic way to find—such was Paracelsus's faith—at the centre a seed and, in that centre, a magnifying glass would show the 'homunculus', the little perfect microscopic manikin which would swell into full-scale man. When the microscope came it showed that that hope was vain. Descartes, with an even simpler but quite as influential imagining, fancied that in the heart was a hearth on which burned 'the vital spark'. The body essences poured in on this. When flame and essence were in balance then we were rightly conscious: when flame blazed up we had fever and finally delirium: when essence flooded then vapours rose to the brain, and we swooned. This was the basis on which during the age of sensibility ladies who found swooning the best way of getting out of any awkward situation, claimed that they had been attacked by The Vapours.

The nineteenth-century biologists showed that there was no more flame in the heart than there was homunculus in the seed. What then ran man? 'Chemical reactions', was the standard answer. In the eighteenth century the brightly silly physician of the cynical Frederick of Prussia, Le Maître, had made his *mot*,

'The brain secretes thought as the liver secretes bile'—one of those false analogies that put off true exploration for quite a while. Meanwhile, as the next century matured, bile and urea and many of the other secretions of the body had been analysed and one by one synthesized. This was important, because the Vitalists, fighting for the uniqueness of man, had taken up the bad position that there were vital fluids in the body, special secretions that could never be made artificially. To have proved that they could, seemed then to bring nearer the day when thought would be able to be made in a test tube as bile could be.

So the current thought of the time was made ready for the Darwinian explanation. For was it not inherently probable that this curious bag of chemicals really blew and bulged into its present size (and finally suffered from a ferment at the top which made it think it was conscious) because it had been rolled about all these millions of years by the chance buffets of geology?

But the study of the body did not stop with the chemistry of this queer vat. Gradually it was found that a new science would have to be formed to deal with its actual complexity. Biochemistry appeared. The behaviour of chemicals, drugs, etc., *in vivo*, actually in the body, and *in vitro*, in the test tube, were often disconcertingly different. Drugs—such as quinine—did not work simply as direct poison on the germ, but with immensely complex circuitous reactions. There was a *vis medicatrix naturae*, a vital and very strange element behind the play of the chemicals. Pasteur with his discovery of germ life was thought by some to have simplified the picture. True, germs had got into the bag but with proper disinfectant chemicals one could get them out, as moths out of a velvet lining by naphtha, etc. But Pasteur himself always held that he had proved that Life only comes out of Life and that the notion of 'spontaneous generation', that muck breeds flies and not flies breed in muck —a notion naturally dear to materialists—was demonstrably untrue. And as the fight with germs went on the clearer it became that the germs could never be got rid of, and if they were the man would die. Some germs are as much needed by the body as others are disliked; some are neutral and to poison them out would be only to poison first the host. And finally, the theory began to appear, and has steadily gained ground, that the germ isn't and hasn't the last word. That lies with the body as a whole. It is *general resistance* that counts. And what is that? Well that is what the body knows; but it and its Maker alone seem to have settled precisely how it is to be summoned and maintained. One thing, however, seems to be clear and that is that the germ may actually be in many cases no more than a symptom, not a cause. For in many cases bacteria which are present in great numbers and doing no harm, perhaps even some obscure good, only seem to become dangerous when the body has already made a slip.

In short two things were emerging: We had to go deeper than chemicals and below the microbic living bodies if we were to discover the basis of Life—we had to go beyond the microscope. And, secondly, we were involved in an inquiry in which we had to take the body as a whole and not try to understand it just by its parts. That, of course, told against mechanism. The next stage was the discovery and study of the body as electrically charged. This problem had occurred to researchers for some time. For once the chemicals were known which made up the cell—which composed the whole body—and once these were found to be common chemicals, why then not recombine them and make a cell? You are no more than a destructive child if you can take a watch to pieces but never put it together again. But that is all we have been able to do with the unit of life, the living cell. That led to further inquiry. What held these common chemicals together? They were strongly reactive against one another and as soon as the cell 'died' they proceeded to push till they were apart and had destroyed their house. Research soon showed that what held them together was a curiously strong electric field. Then came the discovery of the electric field in the spinal column, that all nerves sent all their messages by an electric current and finally, with the 'brain-waves',[1] the dis-

[1] The knowledge of the electric charge of the body through the brain waves by electroencephalograms is the most advanced point of our physiological diagnosis of man. At present three specific patterns of such waves can be

covery that thought and all brain functions are always attended by specific electric rhythms. All the senses, sight, touch in its three or four forms, sound, taste, smell, all reach the central consciousness—or rather they are all translations made into modes that consciousness apprehends—from pulsings of electric currents that reach us from an outer continuum otherwise unknown. We suspect, with some good grounds, as was pointed out in the previous chapter, that what is 'out there' is a series of wave-lengths of electric vibration. But there is no doubt that it appears as a coloured sounding world because we have the power of taking electric currents that reach us through the body and making them into the world we then assume to be the world of common sense.

Man, therefore, as far as he is a body, is called to-day—as are all living creatures—an electromagnetic instrument of immense

correlated with three main states of consciousness: (1) sleeping, (2) waking, (3) concentrated thought. In man the 'alpha' wave rhythm is in play as long as sight is not being used. But the alpha rhythm can also be stopped if in total dark one 'strains to see'—until one finds that impossible, when the alpha wave resumes. As Dr. E. A. Adrian, F.R.S., has said (Discourse at Royal Institution, London, 4th February 1944), these brain waves show that there is a deep-seated part of the brain which contains the apparatus by which attention is directed one way or the other. And the alpha rhythm is under control of this region. So abnormalities in the rhythm are often associated with abnormalities of behaviour. This permits diagnosing brain disease and tumours because of changes in the rhythm. And also the oncoming—often long before any other symptom—of epilepsy. Further, abnormal rhythms which simply show a slower or faster rate than the average, or odd-shaped waves are significantly correlated with odd conduct in the behaviour of their producers. So in appointments other things being equal, 'it would be safer to exclude the 5 per cent whose electroencephalogram showed the most unusual features'. Perhaps through this non-sensory method of diagnosis we may hope to get a 'profile' of man's field of consciousness which no dissection of the brain can ever give. For not only does it now appear possible that each person may be found to have his particular distinctiveness of brain-wave pattern—analogous to his finger prints (see Dr. R. J. Williams, *The Human Frontier*)—but his whole range of emotional and intellectual life may be 'graphed' in the fluctuations of his electric tides. Here would lie a method of examination and vocational guidance surer and more delicate than now in use.

complexity.[1] That is certainly not the old materialistic picture. For, if nothing more, a thing that is composed of electric charges must be subject to the laws and freedoms of electricity and as no one can say that the electron is material or indeed rule what it may do, why therefore rule that man is material or mechanical? Further, he is made of protoplasm, and, as we have also seen, a protoplasmic creature might also have power of the initiative which seems to reside in every amoeba. It remains then still to be proved that his belief that he is free is man's pathetic delusion.

We are back then at the question, What is Life? In his brilliant essay *Reality* Canon Streeter rightly took exception to the amount of somewhat commonplace poetry that has got mixed into much that passes as scientific thinking and a realistic outlook on life. One of the commonest phrases, and one to which he rightly took exception, was that Life is a frail flame. This gives an idea that it is easily extinguished and also that it must anyhow go out because it eats up its fuel. But as a point of fact this is another of those false analogies that check understanding.

This analogy was taken from the old molecular physics. As we have seen, in the preceding chapter, this notion of the 'heatdeath' of everything had already in the nineteenth-century physics run up against the problem of the sun. Why had it not

[1] This phrase has been used before in this essay's attempt to deal with the issue of epistemology, the basic problem and study: How does man apprehend? i.e., the problem of Perception and Understanding. It may help, therefore, to quote here from an authoritative and comprehensive book on the problem of the senses and their power to grasp the outer continuum. Professor Henri Pieron in his masterly volume *Aux Sources de la Connaissance* (Paris: Librairie Gallimard, 1945) sums up: 'The special senses, far from being windows opening on to the outer world, are complex apparatus for the detection of minute chemical, mechanical and physio-electric *changes* in the environment. Once detected these changes are translated (almost instantaneously) into conscious sensations and perceptions, *forms of symbolism* universal through Life because of the essential similarity of all the organisms that we know in Nature. Though each of us has a unique consciousness, we approach through it a common universe by the universal symbolism of sensory functions.' Professor Pieron has made perhaps the most comprehensive study of the senses of animals and man yet achieved.

already sunk to an ember? How had it kept blazing, even through the past ages of geology, still more through the still longer aeons before this world itself ceased to be incandescent gas? Lord Kelvin had been puzzled by this seeming solar exception to the Second Law of Thermodynamics. And though Kelvin could not be so unorthodox as to suspect that the sun might be able to recreate its spent energy—and therefore he charged the geologists with taking too much time for their lay-out—he did suggest that perhaps Life might not come under the 'Law'. With that problem, as to whether Life may be, not merely a ruthless consumer—a more rapid way whereby the universe brings on its ultimate exhaustion, as the last water goes with a headlong rush down the drain—but might be actually a constructor, a creator, we shall be dealing at the close of this chapter. Here, however, we must first see what has been known about the economy, the inventiveness, of Life for almost a generation now. For if Life be no more than the electric current round the cell, it is certainly a wonderful manager, in a way that a flame never is. For we have seen that Life actually manages to get more work out of chemicals—and smaller quantities of them—than any other device can. We are so often used to talking of ourselves as failures, weak, frail, ill-made things beside our own machines. It is not true. No one has made a machine that will run on as little fuel as our body. And when we add to that that this 'machine' not only repairs itself ceaselessly, can stand prodigiously clumsy handling and rough usage, and when it begins to wear badly proceeds to reproduce itself and can do so many times over, we see the impossible standard of economy with which we are presenting any machine that would compete with life. Helmholtz used to complain that the eye was ill made, yet few if any lenses will stand the kind of handling we give our eyes or adapt themselves to such vast changes of illumination to which we expose ours. And when we think that that crystal lens has been made from flesh, certainly the wonder is no less.

In an essay of this brevity, trying to scan the vast front of Natural Philosophy, we can spend far too little time on each sector. We must pass then from the wonder of this body to a brief glance at the way it functions. It keeps itself going in three ways. It eats, it breathes and it sleeps. We have paid most attention to the eating side so far. Diet has meant—far too narrowly —what went into the stomach. Breathing, we know, is, if anything, more important. But we have taken for granted that though we can stop eating for long spells but breathing hardly ever, yet breath was only important in keeping the blood clean and the blood was made by food. As to sleep, we have treated that as mainly a regrettable lapse. Yet we cannot understand this odd creature unless we know *all* the things it feeds on. 'A man is what he eats'—well perhaps so, if you really know all he eats. For us air is certainly as much a food as bread. With solid food we draw on the solid part of the universe. With liquid on the liquid. With breathing we draw on the gaseous part. What of the electric? Studies of sleep are many but they are mainly neglected. They all show one thing, a thing which incidentally has been known to every sane man ever since man studied man. That is that sleep is more necessary than food. You may cut a man's diet down till he can eat and live on a tithe, on a twentieth part of what the normal man consumes, and he may then top that with long fasts. Many well-known fasters such as Gandhi have lived to old age. Some well-known physicians believe it prolongs life. But keep any man from sleeping a week and it is likely that he will be close on crazy. It is an acute torture and the results are always serious even to the body. Make a man sleep and actual wounds heal faster. What is sleep? The answer is yet to be made fully. But it seems that it is the body's method of making some touch with some electrical condition which it cannot contact—at least effectively—when distracted by waking activity.[1] We must remember that sleep is not merely rest—it is active repair. As the Colgate research showed, in sleep, for the first three hours, metabolism generally increases. The active repair, impossible during waking, is now being brought into play.

We can say, then, that there is much further discovery to be

[1] Cf. The alpha basic brain-wave pattern is stopped as soon as we begin to attend with our predominant sense, sight, to the outer world.

made about the functioning of this strange power-generator—
the body. More economical than any machine we know in its
use of food, it also manages to live largely on air—on the significance of that we shall have more to say in a moment—and this
oxygen intake is the forced draught whereby it exercises its
supreme power, thought. And it lives most mysteriously of all
by seeming every now and then to do nothing. It recharges
itself basically by going to sleep.

Finally it has wonderful power of lasting. Though it is very
soft and owes such rigidity as it has to bones made of lime, it
will endure generally for some seventy years. Nor is it merely a
thing that climbs, or swells, to reproduction and then, having
discharged young, fades. That is a wrong picture. That man is
derived from an apelike creature is not nearly as certain as we
thought forty years ago. That he comes from a lower form of
life is certainly probable, but can't yet be clearly and unequi-
vocally proved. What is clear is the number of things in which,
though he is like an animal, he is still curiously different. In his
important essay *The Uniqueness of Man*, Dr. Julian Huxley has
pointed out how we have now overdone the picture of 'Man
but an animal'. The likenesses had to be pointed out, for they
had been neglected. And they are curiously extensive and detailed especially with the smaller apes. But likeness does not
prove a common source, still less that the lower form is that
source. It may prove convergence toward a common goal—a
notion which is coming to be more canvassed than it was thirty
years ago.

We can, then, in this space do no more than give a list of
some of these differences. First as to man's lasting power. He
is the only creature that endures for another half of its life when
it has passed that peak at which it is at its reproductive height.
Man is something more than a form of life which repeats itself.
This is shown, too, by the fact that man has no instincts.[1] He
inherits no habit patterns which will emerge as he grows and
guide his emerging organs so that he may find food, find mate,
build a home and bear and rear young. All his needed wisdom

[1] See further in the end of this chapter and Chapter Six.

whereby he may function adequately is carried for him in the
social heredity of his group. Instead of instincts he has a great,
a supreme power of learning and suggestibility and on this
plastic matrix is recorded the wisdom of his society. Hence man
can change at a speed which no animal can change. Further,
in this second part of his life man becomes increasingly interested in understanding and no longer in mere action and as
Professor A. S. Warthin has shown in his book on old age, *Old
Age: The Major Involution*, the incessant activity needed for the
growth of the child, the absorbed interest in a mate needed for
the young adult to breed, these two animal phases are succeeded
in man by the fully mature interest in society. And, finally, they
are crowned, if the life is healthy, by that quiet, detached,
serene attitude toward the whole of life, nature and the round
of experience, an attitude which takes away from the young the
fear of death and makes them able to understand and revere
the faith that comes with life's completion.

So we see the extension of life is not mere extension but an
advance to the very end

> *Till old experience doth attain*
> *To something like Prophetic Strain*

and there is not merely an increase of mass and activity but a
wonderful modulation into finer harmonies, a spiral process
whereby we evolve and then involve, implicate and then ex-
plicate, inliminate and eliminate.

If we did not rule out the possibility that—as our first
scientist Heraclitus said—'here we are as in an egg', if we
should, as a hypothesis, look upon man as a growth not yet
finished, then we might see our span of living as something
best to be understood as an embryo stage of the soul, of consciousness. And as the foetal stage of the physique takes nine
months for the prenatal child, after which it has become wholly
detached from the womb and has ready a number of senses and
organs which can only come into play when it is born, so too
with detached consciousness. That consciousness is first identified with the body as the foetus is with the womb. Then it is

detached, only holding on by an anchor connection and with an increasing number of freedoms from sense and (if it will continue to grow) concerns and interests with purely mental and spiritual living. And, as with the child it should stay in the womb for its full term but then as emphatically it should and must emerge or be frustrant, so with the pure consciousness we call soul or spirit. It too should stay in the body for its full 'period of spiritual gestation'. After that it should emerge through a healthy death. The physician—the man who really understands the mysterious sheath, the physique—is one who wishes to avoid a premature birth of the psyche and so keeps his charge in health and full possession of the body until the man himself is psychically fully grown. Stage by stage, by diet and exercise adapted to the stage of the spirit's growth, the true medical consultant brings the growing and detaching consciousness up to that stage when, held only by the thinnest veil and thinnest thread, the soul may detach itself and emerge, as the sun from the mist that it has wholly drawn up and absorbed into its own brightness. Nor is this merely an attempt to solve the individual's problem faced with the growing physiological limitations of ageing. A society which contains its proportion of persons so complete and matured is one that is properly balanced and enriched. So the right stations and *tempi* are given to each of the age groups that compose a complete social organism.

This may seem both too speculative and even too narrow a picture of what Life is. Let us then for a moment examine more closely the findings of modern anthropology as to man's actual frame and then tracing back as far as we may the process whereby it has taken shape (so that we may the better understand to what end it is directed) we may have a glimpse at the whole Life Process, the force at work in it and ask, What meaning does it show? We have seen that we are now, with exacter knowledge, experiencing a reaction from the view expressed in the dismissive term: 'Man is really only an animal', to which was usually added, 'And a pretty poor one at that'. But his eye is not as crude and botched a piece of work as Helmholtz thought. His abdominal wall has been mocked at, the veinous system of his legs and the metatarsal arch of his foot. 'What a ramshackle structure,' some of the nineteenth-century anatomists used to jeer. But the more muscular tonicity is studied and with it veinous resilience and tendon-binding of bones, the clearer this becomes, that here a simple problem of engineering is made much richer and more complex by the electric condition of the whole body and the tonic or atonic way that body is used. The foot is not ever very happy on flat artificial surfaces; its muscles can only be at full resilience if regularly exercised to their full play. Boots—and such exercise as pressing an accelerator lever—do not give that play. So, too, with veinous elasticity and the abdominal wall. If we distend the body with over-feeding and weaken it with under-exercise, no wonder it works ill. If we will not taper our diet when the body requires less crude bulk for physical output; if we increase instead of reduce our load—why blame it on the structure? That structure is a marvel of economy, devised for a purpose—to be a launching-carriage for an emergent consciousness. If we, instead of co-operating with that process, actually try and reverse it, then we should expect breakdown. If we did not find it failing when so treated we might doubt its real purpose. Man is an amazing work even materially. Even as a matter of engineering it is a supreme wonder to have made this object and lovely instrument to be able to do what it does. The head weighs as much as the leg cut off at the thigh. Yet it is carried right at the top of the spine. The spine itself is made of a number of dice set on end, giving amazing flexibility and yet at the same time rigidity. How long that achievement took we shall see in a moment and so appreciate further what a triumph of skill it is. For man is certainly the highest peak of physical efficiency so far. And if he lived up to his full capacity, with the full wisdom that might be his, there is no point on which he might not show a superiority to all the beasts, a superiority which at present he chiefly shows by his power to kill them and outwit their natural fear and unfriendliness toward him.

These are not vague generalities, in fact they only came to light when we stopped making sweeping statements either about our nobility as gods or our baseness as beasts and settled down to answering the riddle—what is this the most mysterious of the creatures? Dr. William White Howell in his summing up of present-day anthropological knowledge[1] draws our attention to the following very important points—points which make us realize at what a crisis we are physically and what opposite forces are somehow combined in us. For we have become a large species among the apes—indeed we are the tallest of them all. At the same time we show an increasing delicacy. The jaw draws back; the hands become more delicate. This is a very important consideration, not only in its particular bearing on the refinement of this giant creature, but on the whole theory of evolution—of how Life moves and whither. One such 'Law' of evolution used to be that of 'Irreversibility'. A process once undertaken, an organ or structure once emerged, cannot be re-taken, re-absorbed. But, as Dr. Howell points out, man's record shows this being violated, violated we may say by that creative refinement whereby an inventor improves away the crude mass and complexity of his first model. If we have come from any sort of ape then we have to own that certain skull bones and the canines in the teeth *have* been reduced. Either we do not come from apes at all or we have within us the power to get rid of the *damnosa hereditas* of a too bestial past. This is such an important issue, especially the second possibility—that we shall return to it at the end of this chapter.

Sir Grafton Elliot Smith also showed in his highly specialized studies of the human brain and head the amazing fact of the gradual drawing-back of the snout, so that the jaw was contracted and so man's head could be upright. For as long as the jaw is massive it tells against the head being fully human in two ways. In the first place, the thatch of muscles that have to be woven over the top of the skull—as is shown most strikingly in the gorilla—actually strap down the cranium and confine the brain. In the second place, a big jaw has to be slung forward—as in Neanderthal man—to allow its action. If drawn in, its action interferes with the two main neck arteries and their flow

[1] *Mankind So Far.*

of blood to the brain. With this drawing-in of the jaw—reduction of the prognathous profile—the nose became a delicate duct for getting oxygen to the brain and simultaneously the eyes could be swung into line so as to bring them to a fully common focus and so permit binocular vision. Hence an immensely extended range and accuracy of vision. And, most amazing 'convergence', while eyes were brought into play so as to give an outlook which no animal has, smell was reduced. As long as smell rules a creature it is the slave of its passions and, further, cannot follow even the clearest dictates of sight, as anyone who has watched a dog hunting will have seen. Only study of the brain has shown this unsuspected co-ordination: that while the neo-pallium, in which conscious thought functions, came forward, in the enlarging and heightening brain case, this new brain eclipsed and put out of action the olfactory centre, which till then had ruled the central nervous system and dictated action.

Yet as far as we can find out by these studies this was not done by man 'taking thought'. Some process was guiding the creature to its advantage. For, as Dr. Howell shows, the brain did not lead. In man the legs advanced first. By the upright position his hands were made free, a free and upright head was made possible and the big brain followed. No doubt, as Elliot Smith points out, then the new flood of new senses did make the brain grow further. The problem, of what gave it its initial start and endowment of advantages, remains. The ordinary man in the street still thinks that 'Chance' will do as a reply. Fewer and fewer of those who actually work with the material do. For example, here are facts which show the complexity of the question: Whence and how did man arrive? Neanderthal man is no ancestor of ours.[1] He is a specialization—to cold, was Sir

---

[1] So says nearly everyone capable of giving an opinion. Dr. Franz Weidenrich, however, believes that Neanderthal man is *Homo sapiens'* ancestor. If that is so human evolution must have gone far faster than anyone has yet suspected and the stranger power of de-specialization must go far further than as yet we have any other evidence. The huge brow-ridges that mark Neanderthal man, the 'bun-shape' of his brain case—broad and low—the peculiar formation of his teeth—mainly taurodontic—cattlelike teeth—so

Flinders Petrie's brilliant suggestion, a suggestion to which the Gadara skull from Iceland gave considerable additional weight. Sir Arthur Keith thinks that that race whose burials have been found on Mount Carmel was a short-lived variety arising from the type. Certainly, this, the commonest other type of humans to be found in Ice Age deposits, we can see becoming decadent. The full Neanderthal skulls, the later ones, have sunk down, become more brutish than the earlier, such as that from Steinheim. The high and narrow brain that is our mark against his, appeared before the mid-Pleistocene. Professor Le Gros Clark, and many anatomists who have followed his thorough knowledge of human skeletal structure, believe that man could never have been derived from a heavy animal and cite the fate of premature weight as shown in the depressed legs of the gorilla. We must have come from something light to have grown so tall. So he favours our going right back to the little tarsier, that can cower in the human hand, to find an ancestor up in the trees, or perhaps back further to the Tupaia—the tree shrews. All experts seem agreed that new forms do not grow from the crest but from the root of previous forms. No giant gives rise to a giant. For the force lent the creature is then spent. The creative force works best with that which is plastic, which yields to the force rather than carves its destiny. He who carves digs his own grave. He who yields rises. Anatomy is increasingly on the side of Lao-tzu on the question of Who wins?[1]

markedly different from ours which are mainly cynodontic—doglike—all these striking features, not to speak of the different curve of the spine, the shape of the leg bone and the general jutting of the face—prognathous—that such a sum of changes should have taken place in so short a time seems not unnaturally impossible of belief to most authorities.

[1] Dr. F. Wood Jones has lately given it as his opinion (*Nature*, 29th March 1947) that the Taungs and Sterkfontein skulls—skulls which have given rise to the names Australopithecus and Plesianthropus and are held by Broom and Keith to be possible ancestors of man or very close to 'the line of ascent', cannot be so. They are neither human nor hominid because they show definite simian facial maxillary-premaxillary sutures. Professor Le Gros Clark, however, still believes that this is not an adequate objection (*Nature*, 19th April 1947).

We can then say that man as we have him is certainly neither finished nor done for. He is a trial piece still under trial. He is shaping and perhaps shaping well. But he has great risks in both his structure and in the type of mind that goes with it. He is still experimental. And he is not only a frail trial, there can be no doubt that he has already made grave mistakes. But one of the characteristics of life is, as we have seen, that it can remedy mistakes because it can learn from them. More on that issue will be said at the end of this chapter, for it is the final question and biggest issue. Meanwhile we have to note that man is made outstandingly unique by a thing which is hard to put in a phrase. We may call it—for it is impossible to point it out as a feature—a triumph of specialization in unspecialization. The brain—and certainly in that we have the human organ *par excellence*—the brain is, Sir Arthur Keith has pointed out, the largest mass of unspecialized tissue in the body. And further, we know from the research work which was so largely initiated in the Kaiser Wilhelm Institute in Berlin that the brain works as a whole, a field, and not, as a machine works, by clearly and finally differentiated parts.

Yet if we grant that the latest evidence would seem to show that man is a potential triumph, is that enough? Granted he is a creature that has defied all the risks of a long ascent and now has managed to attain a platform whence, unweighted by too much armour, he can turn himself to new creative tasks, and untied by automatic reactions which served well and only for survival, he may look out with understanding on the future, does this show the process to have been good? We have seen that he did not bring himself to this position. We have to ask what did? We have to question further, Have the means been good, has the cost been proportionate to the result and the prize? Our concern in this essay is to see if the traces we find might suggest the possible handling of a power, wise, and good as it is powerful. An ingenious demiurge, playing with living suffering plastic, seeing how much it will stand, what odd shapes it can endure taking—such a notion could be a worse nightmare than blind chance. We must then ask: How, from our present knowledge, can we see that Power has treated Life as a whole? What has been the cost, in sentience and suffering, of raising this spire and finial which we call man the self-conscious?

First, we must allow that here we are stepping outside the clear line of what we actually and directly can study. It is always necessary to point out that all science and especially the Sciences of Life are composed of two parts. The one is observation, the other speculation. The one deals with data, the other with deduction. Such speculative deduction may be sound and is unavoidable, but we must always be aware—as some researchers have not been—where we leave the rock of fact for the brick-work and plaster of theory. Evolution—the theory that all life did arise from simpler forms, perhaps from one most simple slimelike form—is theory. Parts of it—as we shall see—such as the section that deals with the development of the vertebrates—make a fairly firmly jointed story. Parts, such as the mystery of the insects and their origins, are a story still to be found in any convincing wholeness. The theory as to why things evolve—Darwinism, Lamarkianism, Emergentism—all this side of the theory of Life is still further away from fact.

Yet that is not to say that even out here we may not decide between two types of deduced evidence, two likelihoods. And certainly such theories bear very closely on our concern: Is there any sign of goodness and wise intention in the life process? And it is here in life that we do come up against the chief difficulty of religion—the problem of evil. As we have seen, it really cannot arise in any real sense till we reach life. The waste of the stars is at worst—even if we can really understand the sidereal method and plan—merely ill economy. The waste of suffering life is surely horrible tragedy. That we stand at the top, that we have reached the dawn, that we may go on into the sunlight of permanent prosperity, happiness, control of our environment at our own wise pleasure—would all that sufficiently compensate the others, who fell, in raising us, for the cost of their failure, their pain, their frustration? 'I am not free', said Debbs echoing the Avatars, 'as long as one sufferer remains gaoled,'

Are we honourably dismissed from struggling with the problem of pain, as long as one in the past died unrequited? Evil must not be done that good may come. That a God did it only serves to disprove His claim not only to be wise but good—and where is godhead left if deprived of these attributes?

It was this deeply sad and indeed terrible thought that threw a darkening shadow over nineteenth-century optimism, at least in such sensitive souls as Charles Darwin. While its effect on the tough was even more distressing. For they, as Bernhardi of the old German General Staff made quite plain, saw which way the wind of doctrine was now blowing. In the doctrine of Natural Selection they claimed—and none was able to say them a sufficiently convincing Nay—a solemn injunction that they were Life's chosen if, and only if, they pressed others to the wall.

But of course the doctrine was worse and less sensible than even that. Natural Selection was really an attempt to give a profile to chaos. The Survival of the Fittest, as Arthur Balfour showed clearly fifty years ago, was a telling phrase for Nonsense. For it was a phrase offered as an explanation, but which, by its terms, ingeniously avoided giving any. It was to argue in a vicious circle. What is the Fit? That which survives—not the strongest, look at the rabbit, the house-fly, the skunk, the jelly fish. What survives? Whatever is Fit. Fit is no fitting word for one who does not define what he means by fitness. Like all poets, Tennyson called what had happened, Nature. He made visual evidence—the geological evidence of fossils—auditory and spoke of this apostrophized Female as crying: 'A thousand types—a score million might be nearer the mark—are gone. I care for nothing. All shall go.' The whole story was senseless. And the whole process was as utterly brutal. 'Nature, red in tooth and claw with rapine, shrieked against his creed—' again the dramatization into sound of what was perceived—if perceived at all—as a slow process recorded by visual findings of fragmentary evidence. Wild animals are never as persistently noisy as man. And as to the sanguinary rapacity of the life processes this undoubtedly the poets and moral rhetoricians such as T. H. Huxley, absurdly overdid. The parody on Tennyson's well-known lines is nearer the truth:

> *He chaunted 'Meat must be my mead'!*
> *But Nature green on snout and paw,*
> *Side-lined the cruel carnivore,*
> *And laughed away his bloody creed.*

Whether or not the meek inherit the earth, the violent have never succeeded in making much headway here. As Broom has pointed out, that symbol of malignancy the poisonous snake in all its forms does not seem in any wise more efficient, and in many ways less, than the non-poisonous forms.[1] The evil do turn up all along the line and keep on emerging. They seem, however, as little suited to last as anything else—unless it can be ultra-sensitive man or ultra-unaware cockroach. Even the phrase 'the Struggle to Survive' has in it a misleading suggestion of human drama. For example, the Dingo, the feral dog, in Australia 'drove out' the fierce marsupial wolf, the 'Tasmanian Devil'. But no one ever witnessed a fight between them. Survival seems to have been granted to that creature which, because it was a mammal, was a better mother to its young and, with the mammal's larger brain, more intelligent in finding food.

That of course brings us back to the real problem—not one of poetic and, maybe, emotional rhetoric—but of sense and meaning and the price of attaining purpose.

Is the process so far as we can detect it blind and has it exacted too cruel a cost from its helpless tools? There are, we must note, three questions here, not two: the goal, the cost and the power (or lack) of assent.

So, first, is the process as blind as Darwin made out? To arrive at a judgment on this we must note the the following things. We must at the start guard against sentiment. Once the Romantic Movement became impatient of the poor results that Reason produced on conduct, we have seen it throw itself into a pet of self-pity. Thomas Moore wrote, for a generation going com-

[1] Dr. Robert Broom, *The Coming of Man* (London: Witherby).

placently enough into the factory age, that it was obvious as to Nature, 'The trail of the Serpent is over it all'. This was of course blind and mendacious reaction. To say as the 'Augustans' of Queen Anne's epoch had, 'Whatever is, is good', and this is 'the best of all possible worlds', was easily deniable. But to say that everything was befouled and misery-struck was certainly even less true. This world is not the kingdom of the devil any more than it is the kingdom of Heaven. There is evil in life and no one has to live long to see it. Nor is it merely man-made. The parasites, such worms as the tape and others, the liver fluke, etc., are clearly horrible and cunning degenerations. Whatever drives them has determined that the form or forms in which it manifests its intention shall be one that abandons all effort to keep itself, simplifies down till it is nothing but a drain on any host on which it can find purchase and in finding that purchase it uses a skill that is quite diabolical in piercing its host's defences and resisting any effort he may make to rid himself of this vampirage. Further, as Dr. Swinton of the British Museum has pointed out in his studies on disease as shown in fossil bones, cancer, osteomyelitis, rodent ulcer, arthritis and the signs of other grave diseases can be found to have been present among the Mesozoic reptiles. Yet even with parasitism we find that many forms, which were taken to be such, are, actually, co-operators with their hosts. Commensalism and symbiosis—the sharing of a common table, the actual sharing of life by two organisms which become for all practical purposes one—these two devices are common throughout life and highly beneficial.

An illustration of commensalism is the hermit crab which has planted a sea anemone on the top of the abandoned sea shell in which it lives. From this station the sea anemone does its fishing and the scraps from its meals drift down to feed the lodger in the apartment below. The lodger not only can shift the house to better fishing sites or into more sheltered quarters, he does more as his share. When he grows too big for his shell he must find another. On these occasions—too rare to be a reflex—he reaches up, detaches the anemone, carries it about till he finds a house to suit both of them, then plants the anemone on the roof and gets inside himself. Further, and most strange, is the often-witnessed fact that though sea anemones are some of the lowest forms of animal life and sting with what seems an automatic reaction whatever comes within range of their poisoned tendrils, when the crab reaches out and takes the anemone partner in its claws the semiplant knows its friend from a stranger and lets itself be carried off quietly to their new joint quarters.

The standard example of symbiosis is the lichen. Here an alga which can consume air and thrive on it and a fungus that can eat rock, have come together and facing very different ways toward the problem of diet have succeeded in making a joint life so interwoven that it is hard to distinguish the two original partners and together they have managed to live under conditions of simplicity—requiring only rock and air—that few other living things have managed to achieve.

Nor are the signs of disease among some of the more ancient animals necessarily evidence that Life is mainly a failure, and that the bad and the low always succeed in pulling down the good and the high. As Dr. Swinton has pointed out, disease as far back as the Mesozoic seems to have attacked mainly those creatures in which old age, an over-sluggish life or too great bulk to the sum of available energy had made the general resistance inadequate. Bacteria that clear up decaying or degenerating bodies can't be considered a proof of the evilness of life. Such suffering as they cause can be understood if we see that it only befalls creatures which by failure of vital energy, and so loss of general resistance, become subject to attack. The sun that sterilizes decay is not evil because exposed to its rays a skin which fails to produce pigmentation, burns, blisters and suppurates. Many of the parasites which attack sheep have been found to leave them unmolested provided the sheep were given a diet which sustained their general resistance.

With the further developments of our knowledge of the problem of evil the next chapter will deal. There, when the question of recovery and restoration has to be handled, we shall also have to consider whether in the problem of evil there may not be three possible sources rather than two. In the West we allow that evil may spring from the individual act and will, and also from the entropic collapse of the universe dragging all with it. But there is a third possible source—the mistaken specialization of a species whereby it retreats from life and in which it involves all its special descendants. This would be a sort of special original sin.

Before doing that we must, however, look a little more closely into the particular argument which for the nineteenth century seemed to have made scientifically demonstrable the poetic generalization about the 'Trail of the Serpent'. Darwin's influence has been so vast, his theory has influenced men's minds so strongly toward senselessness as the one 'meaning' discernible in nature, and blind struggle being the only method that really works in human society, that we must deal with the personality and thinking processes of this almost unique figure. No animus can be felt against a man who personally was gentle, courteous, lovable and considerate, patient in study and masterly in demonstration. Indeed that last term is the first thing to recognize about this personality more influential than Newton and Freud rolled into one. This pivotal picture-drawer for modern man, one cannot call him a thinker.

Charles Darwin, though few who have not followed his life realize it, was no cold collector of facts. He was a highly emotional man—of fine, if ill-thought-out and little tamed emotions. He tells us that it was Malthus—one of the seminal thinkers of the ageing eighteenth century who was concerned not with biology proper but with the practical economic dread of human over-population—that, with his formula of 'breeding to the limit of subsistence' had set his mind on the principles which were to harden into his doctrine of Natural Selection. Darwin's feelings are also shown by the letter in which he writes that it is only a few days till 'the Twelfth', when he will be able to go out and shoot birds to his heart's content, and the later record when he tells us that on picking up a wounded bird which had lain disabled for a couple of days he resolved, and kept his resolve, never again to enjoy himself in that way. He had, we also know, desired to be a doctor but dread of the suffering which a pre-anaesthetic surgeon had both to witness and inflict, debarred him. That his nature was torn by unresolved, suppressed conflicts we know from the fact of the severe nervous disabilities from which he suffered, becoming almost an invalid and doing his work from a couch, after his return from the voyage of the *Beagle*. He was, then, no logician, still less a philosopher. Rather he was the great maker of the Mythos that should rule, and finally destroy, Biological and Economic Man. More than any philosopher of his century or of that before him —and many great names are among the thinkers of those two generations—he coloured the thought not only of those who had to think about ethics and the means and ends of society, but those who actually had to make the choices and guide the practical and political destinies of the peoples of the Western world, when that world for the first and last time had the whole of the world in its power. His responsibility, though he certainly did not seek it, has proved to be literally immense. No one can gauge its extent and its power is still not spent. It is important to note that there was a ready market among the informed, till the publication of the *Origin of Species*, for such skilled attempts as culminated in the *Bridgewater Treatises* to order the natural evidence to see if it showed evidence of design. Thereafter these efforts were abandoned, so that to-day men who think they are informed and who as theologians are supposedly concerned to find evidence for God's justice and goodness, assume in the statement of their case that Natural Theology does not exist. It is permissible to wonder what books on this issue they have studied, what experts have they consulted. It is possible that they are taking for granted that the immense ascendancy of Darwin as a supposed thinker still renders any such proofs as unworthy even of consideration.

The first thing we must note is, of course, that since Darwin's day a vast mass of information has come to light to which he could not have access. Nearly every informed biologist can no longer deny that Darwin was mistaken in thinking that change took place through minute gradual change. In their own life-time Darwin's great popularizer T. H. Huxley—a far more accurate thinker—remarked somewhat ruefully, 'I could wish that Mr. Darwin would not say quite so often, "Nature never goes by leaps".' We can see how well founded that wish was. To a degree that Huxley himself would have considered shattering, nature has been demonstrated to go only by leaping. The Quantum in Physics has been complemented by the Sport in Biology. This mistake of Darwin's was radical to the whole structure of his thought. We have seen also that his 'explanation' theory of Natural Selection was no explanation but a tautology. The truth is his immense industry and his skill in ordering his finds made people think that he was presenting them with an unanswerable case. And we must never forget that against the Adam and Eve Genesis picture of creation—which was what religion was opposing to his alternative—he was giving one that did incorporate the geological and fossil evidence, all of which the Churches were passionately and blindly rejecting. Darwin drifted from being a naturalist of genius, an observer of supreme talent, an indefatigable collector and orderer of his collections, into being taken for a thinker. As Professor Charles E. Raven, who is both a theologian and a naturalist of considerable note, has pointed out, Darwin 'was quite untrained in any sort of philosophy or abstract thinking'. Darwin himself wrote to Asa Gray with the greatest frankness about his own limitations as a thinker, 'About Design . . . I am in an utterly hopeless muddle' (26th November 1860). And again to the same on 11th December, 1861, 'With respect to Design . . . you say you are in a haze; I am in thick mud; yet I cannot keep out of the question. I have written a great deal of nonsense.' There is such generous humility in this that it is right to quote it as showing both the greatness of the man and his self-acknowledged unfitness to be used as one who could decide this question. Yet he has, both by those who want to find purpose and those who do not, been taken as the man who proved that Natural Theology was a vain search. But there were times when he showed that under his surface sense of baffled patience there was an animus—and that animus was in favour of chaos and blind chance. When Charles

Lyell, who had done so much to make geology comprehensible and yet held to there being a purpose manifest in nature, had declared that he felt the pattern of things was ordained, Darwin wrote to him that 'the subject has no interest for me' (13th August 1861), surely we may ask, Why? Why, for a man who was writing most influential books to prove a new thesis that man's ascent and the processes of life were due to blind chance and amoral struggle? On the 21st of August he adds: 'The conclusion I always come to after thinking of such questions is that they are beyond the human intellect and the less one thinks of them the better.' This is possibly true and in all likelihood a consistent, if narrow, Fundamentalist position. But surely no conclusion could be less in keeping with one who was making theories about how Life had resulted in man and why the struggle of the process went on? It would seem that Darwin did not recognize what he was doing, that he was philosophizing—any more than M. Jourdain knew that he was speaking, and couldn't help speaking, prose. The question was not whether the one was speaking and the other thinking, but whether they were speaking well or ill, thinking clearly or in a muddle.

Finally, it is clear that Darwin had never realized that you cannot have *both* a 'chance' theory of Nature and one of iron law and mechanism. The one excludes the other and yet he strove to show both were in play. There had to be mechanism or he could not see and trace out the patterns of blind weaving that he depended on to prove his case. But the whole thing also had to be blind chance, for he did not wish to find purpose. It is very important that the alternative which did occur to T. H. Huxley never seemed to have dawned on Darwin's much simpler mind—the fact that there might be an intelligence shown in the world; and the issue was not whether there was a creative word speaking in the universe but whether what it spoke was ill or good. T. H. Huxley could and did write, 'The Teleological and the Mechanical views of Nature are not necessarily mutually exclusive,' and as he went on to think on this terrible problem he comes to his final conclusion. That conclusion was, inevitably, utterly different from the liberalism of Darwin, so

welcome to those who thought that 'Nature' had left them free
to enjoy and exploit the world and the weaker. That conclusion
Huxley gave in his Romanes Lecture 'Defy the Cosmic Process'. The world and all Life is under a law and it is 'the law
of sin and death', yes, and of violence, cunning and cruelty.
Man alone can make his protest and man can make no more
than protest.

There were moments when Darwin himself saw the direction in which his theories were leading him and all reason. Late
in his day, 3rd July 1881, he wrote to W. Graham who had
brought out a book called *The Creed of Science*, 'With me the
horrid doubt always arises whether the convictions of man's
mind, which has been developed from the mind of the lower
animals, are of any value or at all trustworthy. Would anyone
trust the convictions of a monkey's mind, if there are any convictions in such a mind?' Here, of course, he was up against that
reductio ad absurdum which results when any argument even of the
simplest sort is used to discredit reason—that *reductio* which
reached its final absurdity in Freud. Darwin can see that as, according to his dogma, men's minds, being derived from animals,
could have no thought other than animal thought, enriched and
bemuddled by chance accretions of observation and useless
subtlety, so therefore Mr. Graham's attempt to give 'Science' a
creed is probably subjective. But Darwin, being just as much
the son of an irrational ape as Graham, is by his own premises
debarred from making any criticism of Graham. An ape-mind's
preference for nonsense over sense, or vice versa, is itself nonsense, subrational, utterly insignificant. What Darwin to the end
did not see, perhaps in some depth of his mind did not want to
see, was that 'if there are any convictions in such a mind' then
we have to ask what sort of mind is this? And if we find no
convictions in the mind of an ape then we have to ask, what
happened to the ape's mind—if it was the source—that owing
to blind chance—if that is the cause—there emerged a creature
called man who did have convictions, who did reason and whose
reason did lead him to build up a life utterly unlike—and in his
highest attempts incomparably above—any ape's or any

animal's? That power of reason has proved itself objectively valid by giving man, who alone has used it, unique power over his environment. When we have said the best we can for animals, when we have said the worst we can about our race, Aristotle is right—things must be judged by their finest productions—and by that test what animal can compare with the great savant or the saint? And is sanctity simply an extravagance of brutishness or an adumbration of divinity? By that same test, what work of any other creature can compare with the works of supreme human genius? Again we have to ask, is this blind and biologically useless fantasy, or is it in miniature the work of one who in embryo and under humiliating restrictions is still not an absurd over-developed decadent ape but the son of that Father who is the Creator? It is now clear that the doctrine of Natural Selection—a doctrine that preached cruel pointlessness —won't do and must go. As Dr. Howell and many other workers in biology have pointed out, the theory that it is all chance can't account for the fact that repeatedly there have emerged such advancing characteristics of great complexity as (1) warmblood systems; (2) eyes, and, indeed (3) the rise of the primatic types. Convergence is frankly allowed by botanists. Those who study animal life cannot longer resist its evidence. Those who are still fighting for nonsense have to suggest that as the eyes must have taken long to evolve, for a long time have been no use and so its advantage to the user have been none and its handicap perhaps a factor against survival—all forces being needed to keep the creature up in the struggle to survive—hence we must explain it by a special device. It is suggested that there are linked genes and one of these served the animal's actual needs. So, for example, we are asked to suppose there was a factor in the germ which fruited, say, in a claw while attached to this claw factor aeon after aeon was the still useless but growing eye factor. This, however, is an *ad hoc* argument, like those land bridges which botanists used to 'think up' on a speculative fancy map of what the world may have been millions of years ago, because they needed these bridges to bring over plants from the places where they are now found isolated. No, as Henry

Fairfield Osborn made out, we have to allow some type of orthogenesis, some tendency within the animal to grow rightly and not to be a mere plastic that takes the impressions of all its contacts and accidents and so results in being what it is.

We have, then, seen that the view which has so vastly influenced men's defeatism, against there being any evidence for purpose in Nature and in Life, the doctrine which has proved its mistakenness by sanctioning such outbursts of international anarchy that civilization is one step away from suicide, that view was never worked out, is full of inner inconsistencies, is insignificant as a philosophy and fatal in practice. And yet we must never cease to allow that its success was due to what was true in it. Religion was fighting for what could not be honestly maintained—its absurd geological picture as given in that collection of Bronze Age documents asserted to be inspired by a people who wanted to believe they were special favourites of a partial Providence. And to this handicap in the face of truth there was the greater handicap in the face of morality. The God shown in these scriptures was so often morally unworthy that men had long felt a generous revolt against such a fantasy of men's minds. When truth combines with moral outrage and when personal advantage comes in too, promising freedom from strait-laced prohibitions, then the dams burst and good is flung away with the evil and the otiose. But religion is to blame for letting the good be compromised by association with ineffective irrational taboos—such as the veto on marriage with a deceased wife's sister—and with positive evil—such as the doctrine of eternal damnation.

We must remember that Natural Theology has not to prove nor to lend any support to anthropomorphism nor to such base concepts of Deity as would teach, in the phrase made popular by what has been called the Doubly Dismal Dane, that God is capable of 'Teleological exceptions of morality' as when in the early Hebrew epic 'God' is said to have ordered Abram to sacrifice his only son.

On the other hand, neither is Natural Theology compelled to prove that the evidence it handles shows a perfect world, as was stated at the beginning of Chapter One. This need not be the best of all possible worlds. Anyhow that is an impossible proposition. For to establish it the judge would have to have examined all the other worlds—a notion more absurd to the Age of Reason than even to ours. All we have to show is that it is not hopelessly bad, the trail of the serpent is not over all and that here is an opportunity, a favourable environment in which a creature of good will and good sense can grow. We have also to show that man is such a creature. True, he is not always so, no, not in an overwhelming number of cases. But he is so in that majority which secures that the whole does not not go to rack and ruin and that a few men climb to such heights that there is revealed the promise of something that makes worth while much toil and not a little pain, much testing and some temporary frustration. In actual fact this world is neither a Paradise nor a Hell. It shows itself neither the best possible world nor the worst, but the world of *most possibilities*, the world of greatest possible freedom to go up or down, in short the middle world.

We must, then, start our inquiry as to what is the way that Life has moved, all over again. For, first, the conclusions that the School of Natural Selection drew are themselves not conclusions for they are not explanations. Even if they had had the facts, the whole number of facts and nothing but the facts, a theory which would show that all theorizing is invalid, all reasoning merely fantasy bred from unsound biological extravagance of the nervous system, is no theory. Secondly, a vast number of new facts bearing on the problem have come to light. The problem now is not whether Blind Chance made the world and runs life but whether this power is one that can be understood and co-operated with as a friend or is simply an amoral demiurge absorbed in his inhuman experiments. Life must have meaning. To say that it is nonsense can never be a logical proposition. All that such a phrase can mean is that till now I have not had the skill to find the meaning.

We have to ask what may we now know about the How of Life. From that we may be able to form some conjecture as to the Why. We can in this place only mention some of the most striking and, during the last century, utterly unsuspected facts about Life which have come to light in the last generation, and then those from research in the last couple of years. The first stems out from hints which had been collecting for some time. As we have seen, the more living processes were studied the more they were found to depend basically on electric fields of high potency—living stuff was of common chemicals plus high charges. The association of electricity with living matter we have seen, is shown positively, with the work on the brain waves, and negatively by the fact that malignant tumours either emit no such waves or are of the opposite charge.[1] Inquiry has culminated in a hypothesis which is perhaps the most startling speculation as yet made about the mystery of the Living Process. Dr. J. A. V. Butler in his highly important paper 'Life and the Second Law of Thermodynamics' (*Nature*, 3rd August 1946) has produced results of research which in his opinion show that even with the breeding of fungus cells—a low form of life—the so-called Law of Entropy may not apply.

After pointing out that for a century research has never been really satisfied as to whether Life finds a way of evading the otherwise universal dissipation of energy and that Kelvin expressly excluded 'animate agencies' from his statement of the 'law', Dr. Butler continues, Schroedinger in picturesque but inaccurate language says the organism 'feeds upon negative entropy', and most scientists would agree. But G. N. Lewis in his *Anatomy of Science* maintains that living things breast the stream of inevitable processes, which tear down while Life builds up. For the living thing evolves new substances and more intricate forms. Dr. Butler charges such literary scientists as Dr. J. Needham (incidentally a warm sympathizer with Marxian ideology) with dangerously over-simplifying entropy, maintaining that the loose identification of entropy with disorder has allowed 'The Second Law' to be taken as a universal tendency to chaos. He points out that the formation of ice actually shows

---

[1] Cf. Dr. E. D. Adrian's paper on electroencephalograms already quoted and also Dr. C. E. Irdell, *Colour and Cancer* (London: Lewis & Co.).

that this is a false simplification. He then goes on to refer to his work on the growth of *Penicillium notatum*. The spores could not get their energy from light, being bred in total dark. They were fed only on sugar, nitrate, phosphate and small amounts of a few metallic salts. There was nevertheless an increase in complexity of the flask's contents. The question then is: Has the free energy in the flask been increased by nothing but the fungus' living activity? Protein has been built up and protein is a definite and unique arrangement of constituent amino acids. Dr. Butler concludes, after giving mathematical evidence for it, that 'configurational entropy' is not a dominant factor in the free energy of a protein. Further, the free energy to build protein molecules only can come from the living organism's metabolism. Life, then, in its simplest forms, may always be a building up process and not a breaking down.

But, aren't we still free to say that in the end it must anyhow fail. Maybe it is trying to kindle the environment as a flame tries to kindle damp fuel but after a little incandescence, the larger damp and dark will win. But here again we must note a fact, extensive indeed but unnoticed by the mechanist biologists. Granted that the conditions now are less favourable than they were for the appearance of Life, granted that a warm slush is easier for easy and delicate livers than the comparatively cold bare world in which we live, stripped from our blanket of hot cloud, naked to the winds and the stars. Yet the fact remains that as Life has gone on and the environment grown harder, Life has not been in retreat or even doggedly holding its own— it has taken the initiative and kept on winning new lands to its sway—yes and new oceans. New heights it has won, no doubt. Primitive life there can be little doubt was 'littoral'—it hung on in the warm tidal pools, lagoons and marshes, a marginal lodger, a dependant of the fringes. But Life to-day had gone on to the land. This itself was an immense effort and, strange to say, done as far as we can judge for the sake of pure exploration. For the essential act of bringing forth young had to be risked by these adventurers. They did not do it to get better breeding quarters any more than to get more food. Food and nursery accommodation were all on the side of staying in the sea. The first amphibians—as we can still see in that very successful survivor of the stock, the frog—advanced first into their new kingdom by developing legs and arms to pull themselves about under the greatly increased strain and friction of land walking in comparison with sea floating. And with this they had to grow lungs. Inwardly and outwardly, what a strain on physique; and just to endure the weary world of dry land. For when we are really dry then we are done—more than two-thirds of us having still to be water. So we have to learn to prevent ourselves being dried up by the world we have conquered. But our seed remains vulnerable. So first the amphibians had to go back to water if they were to continue their stock. Then came the next master triumph. The reptiles learned—or were shaped—so as to carry their young in an internal water environment till the young could endure the strain and stress of the new kingdom. And so young and old, child and parent, were tied together. In consequence what, physically, might have meant separation—the fact that they had separate bodies able to go different ways—psychophysically meant that they were linked and thus affection could spring up. So its earliest form, parentalism, appeared or at least was greatly helped. We can't be sure that love was simply the child of physical contiguity. The fishes do not even have the affection of mating congress. Yet the stickleback—a simple and common little fish—is a devoted father. It is well known that having no hands to hold them to his heart, if he thinks his young are in danger he holds them in his mouth until the peril be past.

With the vertebrates even fresh conquests are made of the environment and these conquests are also paralleled by a growth in kindness. The highest animals have spread farthest and on the whole have been the kindest—caring most and longest for their young, liking most to live in groups of mutual help.[1]

So two facts are clear—it is true that the climate grew more stern—or if you will more tonic—but this did not check Life; it seemed rather to stimulate it. How that can be so we saw

[1] See Kropotkin's *Mutual Aid,* a much neglected work in our blindly toughening civilization.

in the last chapter that the new cosmology of Milne does much to explain. Indeed the latest meteorological studies of the changes of climate suggest some kind of co-operation between its changes and the opportune emergence of types able to release more energy and to show more awareness both of their environment and their fellows. The environment does not simply stay 'fit for Life', fit for all Life, fit for however long Life may choose to loiter on. No, it takes a hand, not only in sustaining but in urging on Life to ever higher activity, acuter and more sustained consciousness. As before the advent of Life the environment was curiously prepared for it, so step by step the climate and the surroundings are changed as Life must rise to completely new developments—and those who will not must be put out of the path. Some of the new evidence for this we are about to review. The epochs of Life, as far as we can see from the geologic record, divide into three vast stages. Roughly speaking the first, the Archaeozoic, is the age of creatures happiest in the sea—it is a sea aeon. Next comes the middle phase, the Mesozoic, the age of the reptiles when the spinal-structured four-limbed, air-breathing, cold-blooded creatures rule the world. Finally comes the great, though, in comparison to the others, the still very brief, stage of the Tertiary aeon. This is marked by the rise and dominance of creatures with warm blood and large brains. In the first stage—the Archaeozoic—such things as giant squids and gastropods reach a considerable size and skill of being. An octopus to-day is still worth much study not only for structure but because of its mentality. Yet this was as high as the mollusc structure could be raised and its limit was the sea level. The Saurian stage showed wonderful invention. Flight was mastered by these lizards—or by what drove them. But the brain was insignificant. In most saurians the spinal cord actually gets smaller when it enters the cranium. Instead of a single central nervous system in the head most had —such as the Diplodocus—three. By far the smallest was in the skull, the next biggest in the vertebrae near the shoulder blades and the third and largest in the lumbar region. Finally the blood was cold. Such consciousness as there was must then have been divided among three centres of possible attention and further fragmented by all feeling having to lapse as soon as the temperature fell below perceptible warmth.

With the rise of the mammals an extraordinary convergence of new conveniences come together in their structure to aid their spectacular advance. We have seen that the brain increased in size and the eyes became the sense *par excellence* to guide them. The hand, at the same time, began to be the tester of things 'close at hand', instead of the snout. And these creatures were all very small. Further, the process of breeding showed more foresight—if not by the creature—which is hard to think—then by some planner standing back to it. By laying eggs and leaving the sun to hatch them the reptiles can postpone the hatching and the slower you are to appear the longer you will be able to hold your own and the further push your explorations when you emerge. The mammals carry this advance by delay even further. For, by keeping the foetus within them, the new mothers postponed the actual laying of the egg. In fact it is now not only laid in the mother but hatched there also. This animal seems to find all this possible because it has warm blood. It carries not only the water that the young must have as their environment, the mother carries also the heat the embryo child needs—she is both its primal ocean and its primal sun.

But how did these tiny ratlike creatures generate so much greater energy than the giant lizards that had conquered the earth? First, it would seem because these new models of the highest life-form were more focused. When you grow beyond a certain size, the power to live, the inherent vitality, seems to get squandered and diffused. That seems the explanation of the fantastic growths that appeared on such frilled, spined and warted creatures as, for example, Triceratops. These bayonets of bone and of chitin were not of use to the animals. They were splinterings off of unwanted, undirected growth, a kind of cancer of the crust. The endocrine system, lacking a co-ordinator sufficiently dominant to keep the whole glandular series in line, breaks up into an anarchy. Growth, then, like an unpruned tree, leads to a self-strangling tangle. One of the greatest authorities on later saurian development maintained that these creatures are indicating clearly the structural symptoms of extravagant acromegaly.

Can we find any hint why this failure of the mighty, and this amazing success of the weak and small, who not only took the world from its masters but raised themselves to heights the lizards never approached? There was a vast change in climate as the saurian age ended. A vast epoch of lagoons, swamps, huge stretches of semiaquatic jungle and 'sud' areas covering the main parts of the present dry land, came to a close. In Wyoming, which was just such a district, it seems that the vast saurians were actually stranded in their pools as they dried up, having become far too vast to move their tons of bulk over dry land. They needed water to float them and water to breed their acres of lush vegetable mush. And such conditions—the damp warm climate and the vegetation it could produce—in turn needed much carbon dioxide in the air and much less oxygen. That is the breathing mixture which suits a lizard best. But if you have the lung system of a mammal you prefer a much higher balance of oxygen and much lower carbon dioxide. So the climate that is most stimulating to you tells against your old rival and former master. What pushes you on, puts him back. Before his food begins to fail and his water to dry up, his air is no longer healthy —the atmosphere, the most subtle of his masters, has turned against him and in favour of this new creature. With oxygen as its highest form of food this creature can have its brain lit, its energy roused, its blood warmed. It is always aware, always curious, always alive. No wonder it won.

But it is a wonder why that change should have come on in the climate just when the creature that could use it was coming to readiness, and, just when the creature that had spent its vital endowment in getting vast and becoming pointless, was ready to go. Nor is that all that is to be discovered in this odd alliance of climate with the vital effort going on in the life process. Not only did the climate change definitely in favour of an oxygen balance against the former one in which carbon dioxide was stronger, but the ground changed too. The first act of the vast three-act play of Life was played out with the sea as its stage, sea level as its ceiling. The second act was played out on land, but the stage was as distinctly different from stage three as that second act was different from the first, the ocean stage. The third stage is what we may call the oxygen-tent setting and it is a setting which alters the stage properties and hangings remarkably. Not only do the swamps disappear—a new vegetation takes over. A new thing appears clothing the ground, grass. And new beauties—flowers—are seen everywhere. Grass and flowers which we take to be nature's standard background are new things. They came with the mammals. So, though things are more austere, they are not only more bracing but they are more lovely. The ponderous, slow movement of Life is over and it enters on a scherzo of wonderful vivacity.

Nor is this mere light-hearted gaiety. The conquest of the world is pushed forward as never before until there is not an area from pole to pole into which Life has not penetrated and made terms, or keeps on making sallies to win over the most stubborn outposts of death and night. Nor is it merely upward, away from the sea, to the mountains and the arctic ranges and the air that Life has climbed. Until Dr. Beebe had been there and seen, no one could have believed that Life had gone on at the other end, and, in the abyss of the sea, had pushed down into the fabulous pressures that exist half a mile down. There in the dark—where it is impossible to think it could have begun—Life has pushed its representatives. Not only are there frail fishes which carry their own lights with them in that watery dark but creatures twenty feet long were seen cruising in those frontier fathoms where adaptation to environment must have gone to unsurpassed lengths. The atmospheric pessimists have, however, maintained that all this is only a passing accidental phase. Life, all the more because it has trusted so largely to oxygen in this its last daring advance, will be completely let down. For all the available oxygen will be used up. The rocks will swallow it and go red in the face. The earth will become one great rust heap—like Mars—and we shall gasp and die. For what oxygen the rocks don't absorb will evaporate off into outer space.

But lately[1] this pessimistic atmosphere picture has been challenged. We are not the same as Mars, for Mars is not nearly as massive as we. Mars may not have an iron core similar to ours. That means three things. One is obvious, that we have a chance of holding on to what oxygen we have far longer than Mars may have done. The other two are not so obvious and so till now seem to have escaped notice—though perhaps had we been less keen to notice the futility of our position and less unfriendly to the thought that it might have been planned, these considerations might have gained earlier recognition. The first of these two considerations is that the gravitational differentiation which first set free the first oxygen from the earth's iron core is still at work. We can breathe oxygen because it was and still is released from the molten iron. The process now is slow but it is still going on. At about eight hundred and fifty miles down oxygen is being set loose from the iron there. True, it has to escape through the molten basalt that lies above the iron belt. But in this respect the basalt layer only acts as a filter, the iron remains behind and the oxygen filters through up to us. The second consideration is right up at the other end. True, we do lose oxygen at the top of the atmosphere, out into space. But also, because space is no longer conceived of as empty, we, because we are a large and massive body, net quite a lot of oxygen too as we sweep along. Indeed, the objection which the author of this important paper holds out is that we might capture too much, we might find our oxygen instead of getting dangerously low, going intoxicatingly high. It is here he makes his most interesting suggestion. He believes he can show by mathematical chemistry that the oxygen will never be let go too far. It will never increase more than some 23 per cent of what it is at present. But realize the significance of this prophecy. It may well mean that here we glimpse in the future a provision for just that further increase of the stimulation of the air that is breathed which would parallel a further increase of man's capacity to think, to be conscious. This further increase would complement, it would fulfil that increase of

[1] See *Nature*, 27th October 1945, 'Stability of the Earth's Atmospheric Oxygen', by A. L. Parson.

oxygen content which took place when the mammals were to rise and the saurians, with their need of more carbon dioxide, were to fall back and to be cleared away. So, as we see in the past a curious co-ordination of the environment and its chemistry, not to keep Life constant but to raise it up if it would rise and send it away if it wished to stay put, so, in the future we may suppose there is a further promise of a more tonic environment to aid a creature of intelligence and of mainly a lung nourishment against one of a lower type and clinging more to intestinal food. The creature of head and lungs will be the better placed for survival in such a world than the creature of viscera and loins.

Life itself is not failing, we can then assert. The environment may be getting harder—or more challenging—less favourable to rest and stagnation. But the challenge is being answered. And, far from being found desperate, it turns out to be tonic. A stimulating, inspiring, ever more suggestive set of questions is being asked through keying up the climate, and to these promptings Life is giving ever more apt and acute answers.

The whole range of this convergence and co-operation of climate and organism is so comprehensive, so unsuspected and so lately discovered that we must now summarize it before we attempt to draw any further conclusions about Life and its living quarters and what sort of planning and what kind of planner they might together show.

When trying to define man we were, at the start of this chapter, giving the basic pattern of his way of living by attempting to see how this creature draws on its surroundings and draws them in to sustain and figure forth its self. So we attempted to give as it were, the profile of man's diet in the full wide sense of that word. We found that his diet is a threefold power to absorb power: (1) basically he has the alimentary-canal food—solid and liquid pabulum, (2) next he has pulmonary food—the highly oxygenated gas we call air and (3) the nerve-system food—the electromagnetic field of radiation in which his consciousness is best strung, stimulated and inspired and in which his type breeds best.

Now we can see that, in the co-operation of climate with man's psychophysical emergence and advance, all these three appetites and needs for nourishment of a peculiar high energy rate for this, the most advanced and vital animal, were provided at the time that he had evolved to need them. The Dinosaurs, according to Dr. Swinton, lived almost entirely when on land on resinous plants and in the water on lush weeds. Resin is highly unsuitable for our stomachs and we need a compact and stimulating diet. So the appearance of the grasses gave us those grains (wheat, millet, barley and rye) which would give us what is to us the synonym for food, bread. Man's second diet need, for his new appetite in the pulmonary field, was at the same time met by putting more oxygen into the air and less carbon dioxide. While his diet need in his third area of assimilation, his third need and appetite for stimulation was also simultaneously supplied by the clearing sky, freed of the dense fogs, permitting the short-wave radiations of the sun and the stars to reach his nervous system.

Thus the triple change in climate, met, welcomed and sustained the triple change in the emergent and leading creature, the mammal, who thereby was to surpass all other forms, who themselves, *by the very same changes*, were demoted, degenerated and dismissed. So the climate not only aided and drew out one small but responsive creature, and so raised it to heights no animal had as yet attained; at the very same time that new climate removed the new creature's former masters so that they might no longer be even its present competitors. Truly 'to him that has is given and from him that has not is taken even that which he has'.

And here also we should add that later on this same strange intervention—which looked like disaster but was really a new offer of a new life—can be seen again. For when the next great step was to be taken by Life, once more climate co-operated. And much in the same way, though more keenly; maybe because acting now on a creature more keenly aware and therefore capable of a clearer response, a more vigorous reaction. We have seen that when the warm-blooded animals, with their coats of fur

instead of scale and their vasomotor system of blood-tempera-
ture regulation, were ready to emerge and were thereby ready
not only to face, but to profit by, an austerer and more tonic
environment, then the climate altered. So likewise, as will be
noted in a few pages further, when the mammal stock had, in
turn, spent its inventiveness and in all but one species or genus
sold its birthright of general tentative response (wonder and
curiosity) for the ever-narrowing efficiency and satisfaction of
automatic reaction, then another advance, as great as the rise
of the mammals, had to be made. For self-conscious man is as
vast a step up from the large-brained mammal as that is up from
the intermittently conscious cold-blooded reptile. And here again
climate co-operates by causing a crisis in the outer world to
match and integrate with the crisis in the inner world of the
organism itself. As H. G. Wells remarked in his *Outline of History*
the great Ice Age and man as we know him appear together.
Moreover, we can see that that awful climatic austerity again
reacted both negatively and also positively with Life. It cleared
away a vast unknown number of types that had become adapted
blindly to comfortable living and so had come to rest. More, it
seems to have pruned actually the genus of man, if not the
species to which we belong. As we have seen, Neanderthal
(Mousterian) man may very likely be one of the mistaken—
because purely physiological—reactions to the cold. This species
by glandular (possibly pituitary) changes may have altered its
physical resistance to low temperatures—but at the cost of its
other reactions and further mental advance. In true man we get
the true positive reaction—the purely mental reaction: a multi-
form and fertile response, leading not only to solving the acute
immediate problem—to survive under constant arctic conditions—but to a completely new understanding of his environment and the production of completely new powers. Man becomes an inventor and creates a culture of increasing richness.
He himself has become a new thing, separate from and above
all the beasts. Beside him they—whether they be reptile or fish,
mammal or bird—are one group, and he is another. That this
change may be called cataclysmic, a sudden move of the climate

with the sudden move in the species (for man, there is no doubt, was latent and ready before the Ice Age[1]), is seen by the fact, now recognized, that it was a sudden besieging of Life's terrain. No explanation of the Ice Age has yet been able to satisfy experts. It is, apparently, no regular part of the earth's behaviour. There was an Ice Age in the Permian, perhaps to co-operate with some step up and further emergence of Life as early as that. Then, right down in the Pliocene, with the evident exhaustion of the mammal stocks through their all choosing specialization, suddenly and from both Poles came down the cold again at an annihilating speed (we must remember that we must gauge speed as we have to gauge time, not by our clocks or years but by the rate at which living creatures can become aware and can respond—that movement is instantaneous to which I can give no reply or response before it has spent itself upon me). And when the Ice Age is over, as out of a 'freezing furnace', man is found cast and tempered. The Ice Age, having done its work, withdrew, and man was given again a Genial Climate. He had made the right answer to privation, invention, and so was free again and with new powers. And not, until in this decade did he tamper with nature's structure, has she moved against him or shown signs of moving.[2]

And now we must ask, is all this to be accounted for by (1) accident, (2) by unsuspected power of response in the organism alone to blind changes in its environment or (3) is it more probable to attribute this co-ordination to an overall co-ordination—the Life within living forms responding to tests and calls made through the surroundings and, so far as it responded, winning to higher life? That is what actually happened. We must never forget that, whether it looks like chance as we trace the detailed working, the end process has been an unbelievably odd and meaningful result for any chance to produce. We may say the

---

[1] See the work of J. Reid Moir, F.R.S., on the Eolithic Hearths from the Ipswich Red Crag beds in East Anglia, Britain.

[2] For the latest summary of work in regard to simultaneity of the Ice Age at both Poles see *Report of the Committee on Glaciers for 1945* (Transactions of Am. Geophysical Union, 27.219.1946).

method is wasteful, cruel, tedious. The fact remains that those who hold it all to have been chance or the work of a mind incomprehensible because its values are so different to ours, these critics agree with the most optimistic, and have to say, That it started with slime and it ends with intelligence, and an intelligence not yet at the end of its tether, and combined with a generosity and largeness of heart which has no more been achieved by the lower animals than they achieved the huge brain used by the master mind. Pure chance—'no meaning'— we have seen is to say no more than that I do not know.

The last applicant as explainer is 'the power within the organism'. To answer whether that will meet the bill we have first to define our terms—which organisms? We must remember that the whole picture of Life 'evolving' or as Ward always taught, advancing by 'epigenesis'—this chart of Life's story is very incomplete evidentially. We must repeat: we can get the line of the vertebrates fairly clearly up from fish to man, though there are bad gaps even in that. About the insects we know next to nothing as to their history as a whole—for one thing chitin preserves very badly so their fossils are mainly to seek. Even about the birds there is doubt which doesn't grow less as many paleontologists now question whether Archaeopteryx was really the bird-lizard link and whether birds did come from lizards. We know fairly surely that when the lizards had reached their height it was not they that gave rise to the protomammals but some small unspecialized ratlike creature that achieved hair instead of scales, warm instead of cold blood. But of course the birds had managed to get to warm blood. Is this then convergence? Does all Life when it is fully alive strive to be something fuller than it has ever been, keener than it has ever known? We see also fairly clearly that when the mammals took over and the giant lizards had gone—that from this simple small unspecialized stock or stocks, sprang again highly specialized forms which became gigantic. No fish and no saurian yet found compares in size with the right whale and yet this creature is a mammal that went back into the sea. Further, it there became, in spite of its size, so helpless that its tongue is often eaten out by one of the shark-likewhales called the Orca Gladiator. The giant beast cannot put its hand in its mouth to get out its tormentor nor gnash him to pieces, because it has let even the teeth go, the better to live on a weak bouillon of micro-organisms floating in the sea. On the land, also in that first epoch of the Tertiary, the Eocene, there grew a creature, the Baluchitherium, which stood seventeen feet at the shoulder and whose 'hand' bones to bear this weight had to be compounded into a post. It only lasted through the Eocene and then disappeared. We know also that, as with the saurians, some mammals sacrificed the hand (as in the bats) to fly and others by becoming carnivores became parasitic on other mammals. The carnivores seem to be getting stupider[1] as they have specialized on their diet of flesh and blood and have sacrificed the hand to make it a killing instrument. (See W. P. Pycraft's study of the paw of the lion.)

It seems clear then that Life at least in this the third stage, where we can view the story in some detail and see it emerging into our own, the story of man's emergence, shows two characteristics. The first is that at any cost it must hang on to being generalized. It must not lose a power of wide response, interest, awareness, yes, the capacity to be touched by and to be considerate with what it sees and feels. It must not exploit. And, secondly, we know that, though up to the present the process has not failed, and, more, that when stuck to, it has given wonderful extension both of understanding and power, nevertheless, the vast number of mammalian species as well as of genera have taken the easy road to degeneracy. Either through becoming too slack to survive or by parasitism, in one or the other of its cunning-cruel-violent methods, the degenerate becomes finally utterly dependent on the host, to whom it will give nothing and from whom it finally takes away the very life on which itself has become absolutely dependent. In this respect we must remember that the tiger is as helplessly malignant as a tapeworm or indeed as a cancer cell.

We must own, then, that of all the lines of evolution we have

[1] See studies in the psychology of lions in the wild state, Kruger National Park, South Africa.

only one in which a fairly extensive series of dots will show us a process. But that is the one which concerns us most, for it culminates in man. And we may perhaps say it is the line on which the whole meaning of Life has come most to depend, because here and here alone has detached consciousness succeeded in emerging. Further, it seems possible to perceive that all Life starts at the psychological level of Trial and Error—that is the quality of consciousness which seems to correspond to, inform and express amoebal life. Here is no more instinct than there is reason. A blind questing and striving, the power to seek what pleases and shrink from what distresses, that seems original. From this base two courses were evidently open—the course that would end in a continual striving for more understanding and one that would end with a false and limited assurance, the blind reaction which is certain that it knows all that any event can offer, snatches and consumes what it wants, rejects or destroys what it dislikes. Instinct we can see becomes ever more flawless, more complete, more blind. Till finally, when the conditions have become utterly and fatally different, still the same old reaction is made. Once quite adequate to supply the reactor's need and nothing else, now it is equally fatal, fatal because conditions are changed. So it assures the creature's destruction. Intelligence becomes ever more extensive. Rising from that surplus vitality that will take an interest, feel a curiosity in things which it cannot use for its own immediate purpose, understanding goes on ever recognizing wider 'ratios' and proportions and scales between things that seemed different. This type of consciousness is, then, that which is always accepting, never dismissing. The other is always rejecting and narrowing down its response until the response is no longer its own reply to an actual instant but the ghost of an answer to a question that ceased to be asked aeons ago.

We can, then, perceive in these two vast types of living response the shadow trace of a moral issue. Here is a quality of choice. Maybe it runs right down through Life to its base. And the results of that choice, of negative or positive self-creation, are shown and cast in the forms that arise. Nor is it a choice made once and for all. It has to be made continually and always more definitely. For example, after the enormous effort of the amphibians, which heaved them out of the easy water on to the hard gritty land and into the scarce breathable air, the saurians were free to enjoy an expanse of living, an easy, idle unawareness, which the dangers of the foreshore seas had restricted. But they chose to use their new liberty to become large, overweighted and sluggish. And in turn with the mammals. They are all sprung from small, lively forms unarmed with physical weapons, compelled to wonder, to watch, to endure and to invent extemporized responses to varying challenges—both the price and the power of liberty. For liberty is the climate and the soil of which invention is the crop. Yet again, we see during the very first stage of the Mammalian age—the Eocene—there had been huge defections and secessions from the first liberty in favour of captive ease. And right through the Tertiary age—during the Oligocene, Miocene, Pliocene and Pleistocene—we see this defection continuing until it has reached overwhelming proportions, until only one stock, one species at length is still free, free to go on, free to suffer and learn. The cattle are specialized off as we see in the equine story. From a lively little creature, with the original master endowment of the five digits on the hand, the animal sinks forward, increases in weight and the 'hand' shrinks in form and swells in mass till we are left with the horse —a creature of speed to escape from its dreaded 'dark partner', the carnivore that is parasitic on it. The same occurs with all the sheep family. X-rays can now show in the womb of the ewe (which no dissection of the embryo will indicate) the last five-line shadow made by the five streams of calcium out from the foot-bud of the foetal lamb, the last hint that once here was the endowment of freedom and invention. Looking at these faint shadows so soon to fade into the blunt hoof, one feels the pathos as when in the last movement of a tragic symphony an air, once triumphant in the first, now can only just be heard in minor key, a mutilated dying strain. With the Cervidae—the deer family—the same sad truth is shown in another example. The deer now need the carnivores. The ungulates, those whose hands have become blunted into hoofs, have now a dreadful need of the unguiculates—those whose hands have become twisted into claws to satisfy *their* horrid need for the flesh of their fellows. For if the deer are not stimulated by the constant uneasiness that an enemy prowler may be near they become so slack without the adrenaline in their blood that they suffer from disease through lowered general resistance. While many of the sheep, if they are not constantly roused will, to graze the easier, go down on the knees and so walk till the foot rots off at the joint. Could decadence be more clearly illustrated or the penalty that comes from not living up to continual understanding be more terribly shown? Dog and cat seem to have derived out of a more generalized, more 'friendly' form, somewhere in the Oligocene or early Miocene. While at this time we can watch, Dr. Walter Granger (of the New York Metropolitan Museum of Natural History) thinks, the steady decadence of the snakes going on alongside. There seem no snakes in the Eocene—this was a further step downward taken by the lizards in the Mammalian age; and the further decadence of being venomous seems to have been taken in the Miocene, for no poisonous snakes have been found before that. We must repeat, there seems to have been no gain in this, any more than there was gain for the hypertrophied Mammoth, whose tusks grew and curled to fantastic lengths, or for the Giant Elk that hung on in Ireland till the fourteenth century, with antler span so wide that it could hardly push through any close-set wood.

Then in the last two stages of the Mammalian age, the Pliocene and the Pleistocene, we see the same sifting going on among the last few competitors for Life's prize. All the rest have made their choice, taken their temporary reward and gain, for which they sold their birthright of divine striving and discovery, liberty, faith, doubt and wonder. Now only remain the ape types—and once more most choose immediate comfort. A gorilla in the first months in the womb is curiously human. A fully-grown adult may be thirteen feet across the arm span, weigh six hundred pounds and have such teeth that no carnivore will dare attack him. Yet his mental age hovers about two to two and a half of the human, his temperament is melancholy, he suffers constantly from fears and his weight is so great that he cannot safely get into a tree, while he moves increasingly as a quadruped, his knuckles calloused into heels by this way of walking. Again there seem to have been many trial men.[1] We have seen the failure of the one that lasted longest alongside of us—the Neanderthal. There, too, we can trace decadence.

It has been necessary to dwell in some illustrative detail on the actual data of this the last section of Life's story for from it we can see several moral issues arise. We have seen that right through a striving and a choice seem to have been present and we have seen that choice has to be made constantly, and always against the temptation that rest would now be easy, further toil discouraging. The arguments for stabilizing, both positive and negative, are continually strengthened. The love of pleasure and ease, the dread of toil and pain, join to persuade the creature to pause. The Lotus land that has been won seems ever more pleasant, more easy to make endure and the seas that be ahead look rougher. But the Law of Life in this seems unvarying: you cannot stay still. The more powerful you are, the freer you are, you are only free to fall faster or go forward faster. The more powerful the plane, the higher it can go, the more it must keep to a high rate of speed or crash. The principle, He that is not getting better is getting worse, is not one invented by an exacting puritanism that hates Life. It is of the very current of Life

---

[1] At the time of its discovery—1912—'Eoanthropos' was thought of as modern man's ancestor—the missing link at last. But the discovery of a second skull of this species in the thirties in the Swanscombe chalk cuttings on a geological 'horizon' that could be dated by the presence of flints of the second form of the Paleolithic series—some few hundred thousands of years old—showed that Eoanthropos was a parallel species alongside many others and fairly probably alongside Neoanthropic man—our own modern type. The Pekin (Chou-Kien) fossils: the Mount Carmel burials: the several types from the Java Trinil beds: the Rhodesian (Broken Hill) species—all these are apparently different derivations or convergencies of hominid experiments. They may be different genera yet they are all men, all appeared at the later part of the Tertiary and grew alongside of one another. And to all, the Ice Age sooner or later seems to have proved fatal.

itself. This and this indeed is the task of freedom. It is not a vague faith of sentimental liberals who 'like people to be happy', it is and has always been the price of living at all. But we see also that the reward is incomparably great. We have seen that there can be a real acceptance and a joy in the effort. Speaking of the evidence that several types of ape may have converged and given rise to menlike types and perhaps to men, Dr. Howell remarks that it may be true that you can't keep a good ape down. It may be that no good form of Life can be kept down and that as long as it is good, as long as it will pay the price of enduring, it will not be kept down but told 'Friend, come up higher'. The real choice seems to be whether it will decide on understanding and wonder and acceptance—however rudimentary—and against having as its closed standard and canon, Pleasure-Pain. The struggle to survive certainly does go on but it is a struggle fought out in the organism itself, a struggle to preserve a balance, to hold on to the treasure of wonder first given it, while all the time it must grow more in power. How is a creature to become powerful and yet remain sensitive, big but tender, wise but not cunning, informed but not proud, skilled but innocent. The cost is continual effort. The penalty of failure is death: the prize, life eternal. Nor is the struggle in order that a defined and limited self may survive. At its crudest the struggle is for one's group not for oneself alone. No individual can last beyond the tiny span of his actual physical life. And we see that as Life rises it strives to help outsiders ever further and is still more exacting in making itself into a giver not a getter.

We see, then, that Life has not failed, for in man it has won to a higher manifestation than ever before. He has become the most successful of all the species. Even physically he is a marvel. Fishes put in water which he enjoys as tonic warmth, convulse and die. A boar that could rip him open with one lunge, if given an electric shock man treats as a shrewd practical joke, lies dying in convulsions. Even as a body he is a wonderful invention. And now he has overspread the earth. The gorilla that could tear him limb from limb lives at his pleasure and must be kept in safety, for one whiff of the germ-laden air man can breathe with impunity is as fatal to this giant ogre as would be poison gas to us.

But, and now we come to the real edge and point of our inquiry: Granted that man has won headship; firstly, has he won freedom from suffering and frustration, has he really won, or merely pushed aside all other competitors? And secondly, what has been the price of his winning? Can we justify such a victory even should it prove, more fully than it has, that it is a victory? We can first maintain that this human victory has not been won merely or mainly, perhaps hardly at all, by violence. This, of course, is much to say. Dr. W. R. Inge said with some point, 'It is hard to imagine in what form, were they capable of the effort, the animals would imagine the Principle of Good. But there is no doubt that could they make a picture of the Principle of Evil it would be in the form of a white man.' And yet though we have been hideously destructive still we have not advanced by that destruction, but by sensitiveness and curiosity and sympathy. It could not be otherwise, for the Life in us took that choice scores of millions of years ago. All the insects enclosed themselves in armour of chitin and all their sensitive parts are at the centre. So, as Haskins[1] has pointed out, the ant can only see dimly because its eyes are never washed by tears to make them clear. Nor can it feel through its armour and so can never add any experience, be so touched by something as to disobey with a generous impulse the Iron Law blindly working out from within. Man may be decadent to-day; it is too soon to be sure. We can be sure he must repent of much, if he is to go on. But, as we shall see soon, repentance is part of Life, yes and redemption too; creation, at its highest, can go back and salvage what has been lost. Evolution may be irreversible as is entropy, but epigenesis may not be, because, as we have seen, Life may not be subject to the Second Law of Thermodynamics. We are, then, committed to feeling, to response, by our very structure and, though most of us may turn traitor to that law and so perish, a remnant, we know, always does keep the law. And we know from the past that it is from such remnants not only that man's

[1] Dr. C. P. Haskins, *Of Ants and Men.*

history has been renewed and civilization saved, but all the great up-steps of Life have been made at each epoch when the collapse of the mighty has proved the failure of violence. The meek, the trained and the tamed, they and they alone do inherit the earth.

But even if we did not destroy our rivals but took the place they failed to fill, was not the price fabulous? Every other species but man is now imprisoned in a fatal specialization. While the vast majority of all the forms of Life that have emerged have all utterly failed. Their record, where any record at all is left, is simply in the rocks. The fossil casts of their bones are all that their lives have wrought.

We are here now clearly at the door of the supreme moral problem, the problem of evil. No Natural Theology, no attempt to show that the process we are viewing in its setting, in its actors, in their parts, is really a creative play, can endure unless it can face that issue. We have seen that it does not really force itself on our attention as long as we are mainly studying merely the setting. That setting seems to indicate that we are in a world of Lawful Freedom. That is the first requirement. If living creatures were capable of creative choice that is the stage and setting they must demand. Yet that world itself does not suffer or enjoy and it is these things that decide the moral question of the problem of evil. A stage cannot suffer or find meaning; these qualities belong to the actors and their parts.

But first before entering on this issue which is now before us: If Life suffers, how justify all this suffering? We must note clearly what is often overlooked. As has been said above but needs repeating here, this is a moral issue. Many people say glibly, the problem of evil can never be solved. And, assuming that it can't, will have nothing to do with Natural Theology. More often, and worse, even more people will have nothing to do with morality, apart from its present social convenience—which certainly takes one hardly any distance worth going. If, however, we define our terms, which is seldom done in this vital issue, we find the issue is often confused in its premises. Technically speaking the problem of evil has two aspects, its metaphysical riddle and its moral-problem side. Practically speaking—and who doubts that evil is a practical question—the moral issue is what really matters to us. The metaphysical riddle is what—since the time of Aristotle—has been discussed by men who enjoy discussion. And the discussion has never closed. Nor does it seem it ever will be closed. But we may reach the stage when we are ready to put it aside till we are better equipped to deal with it. For one thing the fine use of words has brought out. That is that the Riddle of Imperfection—as is perhaps its exact title—is linked with something that puzzles the skilled mind even more. That is the Problem of Time—what is it? This problem does not interest the moralist and to its solution the metaphysician can give no answer. Indeed, as we have seen, when in Chapter Four we were looking at the evidence of design in cosmogony, it is the new physics that has made what seems the first step toward helping us to understand the nature of Time through recognizing that it is an aspect of that state the complementary aspect of which is Space. The professional philosopher to-day is one not trained to live but trained to think, to use high verbal accuracy and strictly to observe the laws of logic, to define his terms and to argue closely so that in his conclusions there will be nothing but what may be found in his premises. He adds proposition to proposition as a computator adds figure to figure. There is no growth, no sudden insight. A machine should be able to handle the propositions of logic as machines have been made to calculate. And such of course was the dream of that austere logician Spinoza. In fact he looked on man as a machine made to grind out philosophic propositions—at least that was the task of the highest grade machine turned out by the strange cold Necessity he called God. Now the problem that always appeals to and baffles this kind of mind (from the time that professional high-grade play with words began to be taken for 'the love of wisdom' and 'sophia', which had meant a skill at a craft or an art, became skill at argument) is the problem of how it all began. Once people with an economic surplus would keep those who had a surplus energy of words and who could amuse them with this highly skilled play; once epic poetry and great drama began to give out, then the sophists begin to find salaried posts. It is always easier to discuss where you came from than where you should go. For if you decide where you should go, you may have to do something about it. While about the past you do nothing but speculate, and even the speculations cannot be disproved. Besides, with the rise of the belief in the mechanical notion of causality, there was the feeling that if you could trace things back you would find out how they started and so know why they are as they are, and hurt as much as they do. Hence the theories as to how the world began. There are only three possible: One, that the power that started things was All Powerful, Wise and Good. The second, that All Powerful and All Wise, He was not Good. The third, that He was only All Powerful. The third view is held by most people to-day though it is so grim that they seldom raise it into spoken terms. When man has a horrid fear, if it is bad enough, he represses it. It then only shows in increase of mental derangement and violence and despair. The second view appears as a phase in between One and Three—as Venus can appear either at dawn or eve but never at midnight. The first view, to their credit, has generally been held by philosophers who had any full view of Life and the world—it is mainly a hang-over from the time when philosophy was a life actually lived. Through the love of wisdom and by methods that go beyond and fulfil logic, philosophy, then, leads to a direct experience which shows the disciplined experiment that the universe is interpretable in the end as good, as well as a work of wisdom and of power. But this number-one view has in it a profound basic difficulty—the one we are trying to get clear—evil. The trained thinker often leaves aside or belittles the issue of moral evil. For generally it does not bear heavily on a man kept by a rich and prosperous society, or its ruler, and left to pursue what he likes, the company of his own well-ordered thoughts. To be let do what one naturally enjoys, and to be paid for it, surely is a strong if crude argument in favour of thinking that the world is on the whole a good place and things are as they should be. Besides, to a skilled thinker, moral evil is a very confusing term. And finally, surely—and this too must be allowed—if we take position One, that the world is made by a triply right and competent power, then it must be as it is because He has permitted it. But how can He? He is perfect and perfection is not the mark of anything we see. He is eternal, unlimited and here we are subject to limitations on every side, and the comprehensive limitation is that of Time. In short, how did the Eternal ever come to make a world in Time and if He is eternal, the Ever Present, how does He ever 'come to' anything? In other words, not only Why but How does the Eternal create?

Now, as with a kitten and a ball of wool, in unravelling our problem we have got ourselves perfectly tied up. Of course there must be something wrong somewhere. But the keenest use of logical method and defined terms, or ratiocination and semantics has never got us out of this tangle. And now it seems they never will. The position, however, is not hopeless; far from it. To find the wrong way of doing a thing is often the next step to finding the right. Two thousand five hundred years ago, when the rules of logic and the fear of strict causality, when metaphysics and money, when Karma and Caste were beginning to make life hell for ordinary people who wanted to do right and live well, a young squire set out to find his way out of the dark tangled wood. He found that a path of eight steps would take you into the clear. By defining your terms, by study of yourself, by right livelihood, by a settled system of moral and psychological exercises you could come to a knowledge of supreme good, a knowledge that cannot be put in a water-tight, criticism-impervious syllogism, but can be lived. And, by teaching these eight steps, the method of acquiring that direct knowledge can be conveyed to anyone who really wishes so to live and so to know.

That discovery needs making again and again. Indeed, as Gautama said that he taught, it is nothing unless each man will learn it and prove it for himself. And the starting-point of all this practical drive and its constant success when it is followed is just this: Evil is not underrated. Indeed, sorrow—the fact and consequence of evil—is central in the teaching. But the whole method is practical. Do you want to do something about it? Or do you really want to show with a clever smile or a despairing nod that nothing can be done? That is the issue, there is the real crux, your real wish, your power of choice, your belief. What would you wish to have things be if they could, if you could make them? That means that you define your problem by tracing it back till you can find the place where you can act. The Man Who Woke Up—for that is what the title The Buddha means (not a person fast asleep under a large and shady fig tree, but one awake all night hanging on to the writhing boa constrictor of causality till he came to the point where he could unwind it and it no longer strangled him) the Fully Awakened Man, taught just that. And everyone who has taught the way to freedom and the lifelong happy service to set others free has taught the same. About moral evil and its problem have no doubt. You must indeed wrestle till the breaking of the day with the awful angel till he tells you what you can do. He will then show you how you may climb to where you can see right through the problem to the light and freedom that lie beyond. Then go out and tell the gospel to all who are ready to pay the same price to win this knowledge for themselves and their fellows. But, as you have known where to go on to, know also where to stop. Dig a well till you get water but having dug to get water don't become insane with a passion for digging and so dig right through the underground stream. Then you will only lose the water more than if you had never dug. The academic philosopher to-day is all too like that pathetic instinct-ridden bird the sand martin (one of the swallow tribe). Its instinct tells it to dig into sand cliffs some three feet. Then at the end of this tunnel the urge to dig gives out and its place is taken by the desire to nest and lay eggs. But there are places where men have made the walls of their fields of this convenient soft sandstone. The sand martin, finding these, starts to bore. But the impulse to dig is not spent by the time that it has dug right through the wall. In consequence it starts boring through another wall. It never can lay an egg and the walls are ruined by its futile wish to expend an instinctive drive. Although they have already done enough to make a place where the purpose of their life, to raise their brood, could have been accomplished, they do not know how to stop and begin the next process. So is it with many a modern academic philosopher. He digs with his keen intellect, sufficiently deep into the meanings of things so that at that depth he might then go on to master those exercises whereby he might become an actual experient and manifestation of the Good, the True and the Beautiful. So he would not merely have learned philosophy: he would have become a philosopher. But the critical boring faculty cannot be stopped. It goes on boring, and the constructive, creative, integral power is never let come into play. We must know enough in order to be able to live. The process of analysis must sublimate into the power of gnosis.

The practical action is then simple, the practical definition clear. About moral evil we can discuss, the problem is not insoluble, if we are prepared to act on all we know and from all we learn to know more. About the Riddle of Imperfection, the utter mystery of Time—for Time of its nature involves imperfection—we can say nothing. Nor do we need to, for by our temporal nature, we have no control over the past but only over the future. As Plotinus says wisely, 'The way we lost God in the Past is not revealed to us. What we are told is what we do need to know, the way we may return to Him.'

It was, then, a mistake to tack the metaphysical riddle on to the moral problem. It solved nothing. It was a mistake made by professional thinkers who were perhaps unconsciously willing because they were themselves living at ease when others had to endure. It was certainly not so unfortunate for these 'good easy men' to be able to prove that nothing need be done, when they and their patrons found things so much better for themselves than the rest who kept them could find.

We are, then, concerned in Natural Theology, not with the question why a good god made the world at all. Indeed, we must again remind ourselves that at our stage of this discussion, indeed all the while we are discussing Natural Theology, we are not compelled to prove that the world is made by Supreme Power, Goodness and Wisdom. All we need to establish is that it does show a good meaning and tendency, more than a bad one. Then we can set to work and from human history and by living the life which has brought vision to all who so lived—and without which no one does get vision—we may, from this faint light that was given us, begin to see how the full hopes of the soul and the full claims of the conscience, that there should be a perfect God in which man may find his perfection, can be established.

Our concern, then, is just this: Is the sum of evil in the world greater than the sum of good? Is good or is evil showing signs of winning? If good is winning then I should go in on its side. That is the right and rational thing to do. We have seen that so long as there is no Life and no apparent consciousness, then there seems no choice and so no moral issue has as yet arisen. But we have seen that in studying the inorganic, the non-reproductive, the unconscious, there yet seems provision for such an issue and effort. This is the world of Lawful Freedom. It suggests then that when we come to Life that we should find this stage, which has been so set and balanced, does give rise to just such a conflict, issue, choice, creative freedom.

But once we decide that the problem of evil is something that can be handled creatively under its moral aspect we have in turn to define the moral problem. It also has two aspects: There is the problem of suffering and the problem of causing suffering. The one reflects, possibly, on the original planner and maker, the organizer of the circumstances and granter of faculties. The other reflects more on the free agent who causes the pain. And he who causes, he too may be of one of two types; he may cause the pain through his greed and largely unwittingly, when his evil is not of the gravest sort, or he may do it out of malice, out of love to see wretchedness about him. Here is supreme evil, evil in almost a pure state. Still further, when we go back and consider the problem of suffering—which used to be thought by liberals to be the sum of all evil—for to do what you wanted must always be happiness—we see that it too is twofold. There is the problem of suffering among creatures that can learn nothing from their suffering—or supposedly so—and yet are creatures supposedly endowed with a real and full capacity for pain as we men feel it. This is the problem of pain in animals. And there is the problem of suffering among creatures capable through self-consciousness of full memory and vivid foreboding, of such man is the only one of whose capability we can be sure.

In taking this series we had best start at the point furthest away from us. This is generally not a sound procedure. We have tried to avoid it in regarding the great frame of things, the cosmos in which we find ourselves. But with the moral issue there is reason for starting this other way round, from the rim in. The reason is, that we have already found that a number of assumptions have been made about moral evil, and the obstacle that it puts in the way for thinking that God has given any sign of His presence and aid in the world around us. In observing the cosmos, once anthropomorphism was over and astrology had proved itself to make crass mistakes in its actual data and findings, we have acted as observers, without much passion or bias coming into our findings. But when Life came, then we fought that we might not have to surrender anthropomorphism. Indeed, as we have seen, it was when men were becoming dispassionate observers of the heavens and of the stratified and volcanic earth, that they became enthusiastically sentimental about Life. Anthropomorphism actually advanced in the eighteenth century and during much of the nineteenth, because of an exaggerated concern for animals. Many of the biologists who pushed the doctrine of Natural Selection forward, showed a consideration for their pets and for wild animals which was utterly inconsistent with their creed and which would have struck Descartes and the great thinkers of the seventeenth century as ludicrously absurd and 'enthusiastic'. Indeed not until the use of animal psychology at the close of the nineteenth century was it possible to attain a balanced insight and attitude towards animals and to recover from the sentiment which was a reaction from the Cartesian callousness that treated animals as automata.

Of course the great romantic poets had started the retreat to sentiment. It is Shakespeare who declares that a giant can suffer no more than a beetle. We are now aware that there is no reason to suppose that the right whale suffers as much, or anything like, as keenly as a human dwarf twenty-four inches high. Size is not the matter. It is the complexity of the nerve system that can carry and store and discharge the vibrations that can be felt as pain, that lead us to some criterion as to what the algesic capacity of any creature may be. By this test, and it certainly rules in matters of sheer physical pain, we can see that beetles are mercifully out of the running, indeed all the insects are. We have no shadow of reason for supposing that their consciousness is at all like ours. The whole progress that has been made in the study of pain through the progress of anaesthetics, and especially through the even less known progress in the study of analgesia under hypnosis, shows that even with that over-pain-charged creature man we have a problem utterly different from what the ordinary man has taken for granted it must be. And in this issue we must remind ourselves that that weary expert, busy authority, active polemicist, the theologian, is very much the layman. It is hard to find one weighty and well-known theologian who has studied analgesics, anaesthetics, hypnosis and finally animal psychology and psychophysiology. What has it, he might well ask, to do with salvation? The answer is that without it the problem of pain and suffering can't be defined. But that answer, of course, these overworked specialists seldom have time to attend to. They wish to prove too often that Natural Theology is unnecessary and impossible because they wish to show that the revelation to which their loyalty and lives have been given alone can show man the way to salvation.

We must, then, settle first with the insects: that side of Life which, though it is undoubtedly Life and actively contriving Life, is Life quite unlike ours. The first thing about it has already been said. Here is a form of living creature that is made so that with a hard exterior and a paste interior it can obey instinct and never learn from the moment it is hatched to the moment it breeds and dies. To call this sleep-walking would be to bring it far too high into the light of consciousness. The Sphex wasp, as J. H. Fabre and many other entomologists have shown, when it has laid its egg in its carefully masoned nest, goes off to catch and paralyse a grub, as fresh meat for its child when it will hatch. While it is away you may always remove the egg. Yet the wasp will come back and, unable with its sharp eyes to see that everything has miscarried, proceeds to store and seal up the grub.

Sometimes it is true, as Dr. Cheeseman has pointed out, there seems a bewilderment when the actual process on which the insect is engaged under the drive of its instinct is interrupted. But after a little fuss once more the patterns of behaviour enforce themselves.

We can then say from present knowledge that an insect is neither a machine nor a manikin. Until lately we had but two categories into which to place behaviour—it was either that of a conscious individual or it was the conduct of a machine— clear consciousness or none, these were the only possible alternatives. The work in the subconscious of ourselves, the study of conditioned reflexes, tests with hypnotized patients, with sleep-walkers, all show not merely that there is a 'subconscious' but that consciousness is in many layers and those layers are of very different qualities. Further, as with splintered personalities within the same organism, there may be two and sometimes several 'persons' all unaware of one another until they are informed by outside proof.[1] They may have different gifts, and when one is suffering or enjoying the others are unaware as a person under total anaesthesia. A sleepwalker will seem to be aware of what he is doing and to act in a purposive way; a hypnotized person is surely conscious for he attends minutely to what his director tells him to do. With a post-hypnotic suggestion, when the subject has come to, he appears quite normal, pays attention to the things the company is interested in and takes part in their conversation. Nevertheless if the suggestion has been one of anaesthesia, the subject will not feel pain should physical damage be suffered in performing some act. And the same seems true of somnambulism. High attention and the consciousness required

[1] See the studies of multiple personality and splintered individuals in F. W. H. Myers, *Human Personality and Its Survival of Bodily Death.*

for it and the skill to produce finished action, these things therefore are not necessarily correlated with pain. On the contrary, there is reason to suppose that the complete anaesthesia to even the most massive pain which is so commonly induced by hypnosis, is produced precisely through causing such completeness of attention. Once attention is absolute the pain impulse either cannot get through to the conscious centres of the brain or the store of energy necessary to feel to that extent is not available, because it has been drawn off to supply the high quality of attention demanded and commanded in hypnosis.[1]

In brief, then, we may say that an insect is a creature which shows all the signs of being in a state of constant hypnosis to the spirit and suggestion of its race. Incapable of receiving any creative challenge from its environment, because of its complete insensitive exterior, it dreams in its core the invariably repeated story of the race life, and, as a sleepwalker, carries out this command, regardless of risk to itself or even as to the pointlessness of its procedure. Such is instinct at its highest—or lowest. We must repeat, it seems impossible not to feel, that as both reason and instinct seem to have arisen from a primal Trial and Error, that back of this faultless and fatally blind elaborate behaviour of the chitin-imprisoned insects there must once have been a freely made act, full of contemporary awareness, discovery and inventive reply to a present challenge. Then, through its success, this pattern became more polished, more finished, until it ended in nothing but a series of reflexes so perfectly interlocked that no new experience could be recorded, no new response made. What then runs this line of creatures, most of which never see their offspring? The doctrine of the 'Field' so newly powerful in physics may help us here. It helps us with physiology when we see that Speeman's organizer, the field at the growing edge of the lowest form of the embryo, is what actually directs and guides growth. May we not also use it in considering the instinctive life of the insects. A great French apiarist said, suggestively, we must not think of the individual bee as a person, we must see the hive

[1] This subject, very important as it is, cannot be discussed more fully here. For further material on the issue see the writer's *Pain, Sex and Time*.

as the unit. Each bee is a free-moving cell in that invisible field which is the spirit of the hive. Instead of clinging, as does the organizer to the tip of the growing tissue, the spirit of the hive has spread and distributed itself, making the hive itself one of its points of support, the queen bee, reduced to an egg-laying object, another and the rest of the bees like satellites swarming round this nucleus.

With this fertile suggestion as the only one that covers the actual facts of observation, may we not then combine another, very germane to our inquiry. If there is not a 'person' in any individual insect, but the plan and process of its elaborate life is really dictated by an invisible field whose purchase points are the successively emerging organisms as they pass from egg to adult and back again, then have we not here something that links up with the latest concepts of evolution—or epigenesis? Henry Fairfield Osborn drew attention to what he named Orthogenesis, the tendency of the creature throughout the life of its species to grow rightly, in a balanced way that not only avoided extravagancies of growth fatal to the poise of the whole, but also kept it lively, bulk proportioned to energy and structure generalized so as to be able to give a creative response to changed conditions. This is the type that has high survival quality. When these characteristics are exchanged for size and specialization then the species will become extinct. In his studies of the Megatherium and the Mastodons as well as of the horse Osborn showed that there is a speci-al life which grows up from a tentative youth form to an adulthood, and finally ends in an old age of over-complexity. The species has learned too much, has too many answers to experience, is too assured and so must go. Further, studies made by Osborn and his successors have shown that these speci-al lives are evidently always as limited as the lives of the individuals that compose them. Beside the individual they last long but in the end they too age and die. The Mastodons, Osborn once said, might, he felt, be shown to have have gone through their whole race life in some five hundred thousand years. Many of the present surviving species are literally millions and scores of millions of years old. But in the end they all seem to die. This interesting fact has a bearing on our inquiry. For in such cases, yes right up into the mammals, may it not be this speci-al life, and not that of the individual creature, that really plans, and strives and suffers?

This, strange to say, would be in keeping with the earliest philosophic thought of the people of our language. In the Sanskrit Indo-European corpus of teaching it is said that each species is ruled by a Deva—a creative spirit—and these gods, though they lived for millions and scores of millions of years, yet in the end they die and it is they and not the supreme Brahman who create, make great beauty and manifold wonder, and also mistakes and trials, and discoveries and suffer; and finally learn and understand. This is but a suggestion, but it must also be said that it is the only hypothesis that really covers the facts of orthogenesis and speci-al growing and ageing. And with this it also makes a contribution to the problem of suffering, for here the lower animals are not blindly suffering. On the contrary, a much higher intelligence than we at present as individual men have, is striving to work out its destiny. Not by random incarnations, hopping about from man to dog, to butterfly and snake, but by constantly taking its speci-al form could the demiurge of each species work out its salvation.

What we have seen to be true with the insects—that they are not individuals or capable of suffering so long as they are completely run by the faultless precision of instinct—is true too of every other animal as far as it is a creature of instinct. Fishes and lizards may then be left out of the deepest question of suffering. With them there is a cold-blooded system and a comparatively simple central nervous structure. Even when we reach the birds we find again a system run whereby elaborate and varied breeding patterns may be followed—as nest-building, rearing young and migration—but there is not the consciousness that we know. As Elliot Howard in his masterly *The Nature of a Bird's World* has pointed out, from his own observations, one pattern emerging eclipses the last as completely and as quickly as sleep with us puts out the waking mind and waking banishes dream. As Dr. Rowan of Alberta has also confirmed, these changes are due to changes in the endocrine system of the animal and once they arise the response is complete. Conflict is wiped away and the last state leaves no hangover of a pathetic loyalty to confuse present action. So when the migration mood comes on them the birds desert the young in the nest which till that hour they slaved to feed, and the birds which are lifelong monogamists nevertheless with a drop in the temperature fail to recognize their mates. So we may suspect that as 'Wisdom is justified of all her children' so too Life may be justified in its dealings with all of its broods. Many people in a sentimental, uninformed passion say that they can stand human beings suffering but that 'poor dumb animals' wring the heart because they can't understand why they suffer. The converse seems to be the truth. Instinct means anaesthesia. So again we detect the contrivance of emancipation through striving: If you are free, for freedom means consciousness, you suffer, for you suffer in order to learn and by suffering you do learn. If you are not free and so cannot learn, neither do you suffer. Suffering is a transitional condition then. Into this we must go further when considering man specifically and the place and use of suffering in and to him.

Meanwhile we can say one thing further on this specific issue: We must also guard against judging animals by what we see of them when we domesticate them. Domestication is a very mysterious thing. It is in some degree what may be called psychological symbiosis. Few animals seem to be able to be subjected to it. It is possible that a particular type of human being is needed to begin the domestication of a wild strain. Again, we shall be considering this later more fully when considering the evidence of anthropology in regard to our inquiry. In the wild state animals seem to have a different consciousness from that we see in the domesticated because their Time-sense seems to be different, indeed non-existent. While the domesticated species have caught much of our sense of before and after, in the wild there is a lack of expectation and a fading of memory that removes from sensation nearly all that quality with which we associate it. What pain can be to a creature that has no foreboding and no remorse, regret or clear recollection, we cannot imagine and when to that is added the fact that the unit or field of consciousness may be so fractionated that each impulse of sensation may be separated off from the rest, there may here be very considerable anaesthesia, though associated with power of attention to those things which stir the instincts.[1] Nor is even that all, for the various drives of emotional impulse may run in separate channels, though in the one body, for no reflective self-consciousness may be there to combine them. Pain, then, would be present but in that utterly detached quality which it takes on in some threshold anaesthesias, such as when the patient has been given some five to ten grains of Nembutal.

We see, then, as Dr. Clement Webb remarked some thirty-five years ago in his essay on theodicy, that the problem of pain as it approaches us becomes more clear—we can and do learn from pain. His remark that it is most baffling where it is furthest from us, in the suffering of animals, we have seen that animal psychology and the many studies of natural history are doing much to explain. As the problem of human pain is then one of human consciousness and of human intention we should leave it to the next chapter. What this chapter had to attempt to show was whether Life in itself left any freedom to its suffering creatures and especially to its supreme creature, man. If we were run by instinct then we were helpless to avail ourselves of the world of Lawful Freedom in which we found ourselves. But we have seen that we are not run by instinct. And further, we have seen that the creatures that are so run and so cannot learn now by experience, have evidently degenerated by some speci-al choice. Here too, then, there is no case against there being a good Creator. For though they have lost their chance for the time being, by losing their chance they have also been freed from the price that has to be paid for freedom—their capacity

[1] Animals have often been observed eating steadily and with apparent satisfaction when very gravely injured. And in human pain the problem is far from simple or solved. As Dr. H. Cohen, addressing the London Medical Society, pointed out (*Lancet*, 10th June 1944) on the problem of abdominal pain, it is necessary to postulate a constant stream of subliminal impulses which cannot enter the central brain unless central inhibition (outer attention) is lowered.

for suffering. Indeed, it would seem that here we have a very just and exact sliding scale: For precisely to that degree that you can feel and suffer can you have choice and freedom to learn, and so to become, not merely free from suffering, but to enter into the much higher joy than any physical pleasure, the joy of understanding, and creation through understanding. Conversely, in exact proportion as you lose the power to learn and understand, do you lose the power to suffer and finally to feel at all. Incidentally, this is a strong argument from Natural Theology against the worst of all the perverse deductions of Dogmatic Theology, the doctrine of Eternal Torment—for we see that all we know of pain is that it is of its nature evidence of a transition. There will be more to say on this in the next chapter.

We may, then, summarize this section by putting the conclusions in threefold form. Life is divided in three great divisions: (1) There are the creatures of complete instinct such as the insects. Such seem to be not individualized psyches but rather materializations of a race life. That which feels, knows and learns is the race life not the insect unit. (2) There are the creatures of partial instinct such as the mammals. They partially learn by experience and so partially suffer but mainly forget and fail to foresee and the power of their instincts mainly anaesthetizes them and causes rapid amnesia and finally degeneracy and extinction. (3) There is man without instincts, with great power to remember and to foresee. He suffers and learns by suffering. But with him also, he suffers only in so far and until he can attend wholly to meaning and intention, when suffering ceases.

The two questions with which this chapter opened are then answered. (1) The Life that flows in us and all creatures gives us a chance of creative choice. (2) And the price that it demands for such liberty is not too costly. We have seen that man pays most—in his capacity for pain—and has certainly gained most in creative liberty. Insects are not paying and are not getting. All mammals, and to a lesser degree the birds, and still less again the cold-blooded, get as much as they pay. There is, then, cost and loss, and frustration, though the gain may outbalance it.

In closing this chapter we might then ask a further question: Is there discernible any hope for the animals who are sinking down to extinction through their having in all their species lost the unspecialized power to respond and rise through creative choice? What is the fate of all the creatures which seem to have miscarried? For we must never forget that though many seem skilled, beautiful and joyous, all save man seem doomed to increasing specialization. That means increasing unconsciousness, frustration and finally extinction. In the next chapter we shall be noting the wonderful dietary knowledge inherited by every rat and used by it. But though the rat is a largely unspecialized species, nevertheless in the acquisition of any fresh knowledge it ceases to be teachable at three weeks old. Here, then, on this issue we give first a possible speculation and next a suggestion that has proved full of promise. The speculation deals with the subject we have already touched on—what is the power that directs the evolution and development of other species than our own. Only two choices seemed possible to thinkers in the West until this generation. Either there was individual intelligence, each animal was generation by generation endowed with that degree of understanding which would permit it to forward the species to which it belonged by its own learning being transmitted to its offspring by some sort of teaching. Or God directly was responsible for each creature. But the teaching so often quoted in this context 'Not a sparrow falls to the ground' does not say that the Father of all actually makes it fall directly. What is said is that He knows—not necessarily the same thing. If the bird does not suffer as we suffer, if the bird's consciousness may not be an individualized consciousness at all but is a temporary extrusion of the bird-consciousness of the species or the genus—then the discarding of one body would not mean frustration to the intelligence which for a moment partly informed it. A crab is not damaged by the loss of a claw but grows another. We see then, and have suggested above the Sanskrit idea on the subject, that there is this third and middle alternative to the two possible explanations which seemed to exhaust possibilities to our earlier Western thinkers. We may say that all the animals up to man are not truly individuals, at least as long as they are in the wild state. The more instinctive they are the less they are individuals. When they cease to be instinctive and become capable of any level of learning by experience the more they become individuals.

So much for the speculation: that as in all other species there seems no real individual life but rather a speci-al life, so in these levels it is the speci-al spirit that learns and understands and not the physical unit of each animal life—as we spirits learn and not the millions of cells that compose our bodies.

Now we must turn to the suggestion that has far more evidence in its favour and is of far more significance. We can put the thesis as a question: Is there any evidence that we can do anything for the animals and help them out of the pit of unconsciousness into which they are sliding? Many people of high character are depressed by the thought that, of all the creation, 'Man stands alone', is unique in having been able to preserve the primal awareness and bring out from that bud the flower of understanding. Granted that the animals don't suffer, at least most of them, at least now; still there is some considerable suffering, there has been, there has had to be; long-sustained suffering as each sank down into the anaesthesia of instinct and conditioned reflex. And there is—save for man—universal frustration. For though, maybe, the speci-al mind of each species *may* be learning, we do not know. And, honestly, considering the way species seem to be degenerating and the fact that the vast majority have become extinct, there is surely no real evidence that these demiurges are taking to heart the lessons of their all but universal failures.

Yet, as it happens, to the solution of this problem there has lately come to light some very strange evidence. Even if it had not been found, even then the case for meaning in Life would have stood. The problem of the multiplication of vast numbers of animals and their speci-al failures to advance beyond a certain point—when they sink into unconsciousness—is in reality mainly one of economics, the economy used by the creative power. It is, therefore, more akin to the problem of the multiplicity of stars—considered in the last chapter. That problem, which so worried that couple of generations obsessed with the virtue of saving and giving is now seen to have been due to quite mistaken notions. It was based on wrong ideas both as to the age of the universe and the insignificant proportion of it that could be inhabited by protoplasmic animals. Similarly we have seen that we really have no idea what animal pain in actual experience might prove to be. Again we mistakenly extrapolated ourselves. We ourselves can never feel their quality or qualities of sensation. We ourselves have found the nature of our own pain to show the strangest modifications under the influence of minute quantities of certain drugs or the presence of certain endocrine secretions in the blood.

We see, then, that we need not say that God can't be believed in because Life proves such a tragedy. But we have to allow there is tragedy, tragedy spreading wider than man, uncaused by man, uncaused by any individual animal or man. The individual poisonous snake does not choose to be venomous: the individual bird to be callously stupid. And even allowing that there is a speci-al consciousness, that is responsible and could learn, we have owned that we have yet to find any evidence (save perhaps in man) that these other 'demiurges' ever have or will. We have enough evidence to believe that this world gives proof of meaning rather than of unmeaning, of goodness rather than of evil. But that proof could be stronger and, in particular, it would be greatly strengthened if we could find any evidence that the failure of all other forms of life, than ours, need not be irremediable.

This issue is so great that we can only state it in this chapter. Nor does it rightly belong in this discussion of Life in a general way—as an inquiry into the question, What are we? It really comes under the discussion of the problem—the third section of our whole inquiry—Who am I? What or Who am I becoming? We have to ask not merely what is the Life within me, but who is this consciousness which is the first and foremost fact of all my knowing? *Cogito ergo sum* may be a mistaken saying. For because thought is found to be going on, that need not mean an 'I' that is thinking. What cannot be denied is that there is an awareness of thought going on and *that is* the awareness with which all our other awareness starts and on which it rests. Further, this creature of self-consciousness is the only creature that has really helped other creatures—creatures of other species. And it is specifically as man—the creature unique in his power of detached consciousness—that he has helped them. Here is the problem of domestication taken beyond domestication to true taming. Ants have 'domesticated' aphis and used them as 'cows' but there is no evidence that the aphis have ever become more antlike through that care, or more intelligent. Earlier it was said that the whole problem of taming would have to be considered, and now, as this chapter closes, we must add that it has to be considered because in it there seems involved a much greater and grander problem and hope, none other than that of Redemption, or Recovery by the help, by the grace of another being outside one's own race, outside one's own fate. One is salvaged freely (for Redemption means breaking through the grip of Iron Law and giving gratis of one's freedom to one who has lost his) by someone who comes out of his own nature's security and gives it away to give you the liberty you had lost. The salvager takes an interest in the creature rescued, not to exploit it as a tool or slave but to give it his own liberty.

It is no little thing, surely, to find that freedom has been given to the creature so that it can achieve creative choice, each such choice leading to greater dynamic liberty. But should we be able to discover further evidence, evidence that even when the creature had lost its granted liberty, when it had thrown away its birthright of creativity and imprisoned itself in consequence in a body specialized now only to give selfish and destructive enjoyment, even then it was rescued, the argument for a design of amazing resourcefulness would be greatly strengthened. Further, if we should discover that rescue to the self-imprisoned could, did, and did only come from one who had remained free at the cost of self-denial; who at that cost had won unprecedented power and then, there being no necessity or obligation, used its power to release rivals who were not only helpless themselves to escape but hostile to him who was free, then we could hardly fail to see something divinely resourceful in such creative redemption. For this final creativity refuses to allow there to be any ultimate failure. By its immense power not only of freeing itself and keeping free, but by going back for those imprisoned in their own hostile failure, such a redemptive creation pays back the last penny of the cost which till then seemed unavoidable, undischargeable—the final cost that must remain as the price of granting liberty. We need no longer look upon the triumph of the free as that which shall make worth while the failure of those who used their freedom to choose captivity, who chose the short cut of indulgence and violence and when these paths had led to arrest and imprisonment, could not discharge themselves. No, for the free become so free that they are free to go back, they are free to buy back the freedom of those captives who lost their freedom. That is the final achievement of him who has chosen often enough liberty. He may refuse finally, at whatever cost to himself, to allow the other to pay the ultimate penalty of misused liberty. He may continually transfuse his own freedom into that which has lost its own. He may choose for it that it shall live again, choose again, strive again. He may, because he has become perfectly free, be free even from Time and therefore he may redeem finally even those deeds done so persistently that they seem to belong wholly to the irrevocable past and registered and manifested for ever not merely in ingrained habit and instinct but in hereditary physique, in limbs and in organs.

This is no sentimental fancy, a gushing gift from the giver, a soft escape for the receiver. Not only has the giver really to give—not only to give what he need not, but what to give is a real cost and risk for himself. But the receiver, he, too, is not given back happiness, joy, pleasure. No, he is given back what he deliberately lost because he did not like it, because it hurt; not pleasure but the capacity to understand, not happiness but the power to create, not lust for getting but the potentiality to give, not enjoyment but liberty. He is resuscitated, and resuscitation is always painful. He is brought back to live, but not that he may live on someone—as he has tried to—and so die again—but that he may live for others and so through dying to himself enter the eternal Life. It is always easier to die than to live; violence itself is at root only laziness. The power of those who are really free to give back to others the freedom they have lost, is supreme power for a twofold reason: It manifests itself not only in the free through their capacity to transfuse their vitality into the half dead: it can also, because it is not only faith but, charity, make this painful inrush of the new Life seem to the recipient captive worth while all its undeniable pain. This, no doubt, is the grandest of all the great statements of faith that Dogmatic Theology has ever given. It is the twin splendour of the doctrine of the Incarnation and Redemption, as the West has known it at its best, and that same faith, shining as penetratingly if less dramatically, in the doctrine of the Bodhisattva in Mahayana Buddhism. In this the earlier teaching the freed soul does not in one incarnation nor on one cross redeem mankind but to the end of time takes body after body that ever may it be mobilized, staying in this world and away from heaven that it may seek and save, save to the uttermost, save till the last is saved, that which has lost itself.

It was against this splendid doctrine of highest faith that the Sciences of Life and indeed all conceptions of causality—not to say of responsibility and sense—were thought to have decided. There was strict causality; there was the fatal line. Each man can, and must, and only can, reap what he has sown. But this was not a true statement of the actual facts of life. There is linear karma, but as assuredly there are diagonal and lateral karmas as well. Genetically every man is a polymorph—he carries in him indefinite possibilities and debits. He has as ancestors the whole paleolithic population. And on to this plastic possibility of indefinite response is printed the immense ever-growing complex, the body of human tradition. 'Before I gave thee words thou hadst no thoughts'—says Prospero the master mage to Caliban the beast-human. Shakespeare might have gone further and said: 'Before I gave thee ideas thou hadst no thoughts.' In our society we have therefore, unlimited liability, we cannot have less and live. Cut off part and the whole is in danger of death by psychic haemorrhage. Man has grown further than any animal by taking longer to grow than any other animal. For a longer time he remains weaker than any other animal, in order that he may last longer, and in full strength, than any other animal. His childhood is longer. He is born more helpless that he may become more capable. Right into the womb itself the gaining of strength by defencelessness goes. It was the discovery of these facts of embryology that drove anatomists to see that man was in the striking phrase 'the foetalization of the ape'. Man is born retaining that foetal openness—actual openness of the top of the skull, psychological openness in being plastic—mentally and emotionally—even when out of the womb. This openness the ape loses before it emerges.

These facts are well known, though not sufficiently built into our thought when we would ask, Is there meaning to Life? Nor have we finished in finding out all that such research has to tell us. About the prophetic side of embryology, about its correlation with the freedom from instinct and the dependence on social heredity we shall have to see in the next chapter. Here we must conclude by saying that this freedom by becoming like a child goes still further. Confined to our own species this might be seen simply as a master trick, the strategy of retreat in order to counter-attack, whereby we became in the end more cunning than all the strong beasts and so mastered and destroyed them. But in point of fact this is not so. The salvation by simplicity and by being disarmed was not confined solely to give speci-al and biological victory. It was extended to other species, far from man's line and once enemies dreaded by his line. Such a fact is so remarkable that we may rightly say that it belongs to man in his right. It belongs to him, it has been granted to him, not as an animal but as the unique creature. It is his because he is the creature that won through to real freedom. And, having won that freedom, he used it neither for escape nor to tyrannize over his more mistaken fellow creatures, but to give them of his creative liberty, to give them back the freedom they had lost and were themselves helpless to recover. Were such a thing provable then surely the argument for purpose in Life would be mightily strong. To show that it can be established is then the first part of the chapter that follows.

Note on the Double Nature of the Life Process and Its Relationship to the Environment

It may be worth while, because of our present unprecedented behaviour with our environment, to make a possible deduction that well may follow from our present knowledge of Life and of the specific and peculiar means whereby it has been permitted to achieve manifestation in solid material form.

We have seen that our present knowledge shows us that three things—each of them peculiar—are required if physical life is to appear, be maintained and develop.

The first is a particular condition of 'screening'. Only thus, it would seem, is it possible that there shall be provided that environment which only admits a certain, very restricted belt of radiation wave-lengths. This screening is devised by an elaborate arrangement of atmosphere layers, certainly of great complexity and delicacy and perhaps unique. We may add, and pretty certainly, like most of those arrangements made for our provision—e.g., soil coverage—able to be destroyed by our energetic interference, though immune to the meddling of any animal. Further, it would appear that these filter screens are, aeon by aeon, geological epoch by geological epoch, rendered less dense. Thus it is provided that as the organism develops— and only if it does—greater tolerance and response to higher stimulation, it may be exposed to radiations which will now rouse it to greater capacity and reaction, though these radiations, at the beginning, could only have overwhelmed it, and indeed will and do overwhelm those forms of Life which will not advance. So we see that, as in the individual there is from conception to birth a progressive change in environment, so that the infant at last may sustain and grow by exposures and stimulants which would be fatal to the rudimentary foetus, so too is this true for the entire history of Life. And so too as the foetus (see Chapter Six) prophesies what man may become, so, further, our individual physical development from womb to and beyond birth, prophesies what further exposure to more highly stimulating environment and atmosphere the race may yet achieve and by this become a still higher type (see end of Chapter Seven). The world, we may then say, has been the womb of Life and still continues to be so if we will let it.

The second factor that we have to note in the condition of Life is the materials out of which living creatures have to be built. The living cell is composed of common chemicals, we say. By that we mean that they are common if we choose to confine our attention to this earth. But if we look for them outside the cover of this atmosphere then we have to own that throughout the rest of the universe, as far as we can see, these so-called common chemicals may be as abnormal as this atmosphere of ours itself.

But the third factor, the hyphen term between atmosphere and chemicals, the third requirement for a living form to appear, it is this that is perhaps the strangest of them all. It is an electric field of a particular frequency that holds, and that alone can hold together the common chemicals, the dead matter that composes the outward form of a living cell. These mysterious fields or vortices, like the invisible whorls of heated air that suddenly become visible as desert Dust-devils, can make common, but normally intensely reagent, chemicals combine, hold together and produce otherwise unprecedented energy.

But here comes in a further and very grave consideration. This living field, or these vortices of the radiation wave length which can (and alone can) build up living forms, is strictly limited. It can only exist (or manifest itself in physical form) provided that it is not disturbed by other radiations. For other radiations can easily dissipate it or make it incapable of manifesting itself through the building up of chemicals. Certainly in the presence of wave-lengths—either up or down the scale of total radiation—wave-lengths very little larger or smaller than itself—the Life wave-length seems incapable of taking hold of matter and so making a physical manifestation of its presence. In other words, our environment, this particular and peculiar world of ours, has been so screened by its curious filter atmospheres, that the particular set of wave-lengths, that can build up inert matter into living forms, can function here undisturbed. Everywhere else that may well have been impossible. Because of the presence in outer space of so many other wave-lengths of energy, perhaps nowhere but under our present and peculiar cover could Life have begun to play constructively with chemicals, still less have raised its structures to their present immense complexity and triumph of capacity. Therefore should you once admit past these filter atmosphere belts or generate beneath that cover, those radiations known to be common throughout outer space, then the Life radiation wave-length can no longer function, it loses its hold on matter and is dissipated. Yet no one needs to be told to-day that this is precisely what we have done! Nor did we do it in ignorance. Ever since 1896 when Röntgen gave the world X-rays it was known that these radiations were extremely dangerous to all living cells, even when such radiations were very feeble. For fifty years has Providence been tempted of us and given us long and patient warning. And we now know that by large-scale atomic disintegration we have succeeded in loosing, under our screening canopy of atmosphere, those very radiations from which it had protected us, those radiations that shatter the electric field which is the essential instrument through which the Life principle can, and can alone, build up matter into living forms. Hence we are producing a destruction more direct, more extensive, more subtle and more thorough than any we could achieve by mere explosion. For with this invisible, impalpable breath and blast of death we are blowing away the light invisible of Life itself, we are blowing out the only candle that can kindle the physical world and make it come alive. We were screened from this knowledge and power until now. We were given to eat of every tree in the garden of this rich world save this one. We might use and destroy living forms prodigally. The secret of Life itself, the wave-length that utters the creative word of assembly whereby matter becomes alive, whereby into the clay is breathed the living soul—that was hidden from us. Now we have found it, we have found it because we desperately were determined at any cost to destroy one another and we have used it for death. We have found the formula of creation but we have used it to speak—as in the ancient tradition of Black Magic—the word of Life backwards; we have said the forbidden thing, the uncreative word, not *Fiat Lux* but *Fiat Nox*. We are making the rain which falls on just and unjust to make their fields fruitful, become, as was gleefully reported in the daily press on 27th May 1947, 'literally a rain of death' (see 'the most promising estimates' of impregnation of rain clouds and low-pressure weather systems with atomic energy). So we may cause cancer cell death in all on whom even the mist falls. Further we are piercing the upper atmosphere so to destroy our given shelter and let in the wave-lengths that can drive away for ever the wave-length of Life. What has been carefully prepared for, protected and matured through a thousand million years, we in one span of our minute lives can, and seem resolved to bring to utter frustration. We can now—we must choose whether we will or not in this generation—behave as criminal lunatics and drive ourselves out of the home and vehicle so marvellously provided for us, that vehicle in which the creative power would have nursed us to a birth of true creative understanding.

Since the above was written a report has been issued that 40 per cent of the births at Hiroshima since the bomb fell have been microcephalic. If this is confirmed it would establish experimentally and definitely what had been already calculated before the bomb was exploded—that the release of so vast a volume of intense radiation damages to an utterly unprecedented degree that most delicate of all the links in the life process—the reproductive cell. As it is now more than two years since the wanton explosion, these facts may show that *every* woman in the doomed district who was in a state of early pregnancy (say from conception to the full formation of the brain) was rendered at that moment the mother of a monster. What this means for the stricken district is, that while in ruins and with a vast calamity-rate in deaths and mutilations, such a community must shoulder the further burdens of every two children out of five being hopeless imbeciles. What it means for humanity at large is certainly not less grave. When ex-Secretary Stimson published his defence, as the key adviser who counselled the President that the bomb should be used without warning on a large city (instead, as the scientists believed they had secured, as their conscience-clause concession, that it be exploded over an uninhabited area) did he intend to inflict such hideous, unprecedented punishment on the unborn and loose this anti-Life destruction on mankind? But if he did not so intend, why did he not know? The estimate that such a release of radiation would so make hideous play with future births, by giving rise to monsters, was certainly sufficiently well known. And it was sufficiently appalling to make anyone abstain who really cared for the survival of humanity. Had he acted as the actual researchers, who supplied the weapon, honestly believed had been guaranteed them, then a precedent of restraint would have been established. Nor was the price of such moderate clemency at all high. Japan, we know, was already prepared to surrender. How much less is now the chance that such wise counsels will ever again prevail, when already a man upright, informed, humane—and able to abstain—has made the fatal decision, in order to hasten an already assured event, the decision to deny any warning to a yielding foe and to inflict an unlimited punishment on the unborn.

Chapter Six

CONSCIOUSNESS AS CONTINUOUS COMMUNION

Where am I? We have seen that that question can be answered, In a World of Lawful Freedom. We have seen that the next question that arises, What am I? that, too, can be answered, 'You are vitalized by a Life whose nature is Creative Choice.' By the sustained attempt to accept and embrace its experience the Life within you has not only won control over its environment, but has come to understand its world and finally to understand itself.

We therefore have come to the third question, Who am I? In physics, in the study of the environment, in detecting the path and process of things that do not reproduce, in watching the way matter moves and inorganic, 'dead' things change, we have found that there is a pattern. That pattern is not random: on the contrary, the more it is studied, the more closely examined, the richer it shows itself to be. It is in constant movement, it is the manifestation of fabulous energy, it describes figures and patterns of the greatest elaboration and beauty. And this strangely-weaving base and background on which we live, and from which, maybe, we emerged, permits us just that freedom and play which allows us to learn to create and to become makers of fresh and extended patterns. It is a universe of Lawful Freedom; our particular position in it seems to be curiously optimal and, in that particular spot, matter has been brought both to an appositeness for our needs and to a variety for our possibilities of inventiveness which seem rare if not unique. The environment is strangely fit. In biotics, in the study of Life, we have found that there is not merely an emergence. There is something more than a constant growth by creative striving whereby that Lawful Freedom is preserved and enlarged. It would seem that this process we call Life is actually tending to build up 'dead matter', inorganic chemicals, to ever higher patterns and so to release ever more energy, with ever less exhaustion. Visible Life, living tissue, seems an arrangement of chemicals by an electric field so that from outside the Space-Time continuum there may be admitted into it a pattern-building force which is inexhaustible because it is not subject to the Second Law of Thermodynamics.

And, as physics seems to create that stage and field in which biotics can manifest itself, so in turn biotics would seem to create that stage and field in which consciousness can manifest itself. Life is the environment and matrix of consciousness, as physics is the environment and matrix of Life. The Fitness of the Environment gives rise to Life; the Fitness of Life to Consciousness. If then the answer to What is matter? is The matrix of Life; and to What is Life? The matrix of consciousness; we now have to ask, What is this latest mystery, this final term, consciousness? Everything else points on to it. As Max Weyl has said, this is 'an Open-ended Universe'—it points to something for which it is a portal, an introduction. That, too, is clear of Life; the universe points to Life; and Life points to consciousness.

But when we have said that we have raised our supreme problem—not answered the meaning of the whole—at least as yet. We have seen that if the universe had not been a place of Lawful Freedom, but one of complete irrelevance, incoherence and unlawfulness, or if, on the other hand, it had been one of iron mechanism and necessity, then it would have been no use to inquire further. At death we might be released, but during all our lives we could at best hope only to be helpless spectators of a process utterly frustrant of all our hopes and ideals. We have seen that if Life had not been a process of creative choice but one of blind struggle producing endless confusions of pointless processes, then though we might have said 'Defy the Cosmic

Process', 'Stand by the inner moral monitor', it would all have
served no purpose. The blind tide within us, the Life Force and
Stream, the drive of insensate instinct would have dashed us to
wreckage against the rocks of an unyielding necessity. Between
inner passion and outer indifference we should have been
ground to pieces.

We have, however, discovered that the outer world gives path
and guide—rails on which we can go, and our inner force tends
to drive us along that path.

Yet all this can still prove all the more frustrant unless a
third thing can be established. To the question, What is the
use of a lawfully free world if my passions make me behave like
a barbarian and a brute? We have seen there is the answer that
the energy within living creatures has led them to ever higher
living and fuller consciousness, as long as they did not raise a
sectional revolt against it and deny the price it demanded of
them. To the question, What is the use of the Life within me
tending toward creativity and its discipline if I myself do not
wish to co-operate with Life? we have to find the answer to the
further question, Who am I and what is this consciousness I
most directly experience? Is or is not consciousness co-operating
with Life?

This is the gravest of questions. And it began to be raised,
we have seen, long before civilization or man. It has behind
it a vast weight of support—nothing less, we have seen, than
the entire fossil record and on top of that the whole sum of
every other living species save man alone. Further, as we shall
have to allow in this chapter, man himself, of his present two
thousand million numbers, of his million or two years as a
species (or as something so hominid that he was above all the
animals) what has he to show? Cannot we say, must we not
consent to the verdict, that most of the time most men have
been making such a mess of their lives, their powers and their
opportunities that beside what they have done to their environment, their fellow animals and to their own species (their fellow
men) any animal might be considered preferable, more wise in
its way of living, more lofty morally, less costly to everything

that it contacts? If all the other species are decadent is not man depraved? Nor, as he advances, does he seem to get better. For sheer fiendishness of behaviour man seems to need high mechanical skill, physiological knowledge and psychological insight. With his awful trick of torturing his own kind he seems to have brought to a hellish perfection a cruelty which, in even the largest-brained animal, is only rudimentary. It is in epochs—such as the European thirteenth century and some of the finest phases of Chinese civilization—when his sensibility and taste seem to have made possible a combination of culture and cruelty —that man has appeared so diabolical as to suggest that his self-consciousness is a final and fatal depravity. And indeed that seems to be the precise truth of the case. The animals have all sold their birthright of freedom for some selfish, greedy specialization. Man has held to and used his birthright but to become devilish, not divine. What then are we to do? Have we any choice but to throw in our hand? We must, in honesty, agree that it is little use talking about 'Life Acceptance' and the rejection of 'Escapism' and 'Defeatism' if in point of fact the evidence shows that man at the last, raised to a pinnacle, has chosen to throw himself off it. We are not appealing to some revelation that has access to cheering beliefs and convictions based on knowledge not publicly available, not evidenced by any facts the ordinary man may know. We have seen that ordinarily accessible facts show that this world is all right, that Life too is acceptable, friendly. We have seen that Life brought man safely past those dangerous declines into specialization into which all the other animals sank. Then, having given him self-consciousness, he was free.

To ordinary available facts we must then go to see what man has done with this truly magnificent double offer. Outwardly and inwardly he was free to accept it. But we must allow he was as free to reject it. And thirdly, we must grant that as all the animals have failed to hold on to it but have slipped back, so man—since he became man—shows every sign of having done so too.

We know, not as a *mythos*, a Garden of Eden story, but as an anatomical fact, that decadence can be recognized and is recognized in all species and genera by three things. The descent to decrepitude, malignant stupidity and deadly indolence has been marked by the appearance of three symptoms. The first is gigantism, the creature becomes vast in bulk, seems to trust in its brute strength to crush all opposition and to desert the capacity to be mobile, to feel, to be aware, to respond. The second step is that it confines any general power of response to a few specialized behaviour patterns and that its structure finally becomes shaped to give these and these alone expression and exercise.[1] The third step is no longer individual and physiological, it is social: Intraspeci-al struggle arises. That is never permitted to endure. True, it does appear but when it does it heralds the extinction of that species unless this fatal form of the fatal mistake of 'parasitism' is abandoned. It *has* appeared in the three types of living creatures who have attained the highest degree of social elaboration. The 'warrior' ants practise a true warfare on other ants. The warriors are probably already decadent. Most types of 'soldier' ants are so specialized, with giant mandibles to chop in pieces their foes, that they cannot feed themselves. Some swarms of bees go 'pirate' and will start robbing other hives. Such swarms have to be destroyed. They have lost the wish to work for themselves. Finally, in man also there seems, in comparatively late times (see later) perhaps after the Neolithic, the use of specific warfare. On these three counts man seems already to stand self-condemned. He is a giant species. As we have seen he is taller than any ape, gigantically bigger than what seem the small ancestral ape[2] or hominid types. About specialization there can be no doubt either—he has

[1] An extraordinary finished example of this and evidently late in the line of Life, is the single digit of the strange Madagascar Lemur, the Aye-Aye. This one finger of the hand has become grotesquely lengthened and thinned and is used with its long nail to put into the bored holes of insects, impale them, and, so skewered, put them in the animal's mouth. The hand is thus crippled by the problem of easy feeding being solved.

[2] Dryopithecus, a transitional fossil ape with a bigger brain case (proportionate to structure) than any surviving ape, has a skeleton of some thirty inches height.

specialized in a vast enlargement of the central nervous system
—his brain is his master hypertrophy. Under its rule his jaw
has been shrunken, his sense of smell ruined, his palate with his
sense of taste constricted, his very teeth made unable to erupt.
Depending on this terrible machine he has let his body be put
under almost impossible strains and let slide all its natural
defences. We need not recapitulate the risks of that entire upright position. Strain on heart, on vascular system, on intestines
and stomach, all undergone because the brain must have pride
of place and first call on blood, even when that blood is needed
urgently for digestion and circulation.

And thirdly and finally, who can doubt that as he has specialized in height, and in hypertrophy of brain tissue at the cost of
all else, so he has used that endowment in ultraskill not to enjoy
life—we have seen it ruthlessly starves all the other senses—but
to torment his own kind. This huge brain makes him think that
he can do everything and that he knows everything and that the
only reason for doing everything is to get gear and power into
his individual hands. So he continually assaults his fellows and
they him. And as they are equally clever in means and equally
grossly ignorant of ends they must end by destroying themselves.
These are conclusions to which any anatomist might arrive;
they are conclusions which any historian, especially of the
modern world, would find almost impossible to avoid.

But by allowing (as we should and must) the full weight of the
case against man, by showing that he has been given freedom,
that he did for long retain generalization—freedom's correlate—
and that he has lost generalization and so has lost freedom—
we see where, if there is an answer, it would lie. As has been said
earlier, it is not the slightest use trying to deny that man has
made, literally, the most shocking mistakes—the worst mistakes
that any creature has made.

But when we allow that, when we say, and the term seems
an exact one, that he has 'fallen', we must be precise. He fell
violently because he had been raised high. What we have to
ask are two things: (1) has he fallen so far and so violently that
he has really sunk below all the animals and is gone further to

extinction than any? And (2) has he used up all the vast potentiality of opportune creative reaction with which he was endowed and which was stored in him? Is there any evidence
that he could be redeemed? How far has he fallen and how many
times?

First we must ask. Where should we look for his most serious
and fatal imprisonment? That does not lie in action—such as
crime—for crime is a consequence. The source lies in the delusion that gave rise to the criminal action. Man is not in danger
of doom because he is big—that again may be a consequence.
As to size, he may still be within the bounds of permissible
physical optimacy. The Achilles heel is, of course, specialization.
It is specialization that makes the creature feel it is perfectly
competent and blinds it with its complacency to its real and
deadly ignorance. Now man's hypertrophic specialization is his
brain. But, as we have seen, as it is a specialization in unspecialization, so the rise of the brain need not have been the
fatal step. Dangerous no doubt, it was. It reduced all the organs
to dependence on it. The large-brained creature, and supremely
man no longer responds as an entirety to its problems. The
racial wisdom even when fossilized into instinct, gives the individual animal a deeper insight into its problem than non-
instinctive purely ratiocinative individuality can have. That
deeper insight man has exchanged for intellect, the power which
can arrange its data in many ways but commands fewer data
because these data are for it confined to 'sensa', i.e., to nothing
but what the individual receives through his senses. Further,
when men take analytic, critical intelligence as the only way of
knowing, then a still stricter censorship is imposed. Now unless
we can see how and why we should take a suggested course, we
reject the monition. The brain, no doubt, made man more
widely responsive. Yet we must allow against the forebrain of
man that since he has had it, and through it become absorbed
with managing the outer world, he has lost touch with the inner
world and no longer knowing his own inner nature is torn by
conflicts he cannot even understand.

If we judge the brain by its results we see that this 'specialization in unspecialization' has not made for freedom. Man is supremely a social creature. And the type of society that he has created has been made by his type of brain. He has now become a creature that without its society is nothing. It is his true mind and conscience. It is his organism. That being so we have to allow on this evidence that man appears to be as fatally specialized as bee, ant or termite. For his societies are not merely hypertrophied—showing lack of co-ordination over the highly specialized parts—but those parts are rapidly diverging into ever more specialized and insulated functions. As the society as a whole gets rapidly larger, and requires more co-ordination and service from its varied organs, these fail to receive any central guidance. We are seeing at this moment—as Dr. W. R. Inge prophesied some forty years ago—an actual fulfilment of the myth of Babel: The various builders of the great structure of knowledge are falling into confusion because, owing to their specializations having become so divergent, they can no longer understand one another's tongues.

Man has gained power to analyse his environment: he has lost power to integrate his own nature, individual and social. This is the psychosocial problem. To that we will return in a moment. For first we must examine a comparatively new physiological issue. Here at 'body level' we have new evidence illustrating vividly what we, as men, have lost in essential diagnostic knowledge of how to live healthily. The evidence also indicates both when and how we lost this vital knowledge. Lately it has been shown that rats are far more adequate diagnosticians of their health than any man. They can pick their diet, so as to give them a carefully balanced range of chemicals. If they have not time to eat an apple they will gnaw into the centre to eat the seeds to get the vitamins and the protein stored only there. But further, and far more remarkable, when they have been operated on and made diabetic they will at once select those diets which will give them still the food they need while avoiding that which in their damaged state would now prove fatal to them. Man, then, has lost a power a lowly animal has and one needed for life. Yes, man has lost it, but it seems that mankind has not.

The small child, as long as it is spontaneous in its reactions—under two or two and a half—will pick those diets which its body needs. It still has unspoiled diagnostic taste and though for a little it may seem, when full choice is given it, to sway toward a partial intake, this is corrected in a few days and before any damage is done.[1]

We must, then, look for man's mistake not in his humanity *per se*, but in something added to him since he became man. We see now the question is not, What did Life do to man? It gave him power of creative choice and not till he had become man did he lose his gift. The issue, we have to face, turns on, What did man, as man, do with that gift of choice? Life brought him to a far higher independence of it (freedom from racial urge) than any other creature succeeded in attaining. The issue is, then, specifically human. The question turns from What is the world? and What is Life? to, What is man? On that turns the whole riddle. The problem of whether the world has been a success and all Life been worth while can only be solved if we know what man is and what he might still become. We have to ask, What has he made of himself by his own free choices since he was man? What, now, does he find himself to have made of himself? Certainly his power has not given him peace nor his cleverness, goodness. Something has gone wrong and perhaps—in terms of Life's history—not so long ago. In short we have to ask, Did there take place a fall after man had become man? The evidence would seem to suggest that there must have been a time when man lost his general intuitive knowledge which led to right action, right taste and right choice, when his balanced knowledge of his own nature and outer nature went out of gear. Thereafter the more power he gained over his environment, the less he knew about himself and how to manage himself. Further, it would seem that that sudden breakdown in the psycho-physiological knowledge of himself was precisely at the time—just another aspect of—the same ignorance that made him believe that he was a separate individual. He was, by a threefold darkness, suddenly cut off and imprisoned. He was cut off from

[1] See Appendix note at the close of this chapter.

179

his knowledge of his body as, not his machine and pleasure bottle, but as a wonderful integrated phase of himself, always responding to each change in him and he to it. He was cut off from his knowledge that all his fellows were other integers of the Life and consciousness he felt in himself. And third and final blindness, he was cut off from the saving knowledge that all animals and all nature made the two concentric rings in the vast dynamo in which he spun. His acquired ignorance of his body made him a sensualist and an addict. His acquired ignorance of his fellows made him a tyrant-slave or a slave-tyrant. His acquired ignorance of his environment made him both superstitious and destructive, cowardly and cruel.

We have now made three observations which help us toward answering the final question: Who am I? What may we know of man, as well as of the Cosmos and of Life? We have seen that there can be no doubt that he is the culminating creature. We have seen also that he has made the gravest mistakes. But we have also seen that there is not evidence, as yet, that those mistakes are fatal. About the first two observations we need have no further discussion. The issue turns on the third. The question is, Can man crown the whole or, with him and through his miscarriage, must the whole prove frustrant? Up to this point, up to man, the issue remains in doubt. The universe is not hostile. On the contrary, it has proved a curiously devised situation for the emergence of Life. Life, in turn, has proved a power, not destructive or consumptive but gaining continually in creativity and capacity, until it, in turn, gave rise to consciousness. But, as the universe could be no more than a frame for Life, so Life could be no more than an opportunity for consciousness. With that third term and that alone could it be said whether the whole were to succeed and become worth while or have proved a mistake.

What, then, is the evidence that man can be saved? Only when we have dealt with that can we go on and ask could he become a saviour. And here, too, we must confine ourselves to our thesis—what can be discovered from evidence available to all? We can appeal only to matters of that common knowledge which research and discovery, study and experiment have to-day put at our common disposal.

There are five reasons for supposing that man's outlook, the fate of the human psyche, is not closed. We can dare, because of this evidence, to join issue with H. G. Wells's last and dark judgment—that the human mind is At the End of Its Tether. With these considerations the rest of this chapter will be occupied.

The first thing that we have to make clear is that there is no simple creature such as 'man' to be studied and dismissed. Human nature is amazingly difficult to define. The obvious reason for that is the immense range that is shown by extant human types. It is sometimes overlooked that the ease with which we can define animal species is mainly because these species have become specialized—have given rise to specific limiting features —features which sharply distinguish the group from all other groups and which, as far as we know, are becoming continually more separate. The reverse is true of man. Not only are his organs mainly generalized. His behaviour, too, is not defined because, having no instincts, his responses to challenges of the environment and of other forms of life can never be strictly foretold. Because all men are still mainly generalized types we tend also to overlook the vast gamut of possibility shown by human nature as we see it now. The immense range in mental capacity alone shown by the difference disclosed through Intelligence Testing is only one span of human variety. Besides that, there are the different capacities of the various social heredities. For all men are double in this respect: There is the inherent capacity of the individual to accept and adopt the particular tradition in which he is born and brought up, the personal dynamic plasticity of response. And there are the traditions themselves—some being predominantly religious, others specifically artistic and others again mainly economic.[1] If a man who is highly capable

[1] Arthur Waley has pointed out that a number of cultures, such, for example, as some of the Arabic, have been considered rudimentary because they were uninterested in plastic arts while, as a matter of fact, in vocal art forms they were advanced and elaborate.

in one is judged by the standards of any of the others he may appear a fool. Yet each of these seems to be adequate response to the challenge of life and outer nature and also to their constituents' psychosocial needs. Further, in a single society which is well able to survive, there can be present types of great mental simplicity and ones of the highest intelligence and yet each of these may not only have a place but each may be needed to fill that place in order that the society may function adequately. And among those of the highest intelligence the variety may be as wide as it is between the fool and the genius—for genius has a wider disparity in itself than has foolishness. The impractical mystic with his vast insights is utterly different from the practical executive who clearly envisages all the evident material and can order it undistracted by speculation. Neither may understand the other: both are required in any society that is to be elaborate and advancing.

Human society is therefore of incalculable richness. Though, then, some of the current answers given by one portion, the North-western section, to human problems may seem no longer to be apposite, that is not to say that humanity may not produce other answers, answers provided by other members of this very heterogeneous body. When instinct gives the wrong answer it is done, for it has no other. When intelligence is proved mistaken, it learns from its mistake and gives a new reply.

We discover the second reason why man may not be done when we ask, Why is it that man is so free to learn? That is due to the fact that he does not inherit acquired characteristics. Every generation starts then with a clean sheet of very impressionable paper. On to this, we must repeat, is printed the record of the social heredity up to date. As we have seen, some social heredities emphasize one side and others another but they all seem to stem down from a common social code, a code which combines a psychology and a physics, an ethic and an economic. That basic social heredity from which all present patterns of living are variants, has in it, as its psychological and ethical, half the answer to the five Natural Moral Laws or Questions: What is Force? What Wealth? What Sex and Appetite? What is your Word? What is your Thought? Into the development of these Laws we cannot go here. The present writer tried to sketch the three stages of the answers man can give in a previous volume, *The Eternal Gospel*. Here it is enough to say that man's social heredity, his power to respond to these Laws is very plastic. For a time he may—as he certainly seems now to have done—tend to favour the economic against the ethical, the physical against the psychical. Indeed, he may try, as secularism often does, to show that that psychology is based on ethics. But he is not tied to the mistake and once he recognizes it he is free, free within a generation, to remedy it.

We cannot, then, say human nature is doomed because human beings lately have shown that they have behaved wrongly. As we have seen, even the small child who has an unspoiled and diagnostically capable palate, may err in its diet for a few days. But after that it learns its mistake, feels its 'unwellness' and eats to correct the disbalance. Our society seems not less capable of rapid remedial change than is a two-year-old child toward its diet.

The third reason for supposing that man is not done is one of which we have specific physical evidence. 'Man is the foetalization of the ape.' By his inherent vitality and that of the human family and the human society, the child is born in an unprotected state and stage. So it emerges into the outer world where it must begin to learn in a condition of undefended potentiality, of unlimited impressionability and response, which no ape dares risk. The ape child dares not take the plunge out into the world of learning and suffering until it has shut itself into a specialized body, made itself advance some way toward toughness, lost considerably its full capacity for impressionability. Before it is born it has come down and retreated from the full height of its possible openness and receptivity. Man, as we have seen, takes the plunge, as it were, from much higher up the slope. He does not creep down—or only a little way—so as to break the shock between his high potentiality and the actuality of the outer environment. And this is a joint endeavour, of the infant itself, of the parents, yes, and we may say of the human group too. Professor H. Fleure has suggested that the final stages of this advance were due and perhaps only possible through the domestication of animals—an issue with which we shall be dealing in a moment. For, he points out, the longer the child can be kept on a milk diet the longer the cranium bones can remain unrestricted. For as soon as the jaw has to be used for true mastication of a solid diet, so soon the muscles that run up from the ramus of the jaw have to be strengthened, and, as these ultimately run over the top of the skull, they bind in and close the sutures constricting the area free to the growing brain. This decadent development is seen in full degree in the skull of the gorilla, where a keel has formed on the top of the skull confining the brain case, so that on the sides of this keel the huge jaw muscles may find adequate purchase.

We have no reason, therefore, to suppose that man's psychological development is over. Three freedoms are still open to him. The first is that his period of responsive learning may be developed—he may take longer in growing up and when he is grown up he may be less of a prematurely developed creature than he is now. He may be less knowing and cocksure, and more wise and humble. Nor is that fact maintained here in order to advocate that more years be given at the upper end of education. That would be wise but of secondary importance. It is a matter, at the end, of adding to information rather than expanding real education. It is advisable that as medicine takes more and more years from the student before he can be called a doctor, so, before a man becomes a citizen he should be given more information, and more time for getting it, than we now permit. But the actual argument—the need and hope of real education—moves the other way round. It does not seem that it is much use giving more information to those whose emotional and creative responses are no longer open, or are misshapen. And it would appear that the basic pattern of such responses—the basic direction of the impulse of the human psyche—is settled in the earliest years. After three, most child psychologists seem to think, the

child's emotional response—either of withdrawal or acceptance
—has largely been laid down. We shall be seeing at the end of
this chapter that redemption is a real thing and salvage of character is possible. But it must also be allowed that it is costly and
slow and of course depends on the existence of salvagers. On the
number of those who have a plus amount of goodwill, trust,
confidence and acceptance depends the number of failures that
can be reconditioned and put back into dynamic service.

Therefore, redemption (as has always been taught by those
who knew of it not as a wishful piece of uplift but as a fact) depends ultimately on the number of those who have not fallen.
Education in the deepest sense of the word depends, therefore,
on preventing the child from falling into mistakes and making
wrong reactions to strains which it finds unbearable to its 'faith',
its power of acceptance, its capacity for interest and creative
response. And that means that education must be put back
earlier and earlier. Beside the possibility of, and gains that might
result from beginning education earlier, the possibilities and
gains from extending education to later years are as nothing.
With the former you may get a new mind, a new spirit. With
the latter, at best you get but new tools for a mind that has
already made itself up and a spirit that has already accepted
the current view of the universe.

We therefore cannot say what would be the response if we
could begin education at birth. We know that it is this 'putting
back the clock', this recovering once more the freedom of the
uncommitted creature, that has made man the complete superior of any animal, even of the largest-brained of all the animals, the ape. If man went back still further then he might
advance as much beyond what he is now as that is beyond the
ape. For, of course, by education, at this depth of power, is not
meant the acquiring of physical skills or domestic inhibitions—
such as house manners. Here, as has been said above, we are at
the basic level of fundamental response. Here we are deciding
at what basic angle shall all the further growth be projected.
The education at this level is taken in as a general response, at
a depth well below and more powerful than any rational per-

ception of deduction. Therefore, the educator does not instruct
with words or rewards, but teaches by keeping the child surrounded with an atmosphere of confidence and response which
gives it both trust and a desire to understand and co-operate.
So it is that the security climate of the womb is kept round the
psyche of the child, though the physique has already to be exposed to physical conditions more exacting and more stimulating than those of the womb. Such educators, it is clear, are the
parents, and specifically the mother. But it is also clear that such
educators cannot be so raised and so kept in the right teaching
state unless the community can give them the backing they need
for their faith. They are the medium between the child and the
community. And they can support and keep the child raised to
that height only so long as the community permits them to have
that purchase and support. The community by its common
knowledge, faith and high social practice, so secures for the
parents the necessary purchase, allows them to stretch upward
to their full capacity. For, it must be said again, what the parents
have to supply to the child is not information or instruction in
the ordinary sense of those words, but a climate of dynamic
security, a faith in the deepest sense of the word, a triumphant
banishment of fear through the conviction that all experience
is simply an opportunity for creative response.

Now that attitude of mind and heart cannot be extemporized,
still less 'acted'. It is not the slightest use pretending that these
things are felt 'because it might be good for the baby'. The baby
is so powerful, so capable of being instructed just because it can
instantly diagnose sham and dismiss a synthetic substitute. The
child's mind is so totally powerful because, and as long as, it
makes such a total reaction that there is (until long after) no
outward sign that it has noticed. As a photographic plate does
not make an exclamation as it takes a total impression, but
afterwards when developed shows the whole record in a way
that the human eye and mind would fail to register, so too with
the infant mind. Only afterward when the growing mind develops do we find the full depth and size and terrible completeness of the impression which was taken in, in silence and en-

tirety. Any expression of shock is to some degree a defence against assault and a rejection of outrage. Therefore, the parents must have reached the point—not of high factual information as to infant hygiene but of something far higher. They must have come to the point when they so understand the promise—and the threat—that each new life brings with it that they themselves become incapable of greed or fear in the presence of such a terrible recorder, amplifier and creator. And, of course, if they are never to send out fear and greed into the child's climate, then they must never feel these destructive powers themselves at any time.

This, we say, is an impossible ideal. But that has been said whenever any demand of hygiene was made for the first time to a new generation. If we once felt, as those who are informed now tell us they are assured, that this matter was of vital importance, there is no reason why we should not do it. When bacterial infection was recognized then the standard of physical hygiene in all children's and maternity hospitals and through most homes was raised and the death rate brought down at such a pace, that, as every population record shows, the history of man in the West has been altered by this one fact more perhaps than by any other. For the death rate in the first year of life has always been man's highest casualty and the lowering of that has utterly changed population outlooks. But this danger of psychological infection, of the *damnosa hereditas* of our passions being printed on the minds of infants, seems far more serious than bacterial infection. The latter may poison the body, after which many gain a complete immunity. The children that survive may actually be hardier. But with psychological infection, not only does the poison spread but the damaged live on. We have a twofold, deadly danger. This not only ruins millions, by turning them into neurotics and psychotics that can neither accept life nor do anything but drain the energy of those striving to live creatively, the damage spreads far wider. From these failures are drawn the social toxins, the hatreds that now endanger civilization as a whole. Those who are so weakened by their sense of wrong and despair—gathered in infancy—that they are individual failures and fill asylums, these we now see are the minor casualties. The major and incomparably graver casualties are types that respond not negatively but with positive badness and have given rise to those fanatics who can fill whole populations with their sense of wrong, can league the highest development of destructive physical force to their insane dreams of revenge, and now can—and if not stopped assuredly will—destroy the world.

The three freedoms are then: To leave the child free from all fear and greed, to keep it in a climate in which from the moment of its birth till it is three it will only be with those incapable of a response in which there is not courage and generosity, peace and creativity. The second freedom is to see that parents see the need of acquiring such a frame of mind—that on it turns, not merely the happiness of their child and of their society, but of mankind —yes, its very survival. The third freedom is that society, seeing that its future depends on the parents that can be provided and the infants that shall be born, will provide these conditions of psychological hygiene and education without which man has no future.

It may be said that these three requirements are really three points on a closed, a vicious circle. Society is going mad, no wonder parents are irresponsible, no wonder child delinquency (to grow into adult delinquency) flourishes. Where break into the closed line? Again the reply seems to be found in past experience. For centuries there was a general conviction that cleanliness was a good thing. It is a historical mistake to think that men did not try to practise hygiene. Primitive codes nearly all have much to say on it (e.g., the fear of excretions, of blood, especially menstrual blood, etc.). The dread of washing in the late Middle Ages and the early modern was due to the fear of the spread of infectious diseases, especially the horror of the great 'Leprosy' plague of the thirteenth century and the even greater dread of the Pox—Syphilis—in the sixteenth. But only with the nine-teenth century's new power of understanding the nature of many of the infectious diseases was there able to be roused sufficient energy to make the immense effort to combat such infections. It was because the proof was clear that many diseases are carried by dirty water supply that there was able to be made the huge endeavour necessary to give cities safe water. And the proof of bacterial infection through contaminated food and through disease carriers led to sterilization of hospitals and the use of disinfectants. So, too, as we discover the psychological infections, we shall be able to get rid of psychotic and neurotic disease —especially as the urge to do so is so strong because the threatened peril of total destruction is near.

At this point perhaps it may be questioned: What have such speculations as to man's possible future to do with an attempt to show that God exists? How do such hopes support the proofs that this world is planned to environ a moral being, Life to produce him and consciousness to guide him to his goal? The answer is: What may be expected of man is part of his nature. He can only be understood through judging his capacity as well as his present output. In every animal there is (however overlaid by blind adaptation) a striving toward a goal greater than itself. In man, and because he is man, that teleological capacity is far stronger than in any other animal. It is indeed his distinctive, special characteristic. For man's peculiar, hopeful significance lies in his power not of actuality but of potentiality, in his reserve of unspent creativity, in what he may grow into and not in what he now is.

So far, then, in our attempt to find design we have seen that man *qua* man, our third line of inquiry, also gives evidence of a shaping purpose. We have found him in a world of Lawful Freedom, vitalized by a Life advancing by Creative Choice. And now we see this specific creature has been granted the Lawful Freedom of that 'secondary environment' the social heredity, the psycho-economic tradition. Instead of the iron necessity of instinct he is offered education which can advance reciprocally both the individual and his society by constant Creative Choice.

Nor is that the extent of our hope—that man's nature is not yet fully developed, that he is still plastic, has still unspent power of response in him. We have reason to suppose that if we could bring up children from birth in a home climate where they would not ever feel greed or fear, they would be a new psychological seed, a new social departure for mankind. But we have also reason to suppose that education could start before birth and therefore lead to even more wonderful results. We have seen that there is clear evidence that the human child is born far less committed than the ape. We have seen that because of this, the human child is so much superior to the ape, and human society has gone so much further than ape society. Further, we have seen that the human foetus development is so remarkable because when the ape—during its almost equally long gestation—has during the latter part of this womb life begun to toughen up and contract—the better to be able to hold its own as soon as it emerges—the human foetus does not do so. It hangs on to its sensitive responsiveness and uncommittedness. But, and here is the second point of such great importance, though it does hang on to much of the foetal uncommittedness, it loses some of it. True, it is born less committed than is an ape. But it has yet to be born with its full uncommittedness fully preserved. True, it does not descend down as far as does the ape, before venturing out into the world. But nevertheless, it has descended some of the way. No child has yet been born and lived with the full cranial development of the foetus at the height of its cranial development. The creature that should fully retain the highest stage of cranial development is not yet born. In short, the foetus is still prophetic, it is still pointing toward what the future man might be if only there could be the environment—the psychic womb (the family and, around that, the society) which would make such a comprehensive incarnation possible.

It may be questioned whether, as the move must come from the side of the foetus—however much we may encourage by making those conditions to which it could respond—can such reaction be expected. There are two reasons for hope, if we do our part. The first is the puzzling evidence—sporadic but nonetheless fairly continuous—of suggestion and other external influences on the formation of the foetus. These cases seem to be much in line with those cases—also at first dismissed and now having to be allowed—of hypnotic suggestion that passing beyond functional effects actually can and do cause organic changes.

That we cannot yet command by hypnotic technique—at least as a current procedure—cures of physical damage, is not, we now see, sufficient reason for denying the fact that such cures do take place sporadically. So too with the emergence of a foetus still at full cranial development. The second reason for hoping that this would be possible if the proper psychological climate was prepared for the child to be born into is the high intelligence of the foetus itself. As an authority has lately said, 'The high degree of perfection to which the foetus attains in co-ordinating its functional activity in the progress of growth and development must be a matter of constant wonder to the investigator'. And he concludes by quoting with approval Samuel Butler's famous remark, 'Birth is the end of the time when we really knew our business and the beginning of the days when we do not know what we would do, or do'. Granted that the foetal intelligence is turned as it were wholly on its task of getting the body ready to emerge, granted that that intelligence cannot be spoken to in our speech, yet as we see throughout this essay, there are words far more telling and penetrating than those uttered by the voice or framed as propositions and it is this kind of communication which the really open mind and heart can utter and the deep creative mind, such as is manifested as working in and through the foetus, can listen to and act upon.

This, then, remains man's hope. With every loving conception, with every healthy gestation the opportunity seems to be offered of such an incarnation, of a child that might not have to retreat in any degree from the full height of its foetal promise but might be born from the highest possible development to which the foetus attains. Then before it has made any compromise with toughness, any retreat toward narrowness or rejection, it might come forth with its full capacity to respond, to accept, to suffer and understand.

We may come, then, to the fourth reason for supposing that man is not finished, that to him is still extended a vast promise. And this, like the third which we have just been discussing, has actual physical evidence to support the psychological hope.

Here we are going to discuss salvage, the question whether with man there is not present the final triumph of Life. Life itself, we saw in Chapter Five, may be a constructive force coming from without and kindling into creative pattern, building up into new patterns of power 'dead' matter. And, at the end of that chapter, we saw further, that with its final production, man, there may be manifested the power to go still further, far further. As Life may be able to take matter and for a while hold it up above the Second Law of Thermodynamics, so consciousness may be able to turn to Life, and when Life itself is failing, draw it back and upwards and restore it to the higher activity, the activity of ever-growing capacity, which it had failed to sustain.

We are now ready to discuss this issue. We could not do so until we had first pointed out the power that man still has in him unspent and the three freedoms that are still open to him. Now we can see that this salvaging of himself may not be confined to himself. Even as Life can kindle dead matter so man, or rather the unspent consciousness in him, can salvage not only himself and his own race, he may also save the other animals. This is supremely important. For, if established, not only would it prove the immense unspent power in man himself; not only would it argue that if he can really tame and salvage the wild beast surely he may hope to salvage himself, it would be the final and weightiest argument in favour of there being 'A Friend behind the Phenomena', a power that wishes well, works well, yes, and watches over its creatures and its creation.

We have seen that if man alone gets through, and all the creatures other than he must sink down through pain, though lessening pain, to unconsciousness and extinction, then, though we can say that the process has won in a way, we cannot say that it has been without terrible cost. We can say that the power which gave free will had to take the risk that it would be misused and we can say that the gift was justified because from that one creature that won through came a species that has overrun and employed the earth as no other animal ever has. But we have to own that that Power could not save any but that one creature from a *final* mistake. That Power had to retake its gift of Life and confess that it had miscarried, at least so far. But if salvage could be shown to be a fact, then we should see that the gift of freedom could be given—a truly creative act—and yet, a still further and greater act of creation—when it had been misused and lost by the user, the power that gave it could buy back the loss. From its own creative-redemptive good will it could restore to the creature the great endowment which the creature had lost of its own mistaken will. What is the evidence for this?

Such a notion has been called the supreme Wishful Thought, the kind of comforting fantasy which proves its falsity by being obviously Too Good to be True. And to our modern notion that takes for granted that 'human nature can't be changed' (because rationalism failed to understand psychology) biology seemed to have added its final ruling. 'Evolution is irreversible' became one of the great slogans of evolutionists. Nor is there any doubt that in the vast number of cases this is true. Once a specialization has been adopted by a species, once a generalized primitive feature—say cartilage—has been specialized into bone, bone cannot be evolved back into cartilage. It used to be thought that once scale had turned into hair or feather it would never revert. Nevertheless there are recorded cases where this seems to have taken place. Yet we must surely allow that specialization, once adopted, is irreversible, by that species, for it has made its choice. It has adopted a specific and closed reaction to the challenge of circumstances and it would seem that the organism has therefore not only imprisoned itself (e.g., the example of the paw of the lion) but has also spent its freedom and fertility of invention by making this specialization. Not only will the specialized and confined limb not let it move again with unspecialized freedom, the creature itself no longer can desire that freedom and strive for it. It is hypnotized by its local and specific success; and its whole pattern of feeling, and satisfaction, is closed in the vicious circle of the limited and extremely finished and expert act. The conditioned reflex specialized the limb and in turn the specialized limb further conditions the reflex.

It is clear then that no help can come from within the species itself. If help there is in that pass it must come from someone outside the species. Nor is the evidence of moral conversion really satisfying. For not only is that mainly only a change of character and a change wrought within the same species—one man being the channel of grace to another man—but, as we know, such changes in most cases have not lasted.[1] The change, in short, has not been a real change. Can there be incontrovertible evidence of that? Undoubtedly there is. It has been strangely disregarded but it is undeniable. It is in the fact of taming. Earlier in this essay it has been referred to. Now we must examine it closely. What we have to establish is nothing less than the giving back to a species, that has lost its generalized state, that essential and basic freedom. We have also to show that this gift has been bestowed by another and higher species, a species which had become higher by this very fact—that it had kept this power of freedom.

Man is the foetalization of the ape—because of that he is man. Is there any other example of this foetalization? Yes, there is one such—in its way as remarkable as man's. That is the dog. As was pointed out in one of those remarkable papers that came in the 1920's from the Hamburg School of Animal Psychology—work so much more remarkable than Pavlov's but disregarded because it did not tell, as his did, in favour of materialism—the dog is the foetalization of the wolf. This is not a matter of behaviour study, as was Pavlov's. These observations are based on the clearest and most material of evidence—embryology. For precisely as we see the ape foetus, as it approaches birth, lose the high human forehead and full brain case and become in skull shape depressed, contracted, massive and brutal, so we can, by examination of the wolf foetus, see the same degenerative process going on prior to birth. And with the wolf—as the wolf is a more degraded creature than the ape[2]—the degenerative pro-

---

[1] This is not to challenge the value of conversion but it is to stress that conversion is not the same, is not the creative act, as is redemption.

[2] We should, however, note that the ape, too, does undergo a degeneracy of the forelimb. The arm does tend to become 'brachiated', a mere sling for arboreal locomotion and the hand loses breadth of span becoming a hook, the fingers so long that it oversets objects it would pick up (see *Ape and the Child*, Drs. W. N. and L. Kellogg). The gorilla, becoming too heavy for tree life, has, on the other hand, as we have seen, turned back the hand largely into a forefoot.

cess is shown throughout the skeleton. For example, the fore-limb—as we see with the ewe foetus—at the height of its womb development is a generalized limb with still a hint of becoming a questing and exploratory instrument. But as the forelimbs approach birth they become specialized. So when the wolf is born it is already 'cast' into the predatory, parasitic form of its species. The muscles have folded round and thatched down the skull in order to give great strength to the long low muzzle armed with the strong canines. Here we have a specialized instrument for catching hold of running prey and pulling them down. And the forelimbs follow suit. In order to permit this carnivore head to be carried swiftly forward after the flying prey, the forelimbs have become specialized so that a restricted simple to-and-fro movement will allow of one thing, a tireless automatic run.

Such, then, is the wolf when it is born. But prior to birth this was not so. Take the foetal skull out and there one finds a short muzzle, a high and rounded forehead and eyes approaching almost to binocular vision, while the long narrow muzzle of the postnatal wolf hardly permits any co-ordinated sight and so compels an almost total dependence on smell.

But can we compare this foetal skull with anything that could live, that is viable. Surely it was an impossible hope? Surely the struggle to survive compelled these degenerative changes? The foetus could not emerge and live unless and until it had sufficiently modified its generalized and unprotected state and condition, so that, adequately armed, it may take and hold its place in the battle of life? But, as a matter of fact, we can put beside the wolf foetal skull, with its high but unborn development, another skull which is just an enlarged model of this foetal cranium. And this cranium is in actual fact the skull of an animal that lives, has lived now for millennia and which there is every reason to suppose will now survive the wolf. That is the dog, and especially that type of dog domesticated for the longest time-span—the spaniel. The spaniel, and especially in its most historically ancient form—the Asiatic spaniel—the Pekingese and the Japanese temple dog—has a forehead which is merely a quantitative enlargement of the wolf foetal skull. The Pomeranian is also another such 'recovery' restoration of the foetal form.

To return, then, to our actual example: Man has given back to a branch of the wolf stock a freedom it had lost. He has taken an enemy of his own race and by bringing it into domestic relationship with himself he has recovered for it the generalized skull and brain which it had surrendered. The wonder of this is further added to when we consider that not only did man do this to the dog when man himself seems to have been backward (the second Pumpelly expedition to the settlements round the Caspian found burials dated at 9000 B.C. where the dog was found buried with the human dead) but that this first triumph of redemption took place with a carnivore. Further, we see that this triumph was not merely a change of physique. Finally, we see that this change in the brain-shape has permitted not only a change in intelligence but in the whole emotional life. Not only has the mind become again generalized. There are dogs to-day tested to show they can grasp the meaning not only of scores of words—said without inflection—but also understand mental propositions. But the emotional life has been advanced and regeneralized even more. It is a commonplace of canine psychology that the dog has transferred to man the loyalty that it once had to the pack—and with that transference there has of course been an immense enlargement of possible response. The dog (as one of the heads of the Seeing Eye, Inc., of Morristown, New Jersey, said to the present writer) wants to understand because he wants to please. It is affection which like a psychological oxygen is always blowing on the dog's intelligence making it strive to understand what interests its master and to share in every way his life.

Finally, we must not overlook what is perhaps the most hopeful element in the whole of this remedial, restorative, redemptive process. It is, we have seen, real, thorough. For it is now 'bred in the bone'. The restored psyche has been able to register its altered, rewidened attitude and outlook, to build it in and through a physique that has likewise become freed. Yes, it is all that; but to that this story adds another gain—a gain as great and even more unexpected. That change of mind should be able to manifest its conversion in change of body is wonderful. But the rate at which that change took place—that is not less amazing. Speed of process and thoroughness of result—these two things are generally in our experience antithetical. You must choose to be slow if you would be lasting; 'quickly come, quickly go.' Any change of physique, that above all must be geologically slow. Surely the evolutionists have shown that. And if descent is slow, how much slower any ascent. The Virgilian judgment, 'Easy the descent to Hell, how hard the return', that all standard paleontologists would maintain. Indeed, most would change the word 'hard' into 'impossible'.

Yet as a matter of fact, this change up, this delivery from anatomical captivity in a degenerated form into a largely freed physique, matching the freed psyche, that miraculous bodily transformation (and one that is now racial because inherited) has taken place certainly in not more than ten thousand years and maybe in two-thirds of that time. If, as seems probable from fossil remains (see Museum at Lincoln, Nebraska), the dog lost its generalized form in the Oligocene—twelve to eighteen million years ago—that must mean two things: (1) For twelve to eighteen million years the species was degenerating; (2) It was redeemed in seven to ten thousand years. That would show the recovery speed has been fourteen hundred times faster than the decline. Redemption, even when as casual and sporadic as may well have been early taming, is at such a rate that we can say it is never too late to mend. Here we have the answer to that final sad defeatist objection: Maybe salvation works, but, if so, to be real it must be so slow that it will be too late to save us from our cataclysmic follies. Redemption, we see, is not merely creation working in Time but creation working on Time itself, able, because it is creation to unbind, redeem, even Time.

Of course domestication is not confined to the dog. We may leave out of consideration those animals which we have confined and conditioned, harnessed and castrated for our own economic use. Truly to understand the power and effects of domestication

—the taking of a wild animal into one's home and teaching it one's *mores*—we must confine our attention to true pets—animals which are kept purely for the joy their companionship gives to their keeper. The next animal we then must glance at is the cat. It, too, has for perhaps as long as the dog been a companion of man and it, too, as we can judge from its worship in Egypt at Heliopolis under the name Bes, was probably first a religious object, a totem. And here we touch upon a further side of this mystery of taming. As far as we know only twice was it possible to take one of the smaller felines and turn it into a companion. All our Western cats are derived from the Egyptian cat —none from the races of wild cats that still exist and formerly abounded in the West. The wild cat remains singularly intractable to training. The Greeks had no cat, using a kind of ferret for their 'mousing'. The other tamed cat is, of course, the Siamese—also a temple product and with obvious physiological differences from our cat in length of leg, etc. Yet, and this is the next point, though the cat has been domesticated for perhaps three or four thousand years and though we have two distinct varieties, the physique of the cat has proved itself stubbornly resistant to breeders' changes. Consider the alterations of physique that breeders—often quite wantonly and against the animal's chances of good living—can produce in the dog, and we see how stubborn the cat form has proved. And with that stubbornness is a corresponding inflexibility of temperament. The same 'Seeing Eye' authority on dog-breeding for intelligence remarked of cats—of whom he had also great knowledge—that they never really wished to co-operate out of a wish to please, out of 'kindness', but only when they saw that their own interests, their appetites would be served. The form then remains inadaptably predatory and so does the psyche.

This raises the important question as to whether there can ever be real redemption of the psyche if there is not shown also a change back to primal liberty in the body too. It is known that the cat physique is in some ways a 'fiercer', more carnivorous form than the dog's. The tribe of Felis has developed types such as the tiger and its most extravagant form the 'sabre-toothed tiger', which are more obviously specialized flesh-tearers than any of the canine races. Further, endocrine study has shown that whereas, with man, the thyroid is a giant gland and the supra-renals small—in the cats this is reversed. Their endocrine system is geared to anger, rage and fury—man's to reflection and sus-tained effort. Indeed, it is often said that we have 'domesticated' the cat, that is brought it into our homes, but only of the dog have we made a friend, a true companion. There are, of course, exceptional cases and there are exceptional people who can draw a rare response from the cat, making it a real friend, as real as is the dog.

That, then, brings us to the further question of redemption—the question that interests all naturalists: Why, considering that we have domesticated some races of wild animals, why cannot we extend this kingdom of kindness? It is indeed strange that our two pets are fully developed carnivores—both, when in the wild, fierce and dangerous to our species. All our efforts to tame the apes have given pretty poor showing. The usual judgment is that they remain tractable—whether they be gibbons, chim-panzees, orangs or gorillas—so long as they are children. As soon as they become adult they are dangerous—indeed, most become so at puberty. This observation, too, may give us a pos-sible line of thought which will be considered at the end of this section on taming. Meanwhile, we have to own that our record of taming does not compare at all well with that of the ancient Egyptian. For we know that they tamed not only the dog and the cat but also the cheetah, the jackal, an antelope and the dog-faced baboon. The last we have found very difficult and dan-gerous. The cheetah we have used only for hunting—so making it more savage. The jackal is singularly suspicious of us and the antelope has not been made to feel at home in our houses. We have seen also that in the Egyptian culture at least some of these animals, perhaps all—certainly the jackal—'Jackal-headed Anubis'—the cat, 'Bes'—the rabbit even[1]—were all deified and as totems they all were guardians of the path of the soul on its

[1] See the illustrated recension of the *Book of the Dead* by the Scribe Ani in the British Museum.

way to Osiris, Anubis being the messenger of the Gods and Thoth—the Ibis, being the very spirit of truth at the judgment.

We have to ask, then, is it not religion that has enlarged our friendly empire and alliance with the wild beasts? Into the whole emerging subject of totemism we cannot go here. But it seems clear that through totemism there is possible an intuitive linkage with wild life—a linkage based on the fact that you must never kill your totem—except sacramentally—and this may be a later variant—and so you will always be safe with it. There is anthropological evidence of this from West Africa with the panther totem—from the Upper Nile peoples with the lion totem and from the great African lakes with the crocodile totem. While the fact of the snake totem taming is known both in America and through Asia and Africa.[1] Nor is taming confined to the large-brained, the convolute-brained, animals. Birds have always shown themselves as liable to respond almost as highly as the mammals. Indeed, it is one of the outstanding oddities of this psychological linkage that several genera of birds—e.g., the parrot group, the starling (with its outstanding Asiatic performer the myna), and some of the crow species—have responded, though with a strikingly different vocal apparatus, to man's specific non-physical method of contact, speech. Though (to quote again Elliot Howard, *The Nature of a Bird's World*, and as all competent ornithologists have pointed out) bird consciousness is so largely dominated, erased and redrawn by the endocrine alterations which stop one behaviour cycle—e.g., breeding—and start another—e.g., migration—the power of friendship through taming carries on across the basic reverses of attention and perception.[2]

[1] Certain tribes of Pygmies, and not full-stature Negroes, have to be used as carriers by whites who would study the African gorilla. For the Negroes have attacked the gorilla, and so it is dangerous to all with them, while the Pygmy, who have it as a totem animal, are safe with it and can to some extent extend a safe conduct to those they guide.

[2] That birds, because of their high emotional life, retain a power of generalized response beyond the rigidity of the reproductive and rearing cycle is shown by the report of two ornithologists—E. M. Stevens and C. Stewart—

What we can, however, conclude is that only people of great calm, free of fear and greed, unrapacious and selflessly interested —in short, people of the widest generalized response—can tame and domesticate. It is those men and women who have known intuitively that all Life is one who have been able to bring animals with them into the kingdom of human life. We know that even for safety with wild animals, two things are needed and then there is generally immunity to all attack: The first is that utter freedom of fear which causes the body not to smell with the adrenalin that fear and anger release in the blood and through that from the skin. The second now seems as important, that utter lack of tension, that peace, which makes the animal sensing it feel at ease itself. Redemption is, then, wrought by those who have themselves become so free, who have gone so far into the kingdom of liberty, that they have enough to set other and more captive types once more at large.

We can see, then, two things: First, that it is the highest type of man who can tame, redeem. Secondly, that this process need not be over—indeed, it may only have been begun. Every time that highest type of co-ordinated man—the saint—has appeared it has been noted that his appeal is not merely to bad and good men alike but also to wild animals and even dangerous ones. There is no reason to doubt St. Francis's ascendancy with a wolf or with the birds. Birds left with Philip Neri—though he showed no interest in them—could not be kept from flying round his head, the large mastiff Carlo refused to leave him, a cat attached itself to him.[1] And this power spontaneously to attract wild life is noted as a mark of holiness in India to-day—one of the specific Yogas being the taming of some large carnivore—say a lioness. We can certainly account for the fact that we do not at present add to the number of domesticated species because we do not pursue that selfless calm, that freedom from exploitation and anxiety, without which the wild animal must consider us as

on observing for a considerable period that a female sparrow would daily lead its crippled brother to crumbs put on the floor of a room, would watch its ward while the weakling fed and then lead it away.

[1] See Capecelatro, *Life of St. Philip Neri.*

more than a possible danger—and react accordingly. For we have to remember that it is more imprisoned than are we. It is for us, out of our still not wholly lost fund of liberty, to give the lesser creature back its freedom.

We may, then, ask how much further and in what way could that freedom work, what kind of deliverance could we hope to see, and hope to work for the animal creation? To trace the line of possible recovery we should look to the path whereby freedom was lost and the descent into captivity was made. We know, for instance, that in Eohippus the primal horse type, though the head had become equine, with the long browsing muzzle, the five-fingered forelimb was still enduring. With the Pomeranian and the spaniels the high, humanoid skull has been recovered—from the wolf snout—but the paw still remains finger-stubbed. We may, then, assume, perhaps, that in plastic change of physique, the housing of the central nervous system—the head and skull—have first to change—whether up or down—and then the limbs, which are to 'back up' that change, can follow suit. So, too, in the humanoid emergence—or rather the struggle to retain generalization when modern man was to emerge—we can consider two examples from fossil extinct types of 'trial men'. Professor Le Gros Clark has pointed out[1] that the fossil bones of Pithecanthropus have retained the delicately modelled limb bones shown in the skeleton of the modern type, with a low form of skull and jaw, and in Australopithecus there is a simian skull though the teeth are still of human proportions.

Already it has been noted with what striving effort the highly trained dog attempts to use his paw as a hand. He knows already how a door opens and that it needs fingers properly to turn the handle knob. Who can say that that striving will not once more, out of the digit buds, resprout the fingers of the hand, still hinted in the womb.

The primal Neolithic dog-training must have been, we have seen, mainly a casual hit-or-miss education. The early house dogs most probably were more than half mobile hunting traps for their hunting masters, 'conditioned' to obey blindly and to

[1] *Nature*, 28th September 1946, p. 428.

attack automatically—not a good starting-point from which to depart from instinctive violence toward generalized interest and gentleness. Yet, from thence on, the rate of recovery has been fourteen hundred times faster than was the rate of loss and decline. And, as the potentiality is present with each gestation, why should not a psychophysical mutation in a few generations in psychological environment of optimum helpfulness, give back to the dog—yes, and to any other mammal—what has been lost, but not irretrievably.

Nor need we stop there, nor, indeed, can we in any honesty. We have seen that snake-taming is one of the commonest links-across, totem-contacts or yogas—for the word 'yoga' means simply 'yoke' or 'link'. This, however, may be dismissed as 'mere animal hypnotism'—if that phrase really explains anything. Take, then, a specific example. Some twenty years ago a crippled girl showed an odd interest specifically in reptiles. As she would never be fit for fitter work she was let amuse herself by spending her time in the reptile house of the London Zoo. It was soon noticed, however, that the inmates had a use for her. She became so intimate with them that first she was allowed freedom of the place. Then, having demonstrated that she could do what no one else could with creatures with whom one misunderstanding may well be the last, she was given their care. Finally she became curator of that house. When the Komodo Dragons were brought, these two specimens of surviving dinosaurs were marked 'Dangerous'. They had large, quick-snapping jaws. They had brains so small and dim that the connection between cause and effect surely would never be demonstrable to such automatized minds. Nevertheless Miss Proctor succeeded in getting across to them the fact that in her they had someone who understood their outlook. They would walk out in the grounds alongside her invalid chair. And they would actually abstain from eating the bedded-out flowers, otherwise to them an irresistible salad.

Can we form any idea of what this rapport is, of how this interest-affection is conveyed from the higher to the lower, and how the suspicion-reactions of the lower are held in leash while the long-imprisoned, almost dead impulses of wonder and curiosity can begin to flow out in response?

There can be no doubt that our narrowed minds, engrossed in personal identification with our bodies, our possessions and our sense of time-hurry, are least favourable to contacting, soothing and encouraging minds at another tempo and caught in another identification, their speci-al somnambulism. A materialist can never really understand Life—though he may exploit it with terrible power. A sensualist can never help the beast to escape from the psychophysical prison in which its speci-al life has locked it. And here we come across another interesting reference made by a great animal tamer—Bostock of the Bostock Circuses and Menageries. In his memoirs he records as an odd fact that he had observed in regard to the gravest 'performance risk' and 'taming danger' a perceptible correlation between the rise of that risk and a certain carelessness, or to be more exact, looseness. One of the chief cares of a circus master is the peril that is run by his lion-trainers. Bostock notes that he could not avoid the conclusion that if one of his trainers became sexually loose, indulging indiscriminately in sexual congress, the felines in some way became aware of it and he was in danger, danger so great that it was an unwise risk to let him be in the cage with the lions or within their reach. Sooner or later he would be attacked and after that, if the man merely passed their cages the beasts were roused to fury. This may seem strange to us. It would not be to a Sanskrit psychologically trained scholar. He would say that the electric field in the spine (Kundalini) is always affected by sexual action and gravely disturbed by sexual excess. Once it is disturbed then any creature of spontaneous reactions is made restless and hostile by this disturbance. The whole issue of perfect passionless self-control and the power of selfless interest seems central, if we are ever to understand taming and through it have insight into man's wonderful but still hardly used capacity to deliver animals from their blind specialized racial reactions. And the issue of sex appears again and again as part of this question. We can then here further refer to the facts of ape psychology. We have already noted that they become dangerous when they cease to be children, but not because they have as yet (or for long) become ailing and old. On the contrary, it is when they emerge into their full physical potency, when at puberty they become sexually mature, that they become dangerous. On the side of the tamer, man, we have also to notice that psychic power is more freely available before than after puberty. In India, in China, among the Bantus, the prepubertal child is used as the natural medium. Lastly, we must keep in mind, as has been remarked earlier, that man is the creature that has been relieved of his sexual periodicity. This means, of course, that he can become a sex addict. It could mean also that this freed, generalized, basic energy always being at command could be used to give him a sympathy and insight into all manifestations of Life; a range of understanding and of contact which is denied him by the jealous exclusiveness of sex and the identification which it impels him to make with his own body.

What we can be sure of is that the connection between animal and man, through which the redemptive, restorative activity of high taming can take place, is not through the reason, but through the animal sensing the general emotional and psychophysical attitude of the man. We must remember that we are far more 'fallen' in our minds than in our bodies, in our social heredity than in our physical heredity. Our bodies have not yet sunk down from generalized response as far as have our intellects. As Henri Bergson pointed out, this accounts for the fact that the magic calculator and other such types of child genius generally only last on until, say, twelve to fourteen years old. Our social heredity, in this case our method of total dependence on analytic thinking, convinces the child that this earlier integral and instantaneous way of thinking can't be done and must be mistaken. In the cases in which the faculty has lasted on into fully adult life it has after death generally been found associated with an impaired brain structure.

We have now considered the fourth reason and evidence for thinking that in man we have a unique creature. To the third great question—when seeking for any meaning in the world around us—to the query What is man, Who am I—we see we can reply that Man is a creature of immense promise still, that in him the promise given to all Life has not yet miscarried, that physically he is still unspecialized, that though his social heredity has made grave mistakes these mistakes are not irremediable. We have seen also that this species *Homo sapiens* is not supreme merely because it is the most cunning of all the beasts and so most capable of making its own stock survive and driving all others to the wall. Man has been highly destructive and, as he has become more powerful, his destructiveness has increased (e.g., through specific warfare). But we must also remember that along with his growth in power to destroy has emerged a power to co-operate and emancipate. At the faintest dawn of his civilization we find him domesticating a wolf type and making it capable of devoted friendship. Further, from this race of man still come emergent types. And these types have, not merely the power to go on and the power also to bring on not merely their fellows of their own species. They can release and bring forward species which have actually lost their physical freedom of general response. We do not know how far this power of emancipation may spread, how far the emergent higher types of mankind may not only themselves progress, but show the creative quality of their progress by going out to ever more backward types and releasing them, granting them the power to become generalized, free and to take part in the creative effort and advance of the whole.

We may, then, maintain that in this the fourth reason why we should not give up hope in man, the fourth argument why we should see in him clear proof of God, we have stronger evidence of God than in that given by the environment or in the whole of the rest of Life. We cannot deny that from four approaches we may see in man culminating evidence that the whole process, in which Life grows and whereby Life manifests consciousness, demonstrates a just and kindly plan, and that each of these lines is of increasing strength.

And yet there stands in the way of true and full belief an immense obstacle. Maybe the arguments from the Fitness of the Environment, the expanding energy and ingenuity of Life, the growing creativity of man, do make that obstacle tremble. But, to use William James's famous simile of partial conversion, back the massive cube falls again on to its original base. The environment, maybe, is arranged, held open, as it were, for Life. Life, maybe, is using that opening and opportunity. Yes, man himself is, possibly, winning, winning not only for himself but for all. Ahead may lie an unimaginable goal for those to come. The Heat-death of the universe, that last tragic Act may be indefinitely postponed, rewritten. Tragedy may turn into comedy, Divine Comedy. Life, now only beginning, may win such creative competence that joy may be the natural state of living. Man, too, may become not merely the exultant leader: he may become the saviour of all imprisoned and frustrated lives, the beloved friend and emancipator of every creature, the head and heart of a single incorporated creation. Yes, he may, on the present evidence. But, of course, at vast effort to himself: indeed, much cost and even suffering. And (for this is where the shoe pinches so cruelly) I, the actual man, this present generation—we, I have to receive the least reward. This is a sliding scale of pay with ourselves right at the bottom of the slide. I have to live in actual denial—constant and heavy—and die with no more than a distant, a hypothetical promise, a promise that others at an indefinite date will receive an inconceivable reward for my most painfully obvious losses.

We must allow the full force of this argument. It is terribly telling. It has told up to the present decisively, as far as most men have been concerned. It is no use saying that it is unworthy. Evidence does not depend on palatability. Each individual man lives, and cannot help living, in a particular perspective. It serves no purpose to point out the serene beauty of the sunset to a man in the grip of sciatica. If in our own immediate foreground, if in this generation's close-up, there stands the fact of personal frustration, then, even if we could describe with inspired assurance and scientific accuracy the majestic future of Life and man, would the future vision shine through the present futility?

If it does not, then it is no use berating this generation for its selfishness. For not only is this generation all we have to work with; this, our present lot, is all there is of actual mankind. We have had to allow that the future depends on the present. What mankind will and can be, turns here and now precisely on what we are and what we can do with our present selves. If the link breaks here, or can't stand more weight, the chain can never be completed. If this story crumbles the skyscraper will never be reared.

So we are compelled to ask as the most practical anthropological question: Can we expect mankind to believe in God and go forward in His service to fulfil His plan for mankind's future, if the above are all the arguments that can be adduced for convincing us that we must so live in lifelong mobilization? And further, when we would answer this the gravest of all questions (for on it the whole process of Life and man must turn) we must remember two things: (1) As was said at the start of this essay, if we do not think there is real evidence for God here and now in Natural History, in actual present observation, we shall not be able to accept the later more deductive evidence of God in History, in the record of the human past, generally called with considerable provincial partiality by each mutually exclusive Church, Revelation. (2) It serves little purpose to have enough evidence just to make people have a bad conscience. Just to feel they ought probably to do something, and yet to know that they are not wholly convinced and so can't summon enough will power; that state, common enough, is commonly enough known to lead nowhere.

And when we have given due weight to these two facts, we must own that the answer to the question is No. Clear our minds of wishful thinking and face the anthropological fact: We know that when men—our actual selves—are up against our actual personal frustration, then the possible picture of mankind's future becomes not merely shadowed but undergoes total eclipse. And now, having allowed this, we are free to ask, What would have to be added to the proofs of God's existence to make it possible for man to live so that God's indicated promise for mankind could be fulfilled? The answer, of course, is simple, for it lies in each man's heart, indeed, on the tip of his tongue. It is known just as much to the decent who struggle on trying to live up to an impossible ideal as to those who openly state it and openly secede from a venture demanding too much of them. It is the problem of survival. Is there anything but a meta-phorical connection between us, the present living, so soon to be dead, and that future to which we shall have sacrificed our-selves that it may be created, but which we shall never enjoy? What real answer have we to the challenge, Why should I do anything for posterity, what has it done, what could it ever do for me? Havelock Ellis's answer—the only answer the old Human-ism could give—'It has given you a wider horizon', is met with the 'perspective' answer, 'I live here and not on the horizon. A fine view is right enough if you are feeling fine. And the fine view is conditional on my feeling fine. A mirage is pretty enough provided you have drunk enough water before looking at it.' So here is a vicious circle.

Of course, *if* we didn't end with death, or, better and wider, *if* my consciousness is really part of the consciousness of the whole: if by living for others I actually am delivered from my false delusory identification with my body, my personality, my present, why then the question would be answered, the whole process would be linked up, the whole perspective, from my actual present position to the ultimate beatific vision would co-here in an unbroken, inevitable sequence. 'Too good to be true,' we hear the old reactionaries' reflex. And from the other side comes the antiphon: 'How ignoble! How unworthy of true faith!' But, as a matter of fact, a faith must be judged by its fruits. It is faith—and not delusion—if, and only if, it can make men capable of creative action. We saw that clearly in Chapter Two. The saints have always maintained that their faith is *true*, that it refers to objective fact. It is not because the faith is noble or nice that they have come to it and given their all to it. If they believed in it because it made them dignified or decent or was 'an effective personal therapy', as we have seen, they might become dignified, decent or personally 'normalized'—what they would never have been is a saint. And we have seen that the definition that describes faith best is, The choice of the most meaningful hypothesis—it insists that all the facts must be taken and the largest possible meaning they suggest must be taken.

We have, then, to ask one plain question: Is there any actual contemporary evidence that consciousness (1) exists in its own right, in *suo jure*; (2) is greater than the actual body-identified self? There can be no doubt that such evidence does exist and it is the capstone on the evidence for a plan and purpose in the world, throughout Life and for mankind.

There can be no manner of doubt that this is a question so important that all of us laymen must make up our minds on it. We cannot take at second hand opinions given by men who because they are preoccupied specialists in other fields are of necessity often less informed and less inclined to study information in this one. It is also a matter where there has accumulated so much evidence that a layman also is able to form his own opinion. When three such universities as Oxford, Cambridge and London have all in the last five years given their doctorates to researchers for theses specifically on psychical research how can it be maintained that the subject is not factual or scientifically studied? The weight of statistical material obtained by Dr. J. B. Rhine and the department of parapsychology at Duke University—research which has gone on since the early twenties —the ample and extended confirmation that this has met with thorough similar research by Whately Carrington at Cambridge and by Dr. Soal (granted his doctorate for this work) at London University, established at least the following conclusions: The human mind does function independently of the body. As Professor A. D. Ritchie of the University of Edinburgh has written:[1] 'The evidence in favour of telepathic communication is now enough and more than enough to convince any reasonable inquirer.' Telepathy, or extrasensory perception, the direct influence of one mind on another without the connection of any sensory clues, is a fact. Further, this influence does not obey the Law of the Square of the Distance—it is not a radiation in any

[1] *Nature*, 9th December 1944.

sense that physics understands and defines that term. Distance makes no difference nor the plane in which agent and percipient may be to each other. In the tests carried out between Duke University in North Carolina and England the results from England were in a number of cases, if anything, better than those obtained across the Duke campus. Thirdly, the message, the apprehension appears to be 'total', that is, it does not come in sections like a verbal message or in extension like a picture. It comes as a total instantaneous apprehension which is afterwards turned into a message or a vision—a message if the recipient happens to be an 'auditory' type, a picture if he is a 'visualizer'.

Fourthly, and as undeniably, precognition seems a fact of such research. The future can be seen as well as the physically hidden present.[1] Fifthly, if careful experiments made for more than ten years by researchers who have established the above, are not to be rejected on *a priori* grounds, then, too, mind can directly affect matter which is sensorially and physically separated from it. The evidence for the psychokinetic effect must be studied by everyone who does not wish to have a closed mind on the place and power of Mind.

Evidence of this sort has long been ordered and given its full force as far as human testimony can go—the kind of evidence on which law courts alone can work. With F. W. H. Myers's monumental work, *Human Personality and Its Survival of Bodily Death*, what may be called the Natural History side of this subject had been put on a secure and wide basis. The annual work of the London Society for Psychical Research both before that and until to-day has made a volume of witnessed evidence clearly available, and no one can pass judgment on the subject unless he has studied these findings.

Nevertheless those who had a strong wish to reject any such possibility took refuge in saying that the results could not be

---

[1] See precognitional 'displacement effects', i.e., that foreseeing and recording of cards which afterwards were chosen by the experimenter to test the telepathic experimentee. *Journal of Parapsychology* (Duke University) and the *Journal of the Society for Psychical Research* (London), Dr. Soal's report.

obtained under laboratory conditions. And, further, it was demanded that such results must be obtained wherever and whenever any experimenter should choose to test them, under whatever stringencies of control he chose to impose. This, of course, is asking more than can be demanded of much physical research. If the humidity, for instance, is high in a laboratory room, research with very delicate electric fields and conduction cannot be carried out because the air becomes, through the damp, too good a conductor. White light is arresting to certain biochemical changes. Light actually disturbs the electron—the ultimate unit of inorganic matter.

Yet it was, of course, a grave handicap to acceptance of psychological evidence if it tended more often to take place spontaneously than under the control, and from the initiative, of the researcher. It was also certainly awkward if the most striking cases seemed to be witnessed by individuals and not by a number of people, or at least two, and to take place when attention was not prepared. Add to this that for long—long before the outburst of credulous interest in the mid-nineteenth century with the Fox sisters—the whole subject of preternormal psychology has been surrounded by fear, fraud and superstition and there is reason to understand the counter-prejudice, the sub-stition with which analytic researchers met the evidence. We must also add that all Churches believing in a closed and final revelation only to be interpreted by themselves will be actively hostile to any knowledge or explanation which trespasses on what they have asserted to be their preserves. While on the opposite side mechanistic scientists, dreading the return of superstition and so interference with their experimental freedom, discredit any evidence that points beyond materialism. Hence, organized religions fear psychical research, because it might bypass the toll roads which they claim to own as the sole ways to spirituality. And organized science equally fears the subject because it might produce evidence which would show that materialism is untrue. No wonder it is hard to get such evidence examined when such a coalition would repress it. Here, in the world of thought, is the same powerful alliance which in the world of politics ruined democracy in Europe—when the Junker reactionaries and the Communists in Germany united to make the rule of the majority Liberals impossible.

True, each side's behaviour is easy to understand. We may say they have clear reasons for so behaving. There is reason; but still it must be allowed that the excuse, as an excuse, is a poor one. Because smallpox was said to be due to possession by the smallpox demon, that did not prevent medicine from dealing with it. There was a phenomenon, there were symptoms. The explanation given by the sick and the 'leeches', the wise woman and the witch doctor could be put aside. So it should have been with abnormal psychology—the symptoms, the phenomena should have been studied. Then and then only could the superstition be got rid of. This was the course taken by the first Psychical Research Society—the London—and the results have certainly shown that this is the path to take.

Far too little room has been given to this matter and yet in a book of these proportions trying to survey in outline the whole field, the whole evidence for purpose, this one subject has taken too much room. Yet, on the other hand, though, of all the evidence, it is most bitterly contested and opposed—and this may well be the reason for the opposition—of all evidence it is the most nodal, culminating, conclusive. For as the evidence for purpose in Life is more significant than the evidence of purpose in inorganic, 'dead' matter; so evidence for purpose and design in man, in his individual life and in his consciousness is, again, more significant than the evidence drawn from Life and its processes.

The whole issue, we have seen, draws to its climax in man, in the creature that has attained consciousness. Therefore the final issue and question is: What is that consciousness? We have seen that mechanistically-infected biology in the last century tried to 'decategorize' man. It tried to maintain that man's specific activity, rational thought, the activity whereby he made all and every explanation of his experience, was simply an absurd, misunderstood by-product of blind living processes. Thought was merely epiphenomenal—a long word for the short one 'bunk'.

Thought was merely 'the steam given off by the body-engine as it worked'. We have seen the falsity of such analogy and the self-stultifying effect of such an attempt to prove that all proof is inherently invalid.

But if that is so, then we are left with the other alternative —thought is valid in its own right. Consciousness is *sui generis*. We should, therefore, expect that it can and does manifest itself independently. As Henri Bergson said forty years ago in his address as president of the London Psychical Research Society, 'Consciousness can and does use the sensoria of the body but it is not compelled to use them; they are its instruments but not itself.'

We are left, however, with the problem: Granted that man is really consciousness, granted that that consciousness is not cut off from others by the separate body nor destroyed by the death of that body, then why is this functioning of that which would triumphantly demonstrate the evidence of purpose and plan, so sporadic, sparse, yes, even dubious—a hint here, a trace there, and always faint and enigmatic? Professor C. D. Broad of Cambridge University in his presidential address to the Psychical Research Society made a helpful analogy which may assist us in approaching this problem. He pointed out that when, at the close of the sixteenth century, William Gilbert, Queen Elizabeth's physician, and the first electricians were experimenting with the magnet, their work and the faint phenomena they studied seemed utterly anomalous. Galileo and his colleagues were also at that time collecting the evidences from which was to emerge the Newtonian conclusion that the one force in the universe was gravitation. A needle rubbed with a loadstone and then floated on a card in a bowl of water would generally twiddle to and fro more or less toward the north. And also if you rubbed amber, here was another queer little trick whereby salt grains could be made to hop up from the ground, 'defy gravitation', cling for a moment to the amber, and then fall back into the vast stream of Law. What could this funny thing—that amused the tired and tormented old queen— have to do with the magnificent march of Law? Yet, in the end, it was to be proved the basic thing. 'Gravitation' would have to lose nearly all its magic. The ultimate explanation of the structure of all matter was to be found in electricity, in the attraction and repulsion of the universe's basic particles (beside which grains of salt were universes) the electrons.

So, too, with telepathy, E.S.P. What does it matter, asks the big man busy for big results, if the cards do tend in those experiments to show up in orders slightly more frequent than by the law of chances they should be? You couldn't even win a few dollars at dice through such knowledge! Why! you can't even make your tiny increase in scoring keep going for more than so short a time that the practical man laughs the whole thing off as chance—just a short run of odd luck, and so does the 'laboratrician'. Yet, once more the small may beat the big. Here may be the first faint light of an utterly new knowledge, even more striking than that won by the new physics over the old. For there is another analogy here. The new physics has introduced us to the idea—but not the experience—that we live in a world in which, for instance, Time is part of Space. This new psychology owns that it does not fit into the Newtonian picture. But when we ask, Would it fit into the post-Newtonian pattern? then the answer seems to be Yes. For in extrasensory perception that is precisely what seems to be going on—man is then functioning in, and in a way apprehending, the universe not as the body apprehends it and functions in it, but as the mathematics of the new physics demonstrates it is in actual fact, in fact as pure mind should apprehend it.

We should, then, find that as the new physics maintains that Time is not the final thing but there is a state which transcends Time, so the new psychology would say that consciousness can under certain conditions enter that state and there function. And further, that the less sensate, more pure and actual consciousness is, the freer it should be of Time. And here do we not find the very answer to the problem stated above? Why is it that this functioning is so rare and faint? Why, because it can only take place when man is not identified with his body, does not divide the continuum into fragments and lines but gets rid of his obsession with physiological and materialistic Time.

In extrasensory perception we are seeing then the faint dawn —or perhaps the return—of a faculty which can only at present give these very weak signals. But if we will co-operate with it then we shall get them with convincing clearness. When a set is badly tuned-in we hear just the suggestion of a voice speaking and may dismiss it as no more than 'static'. But tune-in and the voice with clearest accent can fill the room.

Of course many people will still ask: How can such facts have been made plain for so long and such a weight of evidence have been accumulated and yet public opinion remain unaware of them? These are issues that really matter: Men fear death; they dread the price that virtue demands of them; they feel that the arguments of morality and religious tradition are generally inadequate to make most men behave sufficiently well to save the world from destruction; they own, if they are honest, that their own devotion is often numbed if not paralysed, made insufficient to its task if not immobilized, by their doubt of these very issues. The facts we have been considering bear with decisive weight on these vital issues and activities. And yet those who are supposed to welcome all new facts disregard them or try to dismiss them without investigation and with sneers. While those who are supposed to welcome every aid to moral and spiritual living behave in the same way. When the Churches and the laboratories behave in the same manner the common man assumes that, as they have hardly ever agreed, now they must be right. But he is wrong. And the reason why they have agreed on this *suppressio veri* is clear. The scientific technician had an emotional reason, as we have seen, for refusing to notice these facts and then for trying to discredit them. He had become unconsciously attached to the hypothesis of mechanism, because of its simplicity in handling the inorganic and its easy way of dismissing anything that did not behave mechanically. The death of Pierre Janet on 24th February 1947 reminds us with particular vividness of this issue and of its importance. As is well known, he worked as Charcot's brilliant assistant. He soon saw that Charcot's materialistic views were being defeated under Bernheim's attack and with evidence gathered in no small degree from Janet's own work. Yet Janet himself writes in his *Principles of Psychotherapy* on this controversy and its upshot: 'The victory of the animists was not well received, at least in the scientific world. They acknowledged it, but deplored it. The doctrine of Charcot, that it defeated, was *clear, definite and easy to study*; it seemed to bring animal magnetism within the limits of physiology, and that looked like scientific progress.' And he dreaded anything that might be used by the Churches as an argument for reintroducing anthropomorphism, 'superstition'. The Churches on the other hand dreaded, as a not less vested interest, the introduction of any fresh light on a subject on which they claimed that their ancient reflections of a long-ago illumination was the only and right guide.

We have now viewed the fifth reason why we can say that in man is shown forth a design, a purpose, plan and goal. So, to the discovery that this is a Lawfully Free World, that that is the Significant Scene, we have seen we have been able to add, as actor on that scene, Life shown using Creative Choice. By that Creative Choice, man, a creature of full consciousness, is achieved. And now we may add to these two terms-of-meaning the third, consistent and completing term. We can see in mankind and his mind a continually expanding and communing consciousness. We can see this consciousness not only transcending the limitation of the bodily senses but also going outside Time itself. We can see that in man there is an aspect of consciousness that is far greater than, utterly different from, his sensory frame, and, what is more, far greater than that surface personality with which he too often, in a world misconceived as material, has identified himself. Here we have at very least the answer to the questions, Why should I do anything for Posterity, what has it done for me? Why should I not, how *can* I not, behave only for my own interests, for is it not certain that, as far as all of us now here are concerned, it will be 'all the same in a hundred years'?

Here we might close our inquiry. Natural Theology, we may here say for the last time, has been discredited largely, not merely because many of the facts were not known, but because the whole argument was made to carry far more weight than it should. Natural Theology is the first note of the chord. That chord has its full and compelling harmony when, secondly, the study of history has given us the story of mankind's search for God and what that record shows, and, thirdly, the study of the individual's spiritual experience—the actual personal experiment to find God according to the knowledge which He has given—has been also sounded. With Mystical, experimental, religion (experiment according to the traditional rules), with that added to the Tradition, to the vast span of the human story, in which the various revelations granted man are all found to be essentially one, we have the two completing terms. Then we have 'a reason for the faith that is in us', yes, and a compelling reason why we should live the life and follow the practices which will grant each of us that conviction which in turn will give our society the moral sanction, lacking which it is collapsing. Moral conduct can't pull itself up by its own bootstraps. It is a consequence of knowing that certain things are true.

And yet, as we close, one pressing question, it is clear, must remain in men's minds. And if it is left unanswered, it may well lead to that inability to believe with the necessary thoroughness which alone can assure the change of living, without which direct experience cannot be won. After all, the smallest leak, the slightest ill fit in the piston of a cylinder will prevent its generating really high pressures. Such an engine serves on the level, it fails on a hill. And we are on a hill.

The urgent question is: Could any change now come in time? Haven't we let our physical knowledge so outrun our psychological that it is too late? This question of course has to answer the old dogma. You can't change human nature. We have seen that that arose in the period of disappointment when rationalism based on mechanism, after making a great success in handling the inorganic, had fallen down hopelessly when confronted with 'making man rational', in other words with the problem of psychology, with which materialism must always be helpless to deal. But we have seen further: that human nature is not an animal thing, a matter of immensely ancient and rooted instincts. On the contrary, we see that though man has made very serious mistakes, those mistakes were made by him as man— they are not mistakes of his animal past, they are not physical, bodily blunders. If the tracing of man's evolution through modern embryology, paleontology and archaeology has any truth in it, it would show that man reached the human body— as the great myths have always said—still 'unfallen'. 'God made *man* upright,' says the old Wisdom text, 'but he sought out many inventions.' The life force in man delivered him to the threshold of self-consciousness—when he had to take over the machine and fly it for himself—with a body freed of instincts, with sexual periodicity put aside and with a skeletal frame still wonderfully generalized. He was, in fact, carrying as little embarrassment of heavy gear and tackle as is possible for such a powerful creature. He was, and is, streamlined for further advance physically as well as psychologically. Indeed, there seems clear evidence that man's body is still as busy in getting out of his way, leaving ever more open his evolutionary path, as ever it was. As fast as the spaniel has 'regeneralized' out of the specialized wolf, so fast has man kept on recasting, refining his physique. The muzzle had to be strongly snouted as long as the creature (say, Tupaia, the tree shrew ungeneralized mammalian ancestor) was dependent on scent. That withdrawal of the snout (prognathous condition) is still continuing. This is shown by the facts (1) that while the Australian aborigine still often erupts three and even four perfectly formed wisdom teeth, the Caucasian now often fails to produce a couple with adequate enamel and as frequently they remain unerupted and even forced up into the ramus (the 'hinge') of the jaw and (2) as Sir Arthur Keith has pointed out, 90 per cent of skulls from early Saxon burials show 'end-on bite' of upper and lower jaws, while 90 per cent of contemporary English jaws are now underhung, the lower incisors, when the jaws are closed, contacting the inner base and not the edge of the incisors above. The retraction of the jaw is a symptom of a more general shift in the whole design of the head, the whole 'facial angle', the change of face from the sloped face of the ape type to the upright face of the fully human. And this involves change in the lower table of the skull on which the master glands, the pituitary and the pineal, are planted.

And when we study the evidence from embryology, as we have seen, there, too, it is extraordinarily hopeful. True, man does not get himself born as yet at the full height of his foetal capacity. He still shrinks back a little before he emerges. But, though the potential promise is not fully accepted and implemented, there is not here a fall—or rather, if there is, it is like those 'falls' in the birth-rate—not an actual drop in numbers but a failure to maintain the rate of increase at which the rise had been going and could have continued to go. The curve is not falling but tending to become less steep and to flatten. There is a falling off but not a falling down. Man's physical fall might then be called no more than a hesitation or a wavering. And, as will be pointed out in a moment, its indication in his psyche, his consciousness, would be reflected in a limitation of perception.

When did man make his actual or specific Fall? Perhaps it would be best to be definite here at the risk of being detailed and say that there would seem to have been three Falls. The first we have seen may be called preliminary—perhaps we should call it only a capacity or tendency to fall, a limitation of perception due to a failure to achieve the fullest development possible for the body-mind—as shadowed forth in, and promised by, the foetus form. The next Fall was very distinctly a moral and social disaster, it was in the mind and will of man, man as full man, man as a social creature. Further, it would seem it took place in man when he had already achieved a culture, yes indeed, a civilization. As has already been referred to, our present knowledge of prehistory would seem to show that during that long primal farming period, which is called oddly the Neolithic, man seems to have had a collective sense far stronger than any sense of individuality. That culture is marked over a great part of the Old World by its distinctive mark, the long barrows.[1] In this vast burial chamber the whole of Life has communion. Round this place, as round a pivot, the whole corporate life revolves. These long barrows are, as it were, antechambers between those who are over the earth and those under it. There meet death and life and they are linked. There man and nature, the seen and the unseen, commune. Death and birth are two aspects of one thing. Both are awful, neither fearsome. And nature and man are equally polar and reciprocal. Certain it is that this simple but balanced culture, this way of life whose psychological cohesion seems to have been perfectly balanced with its economic power of expansion, was destroyed. This simple solution of the balance of power and understanding was shattered by the invasion of another 'culture'. This later social pattern is specifically one of fighters and these fighters are, manifestly, strongly, exclusively individualized. The burial custom of the long corporate barrow disappears. It is supplanted by the round barrow in which, in lonely and arrogant state the big man, the war leader is buried. He alone is given 'the extended presence of sepulture'. The common people are flung away, 'as though they had never been'.

Ever since that time, though man has advanced in power over his environment, he has not advanced equally in understanding himself. He appears increasingly to have used only one aspect of his mind, and as that grew more powerful his latent apprehension of general meaning—and of the laws which govern the power of cohesion—has sunk further and further into the unconscious. Hence, his power to make his *mores* real, self-sanctioning, grows less and less. His ideals, his conscience, his moral standards seem increasingly to be an irrelevant hangover from an instinctive life and to have no objectivity in the actual world he now inhabits. Hence he must attempt to sanction conduct by violence. For to him moral conduct is no more a real fact but

[1] See Dr. C. F. Hawkes's summary of the last ten years of British archaeological research. His conclusion is that the long barrow culture which precedes the round barrow culture was 'a form of the Fertility Religion intensively concerned with the power (spiritual, not physical) of the dead' (London: Royal Institution Discourse, 22nd March 1946).

a social fiction convenient for controlling people when the use of real force—violence—would for the moment be inadvisable. Such a mistake tends to use up ever faster the last reserves of cohesion or consent. While to that essential cohesion no addition of strength is now ever made. The old raider lord and leader, the 'Hero' who smashed the former quiet collective culture, at least awoke loyalty in his followers. He seemed to them their epitome. But there is a state below that and to that we are rapidly coming, if we have not already come. That is the condition of complete disintegration of society.

Now, as we have seen, there has been a physiological limitation. If not a Fall there has been a 'flattening' of man's advance shown even at the physical level. He is a little fallen-off even in his body. And that failure to continue rising at the speed at which his stock had been advancing, that shrinking back from the full boldness of advance, which is shown physically by the decline of the foetal skull as it approaches and finally reaches birth, psyche and physique must mirror. They express and reciprocate each other. The prenatal retreat from the highest possible promise of apprehension and awareness, should then be shown by limitation of Perception. Our perception seems to have shrunk as our skull seems to have failed to expand. Granted that the awareness of the pre-man was vague and ours is much more definite, our fault was that we did not bring into definition the whole of the field he saw. We did define highly one part but left the rest in complete darkness. As the psychologist, Professor Oliver Reiser of Pittsburgh University, pointed out some fifteen years ago, it is a remarkable fact that our central nervous system is only aware of such a small band of the known radiations though our cells may be fatally damaged by many of these to which we are completely blind. X-rays sterilize and 'burn' though we feel and see nothing while they do it. Nor do we respond to electric fields with any sensitiveness. Indeed, as has since been found, some of the rays may have very odd effects—some of the five-metre range having a little-understood effect on the blood pressure. Further, many animals seem much more aware of the 'unseen' radiations than are we. We may well have lost as much Perception of radiation as we have lost direct perception of the dietary quality of foods and chemicals.[1] As Dr. Reiser suggested, we may have sacrificed our power of attending to nonpalpable radiation because we were obsessed with noticing—and exploiting—palpable radiation, in other words what we call solids, matter, the physical objects we so much prize and with which we have chosen to become engrossed. We wished to exploit the outer 'dead' world as we wished to call it, so we did not wish to understand either its connection with us or our own safety. We preferred to disregard the rules under which it is safe and right to move about in this world and to move about the things in this world.

What, then, would be the consequence of such wrong or limited Perception, if it were not corrected? As we have seen, there would first be a wish to exploit the physical world and

---

[1] That a number of animals have retained a sensitivity to radiation which we have lost is illustrated from many varied genera and families. For instance: among the insects, as is known to the Tyrolese and the Chinese, changes of weather can be foretold for considerable periods in advance by watching the precautions against such change being taken by ants whose visual outlook can't be compared with ours. Among the birds all breeders and trainers of carrier pigeons have long known that such pigeons lost their way when passing over certain ranges since found to be highly magnetic and, now that radio stations are common, pigeons loosed for flight near them are seen to be distracted and unable to set off on long-distance flight. That these flights are not sight-directed is proved by such record 'homing' of such pigeons from Saïgon (S.E. Asia) to Paris, the bird being taken in a coop from France to Indo-China. The only explanation that seems to cover the facts of the carrier pigeon's 'homing' intuition is that these birds are sensitive to the earth's magnetic field. Among fishes the catfish previous to the war was being used regularly in parts of Japan as an earthquake forewarner, and research showed that if the tank was electrically insulated the fish did not respond. (If an earthquake is within an hour's manifestation and the fish tank is tapped with the hand the fish goes into a kind of 'seizure'.) There has also been reported in *Nature* by Californian observers that half an hour and more before a shock peculiar disturbances may be noticed among birds especially if it is during the roosting period. The eel's power of finding its way from land-locked pools, say in Denmark, finding a stream, thence making for the sea and thus travelling across the Atlantic to the Bermuda deep, this also may be sensitiveness to the earth's magnetic field or some specific magnetic attraction in the ocean bed off the Bermudas.

then a belief that one could use it for one's own ends because it is obviously dead and passive. This is that *hubris*—that overwhelming pride of feeling that one can do as one likes. Against this the Greek conscience revolted and at this the first of their great tragedians, Aeschylus, aims most of his warnings. You must not treat nature as an alien or a weakling. Though she may seem dumb and distant, she is really in invisible touch with you all the time, for you are her child. Once outrage nature and soon there will be the same outrage against the human *mores*— I begin to treat my fellows as being as alien from me as the earth that bears us both. Now we do find in history this is specifically the mark of the so-called heroic age, the age which destroyed the old peaceful traditional society, destroyed its priest-kingly 'mild' ruler-by-prescriptive-right, and put in his stead the war lord. And as the psychological mark of the physical decline in man was Wrong, because narrowed Perception, so this further shrinkage into ignorance is marked by Wrong Attention. As man, when he became man, began to fail to notice certain moving forces and became obsessed with solids, so in his next fall he failed to attend to even the fullness of those processes which he could see, physically, optically. Hence we get real obsession ending in addiction. This is clearly seen both in sex and in money. Sex addiction and avarice arise from wrong, narrowed and arrested attention. Earlier, non-violent, pre-individualized man knows intuitively that he takes part in processes—'Everything flows', as Heraclitus said. Only to the false individualized wishful thinking of individualized man, fearing the future and death, does anything seem to be still. Nor is it wished that such should be the arrest of Life. Sex, seen as part of its great reproductive cycle, is lovely and joyful. Courtship, marriage, coitus, rest, gestation, birth, parenthood, these are specific names for successive aspects of one creative cycle of experience as known by the nonstrangulated consciousness. So, too, with money or rather goods. The harvest and the planting, they are both aesthetic and economic. The whole agricultural cycle is The Dance of the Year. Everything must be used in time, at its time and so pass into its next phase and manifestation. To-day we are relearning how much more nourishing food is the less it is preserved, the more it is fresh. That means we must go at the same rate as the fruitful earth and not try to hoard. What we can't take when fresh we should give back to her. She will store it better than we, far more subtly, more foresightedly. But man, after his Fall into Wrong Attention, made a series of mistakes: first comes the great effort at storage—e.g., Pharaoh's Granaries—and then the even more foolish attempt to store value in gold, in cash. This has always ruined society. *Miser* in Latin means 'wretched'. 'Man over-saves,' says Marx rightly and he sees that as the central trouble of capitalism. But he does not see that it is a psychological fault, a fissure in the mind. The over-saving is a symptom of a mind which, because it has become individualized, and so fears time, hopes to arrest loss and make a permanent prosperity.

Once this second Fall, or full Fall, has taken place people cannot fail to see that something has gone badly wrong and that in the past there must have been a state positively golden beside the present. That does not, however, make man desist from his mistake. He tries to remedy it by going farther into it. Wrong Perception has led to Wrong Attention, He ceased to see all there was to see, perhaps when he became human. He ceased to attend to all that he could yet see—the full cycles of growth— when the violence of the heroic age—the temptation to think of himself as separate not only from nature but from his fellows— made him turn to be a looter, a pirate, a glutter, and no longer a maker, producer, creator. And at the end he was not merely ignorant, he was neurotic (see Chadwick's, *The Heroic Age* for the manifest neurosis of the Greek Homeric heroes). Then man has further to pervert his consciousness by a further denial and deliberate delusion. To Wrong Perception he added Wrong Attention and now to Wrong Attention he has to add the final folly of Wrong Suggestion. As we have seen, Man is the most suggestible of all animals. Through this power he has been able to be relieved of instinct for he carries his psychological knowledge and his social information, not engraved in his nervous system as a rigid guide, but in the social heredity of his society.

Each individual, in order that he may pick up this growing record fresh every generation, is of high suggestibility. Indeed, as animal psychology has lately shown, all the large-brained animals, the mammals and even the birds, hand on a co-ordinate teaching and training without which their young would be unable to answer their adult experience.[1] But this great power of suggestion, of belief, of faith, may be perverted. As we saw at the beginning of this book, it cannot be maintained that any suggestion will take and stick, however outrageous, but it certainly can be accepted for a time. So, when man finds that his Wrong Attention is clearly ruining things and himself, he may hold, and indeed has held, on to the wrong course. By his power of Suggestion, he may persuade himself when facts oppose him that he can ignore them. He will try to live in a world of complete fantasy. And for a time (as Hitler proved) this is possible. This will release the last reserves of energy and, as we have seen with Germany, it may make for a frantic effort and achievement.

So we have seen and traced the three Falls.[2] And what we have seen, though surely grave, is nonetheless hopeful. For, first, we have seen as already said, at the start of this essay, that false suggestion though powerful does not and cannot last. The Danes

---

[1] 'In a number of cases highly characteristic and constant behaviour patterns of birds—such as song types—usually regarded as specific characteristics, are now known to be transmitted generation by generation by learning' (Dr. W. W. Thorpe, *Nature*, 14th July 1945).

[2] It should be noted that that profound and original scholar, Dr. Robert Eisler, has in his brilliant essay, 'Man into Wolf' (*Hibbert Journal*, January 1946) suggested that the primal Fall was when man ceased to be frugivorous and became a carnivore. The second he sees as the warmonger. And the third when man uses drugs, drink and blood to produce frenzy. So we should have (1) a peaceful rite of joy and union which produced a quiet ecstasy—'the sober certainty of waking bliss'—then, with Wrong Attention, (2) an overstress on emotion ending in orgy, specific lust (Life Religion turning into lust and phallic religion) and then alcohol to keep up lust—a mistake—and finally (3) sadism. The Bacchic religion was, as has been said, a frenzied form of the high Orphism from which it degraded itself and the Bacchic orgy sank to that of Dionysus Zagreus where the women maenads tore to pieces a living boy, drank his blood and ate him bodily.

were in the ninth century regarded and treated as fiends and with some grounds. Within a few generations they became much what they are to-day. Man can recover from a false suggestion as quickly as he falls into it and this is as true of societies as of persons. Secondly, man can as quickly recover from Wrong Attention. Already we see the mistake lies in trying to arrest and strangulate one part of what is in reality a whole process.[1] The recovery can then be as quick as from Wrong Suggestion. If we recovered from these two Falls our society would be comparatively a paradise. But we have seen that there is no reason why we should not go the whole way and recover even from that Wrong Perception which prevents us from being as wise as a child in our diet and as wise as a seer toward our environment.[2]

Note on Dietary Insight in Creatures Unpossessed of Critical Analytical Knowledge and Method of Thought

This whole issue is so important for any understanding of man, of his peculiar position in the history of Life and his present place in the animal kingdom that it is necessary to deal with it as appendix to this chapter. Moreover, the information has so lately been made available and runs so strongly counter to what till then had been assumed by experts in this field to be the facts

[1] There is striking evidence that our whole current way of looking at things may be recovering from our fractionated consciousness and its inability to see things as wholes and as integral parts of the continuum. The great movement in painting which began with the Impressionists is precisely that. Study close up the canvases of such a late and free 'traditional' master as Tintoretto. An actual black line is generally found painted round each figure. Each object is a distinct and separate thing to him and his onlookers. Through the nineteenth century, largely under the lead of Constable and his rule—'there is presented actually to the eye, not series of distinct objects, but only light falling on light'—the great French Impressionists saw and rendered just this fact, they demonstrated the endless wholeness of things, the visual actuality of the one continuum.

[2] It is interesting to note that many people can, under hypnosis, note not merely their own physical condition with diagnostic power and that of others but also be aware of short-wave radiation to which the eye 'normally' does not respond.

that it must be given in considerable detail such as would in the text too long delay the development of the main line of argument. The principal work to which reference is here made is that of Professor C. P. Richter of the Johns Hopkins University School of Medicine (see the Harvey Lecture Series 38–63 [1942–3]). His work was done with rats and showed that they possessed the following extraordinary and unsuspected power of diet selection: First, while in normal health, they would always select from a number of foods most carefully those which gave them the best balanced diet. Next, their power of diet selection showed that its capacity went beyond sight or any ordinary smell. For first mercuric chloride was put into one of their drinking tubes in amount so small (·003 per cent) that it was far too small to produce any physiological effect. Nevertheless that tube was shunned. Dr. D. R. Davis of Cambridge University has also pointed out that rats can maintain their caloric needs on solutions of sugar, alcohol and water. When saccharin was put in instead of sugar then the alcohol was increased. Next Dr. Richter found that during pregnancy and lactation calcium intake rose only slightly during pregnancy but markedly increased during lactation. And salt intake increased during pregnancy and still further during lactation. Then came the further and stranger tests. The suprarenal glands were removed and the rats increased brine consumption hugely even when other beverages were offered. The parathyroids were cut out and so the calcium balance of the poor creatures was overset. They gallantly and skilfully replied by taking more calcium salts and strontium and magnesium—metals that yield similar salts. They were surgically turned into diabetics—straightway they shunned sugars and starches and kept themselves going with fats. When given aneurin but not let have riboflavin, nicotinamide or pyridoxine they knew it was safe to take a little more starch and some fat but shunned protein almost entirely. Evidently they knew—what our research only suspects—that those three vitamins are needed if proteins are to be handled by the body. It seemed impossible to fool or confuse them if they were given a wide choice set before them. As many as twenty tubes were presented them, many of them containing substances never normally encountered in their pure state outside a laboratory, many of which in that state have no scent or taste. Still they chose so perfect a diet that they thrived better, used less and made more growth, than when given a standard diet of non-purified foods. Further, Dr. Richter has confirmed that this wonderful insight into diet is not confined to rats—is not sub-human. It exists in humans if they are below or beyond a certain restriction of attention to sense-warnings—which constriction may come on when the critical analytical method is accepted as the one way of sure knowledge. There is on record the case of the *three-and-a-half-year-old boy*. It was not known that his suprarenal cortex had decayed. For two years he staved off death on his own account by eating handfuls of salt. Put then into hospital, denied such 'improper' food and given 'right' food he died. Another case has just been reported to the present writer of a small child that banged the door of its room against the wall, shook down plaster from the ceiling and ate it because of a diet need only afterwards diagnosed. Richter also draws attention to the fact of a graph made showing that children from five to fourteen like a test taste of cod-liver oil. Then the taste decreased—partly because the need may have been less but partly also because no doubt the palate was literally becoming corrupted.

And here comes in the negative side of the question—the great power of habit to lead us wrong and deny us, blind us to, natural knowledge. From this danger even rats are not immune. To quote again Dr. Davis. Rats can be taught, conditioned, always to eat only out of a pot always put in the same spot—the 'right' spot and the 'right' pot. But when that habit, that social rule, has been set up then they will fail to take a better diet presented in a pot put in another place, the 'wrong' place. Here we see tradition coming in and blinding the creature to nature. Dr. G. W. Scott-Blair has further pointed out the wonderful power of apprehension possessed by the healthy mouths of children who have 'young and unbiased'—we might say innocent —palates. Many of the sensations which go into the joy of food

—and are known to cooks of genius—such as firmness of texture, 'liveliness', 'springiness', etc., which aid actual taste so much—these other factors can now be measured mathematically. But the correlates of these things if they are to be stated mathematically need high arithmetical skill. The mouth of a young person can do it in a trice—like a magic calculator. Indeed such can go outside what mathematics can at present do, the baby can consistently measure viscosity in terms of elasticity.

It hardly seems possible to avoid from these facts the conclusion that man is born with a power of being able to enjoy those foods which will keep him in health, yes, and when injured, to choose those that would still keep him well physiologically and maybe let him recover. He can, further, pick those foods even when the more obvious guides of smell and taste no longer can help him. But he can be easily fooled and spoiled if social suggestion tells him it is foolish to be so intuitively wise and wise to enjoy what the ignorant and corrupt call animal pleasures, and 'having a good time', 'enjoying oneself'. Surely, therefore, we have here a strong indication that we must look for the Fall of man not at all or hardly at all at any subhuman, animal level but somewhere since he became man, since he could choose to obey Life or enjoy himself in private, immediate, over-stressed indulgence. There, somewhere in the dawn of history, man and his society made some mistake, chose the present moment instead of the eternal presence, turned appetite into addiction. Then no doubt he next turned and degraded property into possessiveness ending in avarice. Finally social recognition ended in the lust for power (ultimate hell) and he was seized with the determination, no longer to win the praise and love of all, but their servitude. He would, indeed, prefer their hatred, if only he, the individual—starting from a wish to be recognized—might finally have utter contempt for those from whom he once sought, as the end of his life, approval and praise.

Chapter Seven

THE FOCUS AND FAITH OF
NATURAL THEOLOGY

This brief essay, tentative and temerarious, is finished. There only remains to say what it does not and has not attempted. The writer does not think even if he has shown that there is meaning in Life, that Natural Theology can or should take the place of the other Theologies. As was said at the beginning, it is the first pier of the bridge. It is necessary in order to reach the others. But only by and on the others will the river crosser be able to reach the other shore. For Natural Theology at best— and the writer believes that best is quite good, quite adequate for what it was meant to do—is an introduction, a first step. It is what a man may find out for himself quite unbiasedly, indeed, without undergoing any special training or making even any special inquiry. *It is what he can know without intending to do anything about it.* Man has a right to ask that; he has no right to ask more. He may and should ask that there should be a case for inquiry. Then he must inquire further. He may and should ask to be convinced that effort is worth making. Then he must make it.

The two other theologies then thus follow suit; and they demand more effort. The first is the appeal to history. For Dogmatic Theology, in the broad and generous sense, is the search for evidence of God in History. It asks—and that is the next concern of the man who is convinced by Natural Theology —Is there any evidence that men have risen by the use of religion as high above the average man as he is above the animals? Does religion actually work? Can the rules given by the living tradition, the perennial praxis of the perennial philosophy, actually change conduct, character and consciousness? In history may we see the story of evolution being carried on at that vast acceleration and elucidation—but with the same principles working themselves out—that we have discerned coming to ever clearer, sharper focus throughout the story of Life?

To answer the question put by human history requires more judgment, more decision as to quality and its value, than does the answering of the earlier question put by Natural History. For, in the first place, history is much shorter than the span shown to us by natural history, by evolution.[1] It is far harder to perceive any trend when one has only a few yards to study than when one has many miles along which to glimpse a trail. It is like looking at a tapestry under high magnification; the picture is lost in the threads. And the threads stand out so clearly, particular movements and individuals are so arresting in themselves, that we find it hard to attend to any hints which might disclose their obedience to any general plan. We know how difficult it has been to recognize in the speeches of to-day the basic linguistic roots, say of the Indo-European tongue, that give rise to the seemingly quite different languages; though, in fact, they spring from the same tongue. And this difficulty in etymology has found its parallel in *mores*. We have seen how hard it has been, under the confusion of tribal custom and taboo, to recognize the presence and working-out of the Five Natural Moral Laws. Thirdly, it is so much easier to estimate progress and mark success when we are studying the mergence of living forms than when we are trying to judge whether civilization is winning and what sort of effort really contributes to its victory —and indeed, what sort of civilization is that which should win and would be worth helping win. Life has succeeded in producing a being that can estimate it, and that can consciously find

[1] If human history begins with the first Paleolithic Epoch, the Chellean, usually dated five hundred thousand years old and Life began two thousand million years ago, then history is four thousand times shorter than Natural History.

Life good, and can plan to enjoy life in greater numbers and for longer spans because it so enjoys being alive. That, few can doubt, is proof that Life has succeeded, especially when we see that, with this its final species, though that species appears to be so weak against its better-armed competitors, the world has been filled, all other animals have been made subject and, finally, that they are allowed to multiply and be freed from dangers through the care of the super-species. Yes, Life has won and through its finest instrument, *Homo sapiens*.

But when we go beyond that point, not only do we lose sight of the wood for the trees, we do not know where the new forests are going to sprout, what type of timber really will survive best, which trees are the real trees of promise. In other words, we do know that man has succeeded, so far. But so far, he has succeeded mainly because he was a healthy versatile creature, wonderfully alive, active, responsive, curious, fertile in every kind of enterprise. His further development during the last half-million years seems to have been through the invention of his social heredity. He carries the wisdom of the race in the ancestral *mores*. The question, however, that now arises, is whether man can go on succeeding and if so, how. We have seen that he has already produced a number of signs—in fact the fatal three—that have always marked the decline of a species and its approaching extinction—high specialization, gigantism and intraspeci-al struggle and destruction. That the high specialization is not so much in his frame but in his social pattern does not make it any less grave. For man, as we have seen, *is* his society. Because of his unequalled plasticity, suggestibility, infantile defencelessness, the more potentiality he has to learn the more danger there is, when he learns and is taught wrong. If he is not taught right then he is more helpless and futile than the most unteachable. For then his teachability only serves to instruct him in self-destruction. Man can never become a barbarian again or savage or feral. His only choice is to live in a civilization that is insane or to live in one that is advancing. The life of the former will certainly be very short. And, when once the conditions necessary for rearing this hypersensitive creature, the human child, in the minimum climate of co-operation and rationality, have gone, then the species might easily disappear. As an animal it is not suited to survive and that it can revert to one is highly unlikely. That it could, out of its ruined reason and intuition, derive a number of necessary instincts to take the place of purpose and ideals is surely wishful thinking at its most desperate. There are, we are increasingly discovering, so many psychological factors needed to make possible the amazing unfolding of conscience-charged intelligence, which results in the man who can sustain the pressure of a modern civilization, that we now have doubts whether even now we may not have lost too many of them. For example, the best orphanages are found to have higher death-rates—let alone a higher rate of psychological frustration in the children—than quite moderate homes where motherhood is an actual relationship and environment of the child. On the other hand, the correlation between irresponsibility and frustration in the children and the divorce-rate of the parents is now impossible to disregard.

Further, we have seen that man has to be redeemed, he has to go back and remedy these mistakes if ever he is to go on. And he must go on, for as his society grows ever more complex—through the unbalanced advances made by his partial attention to one aspect of reality—the material—he must become ever more responsible and far-sighted to run it. A society as mechanically complex as ours calls for a *mores* far more elaborate and requiring far more intelligent and exacting behaviour than did one of the pre-industrial, pre-inventive era. To see this, one has only to think of the complexity that has been brought into the morality of wealth—and the law against stealing—by credit systems, investments and banking—into the morality of force by bacterial warfare and the atom bomb—and into the morality of sex by contraceptives, companionate marriage and mental differences as grounds of divorce.

Yet, is there any agreement as to how far man must go back and how deeply he must own that he has been wrong, let alone about the method and the cost of so going back? These are the questions which must be answered before we have a criterion for judging history. Then, and then only, we can say which type of human culture has shown signs of being the emergent type, which type is the proof that this way lies the road to Life. And then, and then only, on the sanction of this type's success, can we accept its system, its praxis and choose it as our way of learning to follow the path and co-operate with Life and meaning. We are agreed that there are supermen. But when we define them we are up against the greatest difficulties. One would say they are the intellectual genius, creatures of pure mind—the Newton or the Bacon type. Others would say, These are no use; they lack will. What would they have done without the force, the nerve, the decisive power of the conqueror—Alexander, Caesar, Napoleon, Genghis Khan—they are the men who shape history and so are carrying on the life process. Still others maintain that it is moral goodness that alone can hold the world together. Pure mind is helpless, pure will destructive. Pure love alone can redeem and make whole (sanctify). And granted that this third case can be made—though this is not the place even to outline it—still we have to own that it is only in the making. The saint is for most people, we must confess, a mixture of fraud and fool. He certainly, we must own, has not yet succeeded in fully emerging. We may call him a prophetic promise, partial, a hint, only half born, carrying features not yet of manifest value even to himself. He is immensely impressive to those who are already willing to be impressed. To the rest he is an irrelevance, a private exploration and departure, an enigma.

History, then, is still a matter of choice—we must choose the type we would have succeed. By an act of valuation we must decide on the type that should, that we should wish to survive. Then we throw in our lot, undertake the way of life that he shows. To do that, we have seen, means that we have decided what this world is. If we think that the will to survive is all—then we follow the world conqueror. If we believe that knowledge is everything then we endow intelligence and put all our money on it. If we believe that goodness, love and self-sacrifice are the real power, then we plump for the saint. The masses to-day vote for number one. The technicians for number two. Not one in ten thousand votes for the third. But even if we choose number three our choices are not over. We then have to decide whether there are many saint types or one. If many, can they be found to be varieties of the same thing, or are they different? Can the Catholic saint, for instance, be equated with the Theravadin Arhant?

Granted that we do decide that there is an Eternal Gospel, a perennial philosophy, and from it therefore can be deduced a perennial praxis; granted that there is a common root and strength in a universal charity (human solidarity), in the highest holiness (complete integration), whether Asiatic, African or European, and that in that lies the hope of the world, of man and all Life, then we come to the third issue—are we prepared to pay the price? For this is certain: Even if it is worth doing, even if, should it not be done, our life and species vanishes and all Life is frustrated, it is very costly. One thing certainly, and without any dispute, all the saints have in common—an immense power to sacrifice themselves, to master their passions, their minds, to annihilate their self-will. One thing they do agree upon with unwavering voice—the way is steep and takes a life-time of unremitting effort. Indeed, they tell us nothing is harder, and also they add, nothing is so worth doing, for nothing else can save the soul and only the saved soul can redeem others, can salvage a fallen world.

That, therefore, turns us on from history beyond history. From out of history we must have made our choice as to the evidence of there being such types as show that a new species is being wrought out. This new species is proof that Life is going on to new heights and mankind is producing persons adequate to sanction and control the forces now at man's disposal. We reach, then, the third theology—Mystical Theology—to give it its technical name. That consists of the methods and technics, the self-disciplines of mind, body and estate that are now re-quired. For with them and with them alone can the individual have the direct personal experience that the higher states of consciousness which Life now shows that it needs and religion says have been appearing, do actually exist. So, and only so, can he have the final proof—by himself actually becoming one of them. This is, as was said at the start of this book, the unanswerable argument. But, as was said there too, this requires the most exertion of man. We have seen the evidence of Natural Theology is at anyone's disposal with practically no effort and no obligation that he should do anything about it. The evidence for God in History, for the emergence of a new species adequate to sanction our new powers, that needs choice, we have to decide what type is that species. And, when we have so decided, we find we are under a moral obligation to say that is the best. This means that we have to alter our lives, at least a little, so that we may not deny too flagrantly the standard we have decided is the real good and the hope of mankind.

And, finally, when we come to see whether God can be found by the individual soul, by my own consciousness, directly, through my humbly and obediently following the rules that have been placed for man to discover, then we come to the final proof and the one which involves most choice, most exertion on my part. For, of course, all the records of all the saints, again agree on this: It will take long, it will cost much, it will hurt deeply. I shall have to die right through to the self if I am to know Him who is utterly beyond the self and of whom the self is the denial and the blind ignorance. Thought, heart, way of life, all must be united. Intellect must be convinced, emotion must be intense to unwaveringness, occupation, right livelihood, must make habit and habitual concern confirm the mind and the feelings. The Perennial praxis, the deduced practices and formulae of living, must be lived out and practised every moment and in every circumstance. The Perennial Philosophy must be decoded, the working elements extracted from those contingent peculiarities, defences, compromises and adjustments which every creed carries as crust and husk and oxide round its essence. The germ, the vital element, the vitamin must be isolated from the local structural material—the unnourishing cellulose. The task is a double one, and mankind so far has failed in one or the other of the two conjoined demands.

The Tradition must not be rejected. There is—we must assume —no dogma that has endured for centuries that does not enclose a psychological truth. Once it expressed it, now it conceals it, as once a dead language made thought clear and now hides it. We have to translate. For, as we must not reject the Tradition, neither must we take over its form unmodified. The spirit it is that gives life and the letter that kills. This is a tremendous task in itself. For can we be sure when we translate that we have not left some essential of the idea behind, embedded in a phrase we thought we had rendered quite well in the vernacular? We say, for instance, that we have to find the psychological truth in the traditional phrases. Now the traditional phrases may be cosmological—statements about the world around us—or physiological and psychophysical—statements about the body or the mind-body. We have to ask, When we render these as and in purely psychological terms, even if our psychology were final, are we really rendering them? Can we assume that all their cosmological terminology, still more their psychophysiology, and physiology is nothing but psychology, not rightly understood by them? That is to take for ourselves a position which is dangerously self-assured. ' "Nothing but" is never true' is a wise warning. Because men in the past did not attend to mechanics as intensely as we do, is it really safe to argue that their perception of living processes, let alone of psychological states must have been less informed than ours? Surely the reverse might be nearer the truth.

The Tradition must, then, be wholly accepted and yet not blindly copied. The true illustration is given us in the history of art. The great Renaissance geniuses in painting did work in and out from the tradition—there is no break from Giotto to Raphael, indeed, from Cimabue and the Byzantines who influenced him right down to Tiepolo when the ancient régime is closing. But none of these men who were carrying on the Tradition tried to paint exactly like their predecessors. That literalist, Fundamentalist mistake was left for the pre-Raphaelites and such archaistic self-conscious scholiasts.

The struggle, therefore, is on three fronts simultaneously, (1) to bring into the vernacular of our contemporary thought every clause of the ancient teaching, (2) to align the emotions by the right psychological exercises, affirmational meditation, alert passivity, integral thought, dynamic waiting (e.g., Van Helmont's key phrase 'The Completion of the Mind by the Prayer of Silence'), (3) and to devise that right livelihood which is both the most powerful form of auto-suggestion—and without which all other forms only set up conflict—and also the most powerful apology for the truth and rightness of the views and convictions to which it gives rise, and without which they must always be suspect. The cost is great, indeed, total. For if it were less, it would not work. For if it were not total, then the whole being would not be taken up, fused and transmuted. Something would be left behind, the new thing would be partial, deformed. For this is the birth-death, this is the metamorphosis. Without such a change Life cannot go on. It remains faced with circumstances too powerful to permit it anything but partial change. Therefore, in the end, circumstances prove powerful enough to make Life helpless to make any creative reaction. Sooner or later it has to surrender to entropy and be sucked back and down with the collapse of the material, the inorganic structure. It must be born again or go down in the second death. And to be born again it must melt its whole structure down into pure potentiality, well below the purchase which blind sinking force has on actuality. So escaping the maelstrom of entropic matter, it dies to rise to the Life Eternal.

The three Theologies are, then, in the end, one. For Natural Theology points to the other two as confirmatory of its hypothesis. Natural Theology has itself shown in its own picture of this that that design is an 'open' one, a picture still in the making, in the painting. To quote again Weyl's remark on Cosmogony: the universe being 'an open-ended Universe'—pointing to something further and beyond its inorganic self, pointing to the organic—so the organic, the living process, is also an 'open-ended' process. Life leads to consciousness and consciousness points out to specific human history. The nerve of that history is the religious process, man's effort to find, walk with and be transformed by, God (Dogmatic Theology). Finally, history points to the individual man as explorer, discoverer. History, too, is an open-ended process. It is waiting to be completed or assumed in that full development of man which alone is possible through experimental religion—Mystical Theology.

Can Natural Theology say more? Does it need to? Surely it has answered the terms of the question put to it; that question which is confined exactly to certain issues? Yet two practical queries do arise. The first deals with the present and the second with the future. Before closing we should try to face them.

The first may be put this way: Granted that Natural Theology shows that the world looks more like having been made for man than having been made by chance: granted that there is a strange Fitness of the Environment making a world of Lawful Freedom: granted that Natural Theology shows that the Life that has worked so long in this environment has produced its strange and spreading success through the exercise of Creative Choice: granted that Natural Theology shows that the consciousness which has crowned that Life is one that can and does function now free of Space and Time, is a constant and infinite communion: granted all four of these things, does all this mean that we now have only to go ahead, obey our finest emotions and we shall be all right, healthy, happy, prosperous, successful, dominant? This is an argument which has dominated Protestantism for over two hundred years. This is the conclusion that the Deistic Century undoubtedly felt to be clear. Right back in the diary of such an active and influential saint as the Quaker John Woolman, right down to the really successful cults of America to-day, this same assumption is clear: If we really lived according to the natural and wise way that God meant us to live, in simplicity, in faith, in love, in the exercise of lawful freedom, in constant creative choice, in constant communion, we should need no more learning or medicine any more than law or arms. Our knowing and our doing would be one. We should be happy and all would trust us and so all would be well. This, of course, is the doctrine of living according to nature which the Stoics tried to teach but never were able to bring to the point that it produced, beyond hard heroism, easy happiness. And later it was brought a step further to elucidation—and to the realization of the difficulty of making it actually work—when J. J. Rousseau taught that all ills are due to civilization and that by *returning* to nature, by deliberately discarding civilization we shall find again the primal happiness. We have seen that here the mistake was the failure to see that the social heredity which gives rise to civilization has two sides—psychological and economic, religious and scientific—and that it is the disbalance between these—not the fact of advance—that leads to civilization becoming self-destructive.

But, if these two sides were balanced, could we then trust Nature, Life and Consciousness to give us a good time just because we trusted them and did not any longer strive to understand them or adjust to them? To that Natural Theology must reply that it does not preach, because it cannot prove, such 'Providentialism'. It does not know whether the World and Life and Consciousness are so arranged, that everything has gone so little wrong, that just one act of good will and trust on our part would then leave us free to enjoy our appetites without risk, our properties without loss, our prestige with security. Perhaps the Fall which we can perceive in many animals and in ourselves goes further? Perhaps the inorganic also has a twist in it. As we saw, the trail of the serpent is not over it all, that all Life is not evil, yet certainly quite a lot is. So, too, though the universe may be lawful enough to let you get by if you walk constantly, awarely and warily, it may need all your skill to get through. And, likewise, with consciousness: It may commune very widely, with all men of good will, but there may be plenty of dark, highly resistant obstructive lumps. The night sky looks limpid enough: we are told that one quarter of it, nevertheless, is filled with black clouds. But we see enough to glimpse the plan of the galaxies. Domestication, taming, deliverance of some species from their ancestral psychophysical captivity is a fact. But he would be a fool who, because of that, would walk into the cage of a hungry irritable tiger. Taming is going on, but it has only just begun with us, takes a long time with every case if it is to be lasting, and needs a tamer who has himself worked for years at the double task, of himself and of his pupil. Certainly a vast number of animals are so sunk in themselves that they cannot attend to anything but the highest developments of vitality. If we are not such, we deserve what we get when we fail to catch their ear and touch their heart. Certainly a very great number of animals are so suspicious and so racially conditioned to look upon other living creatures as either their prey or their rivals that the man who would make himself appear to them other than as a promising meal or an intolerable insult must have powers of conviction and self-transformation that no casual kindness nor earnest philanthropic care can bestow. It is clearly a far deeper matter than that.

In regard, then, to this popular question, 'Won't mankind win to Utopia?' one feels Natural Theology would have to reply, 'With this I do not deal. I have given a case for going forward, not for staying still, content, satisfied. I have shown that there is a case for doing something. Further, as far as I can see, that means taking up a hard training and accepting a hard system.' Natural Theology, we must repeat, opens the door—otherwise closed—not to a perfect world, not to heaven on earth, not to the happy goal, but to the way, to Dogmatic Theology, to the theory and method whereby we may understand—not dismiss—suffering, to the method whereby we may overcome our own wish for our own happiness, change our character and finally, when we have made these methods our very own, change our consciousness. Then, and then only, can we say we shall see the world as it actually is. Now we see in a glass darkly. We see enough to see the next step but not enough to know and see the goal. And this suggests a further counter-question. If what has gone wrong with us has gone deep, deep below our conscious selves; if it lies not merely in wrong beliefs (Suggestion) and Wrong Attention but in Wrong Perception, then what is the exact sense in such a phrase as, 'The world is really all right. It is only our behaviour toward it that is wrong.' Can we say what the world would be if our consciousness were different? We know that it looks utterly different to even many of the mammals. Further, we know that what we assume to be its objective appearance is due to our particular time sense. Were we living faster (as fast as a mosquito) or slower (as a 250-year-old tortoise or carp) even with our present analytic intelligence, our data, our sensa, would appear radically changed. The world, then, may be 'all right' (may present no problems) to animals, to stabilized creatures. But it may always remain a problem to the creature-in-transit, man. Here, of course, is the problem of suffering once more. As long as we are men we may have to endure the striving tensions of the intermediate state between animal indifference and divine comprehension. But that suffering may be wholly worth while. To ask whether it could have been avoided at the start is to raise again the problem of evil, with which neither Natural Theology nor Dogmatic Theology can deal. As long as we have a consciousness which can both think detachedly and feel physically, so long we suffer, for that is the cause of suffering. As soon as our consciousness can function with complete detachment from physiological feeling, *ipso facto* we are free of the body. But it must collapse when we no longer feel for it and with its collapse there vanishes our link, our transmitting set that transmits from the continuum and builds up from that what we call the objective world.

This brings us to the second question. When this book was finished all but these last sections, the writer read Pierre Lecomte du Noüy's *Human Destiny*. In that remarkable essay the author in a number of passages speaks of mankind proceeding onwards for 'hundreds of centuries' and even vaster spans of time, saying that the span before him is as great as the great geological epochs behind. Further, on this vast canvas he draws the prognosis of mankind. In terms of the evolutionary process that he—and all who study it—perceive as the plan of Life—he sees mankind going forward to further moral and scientific triumphs. He holds that what has been, and is at present, only a few 'mutant' higher types, will gradually spread. And so the whole race of man, in the far future is to become great, wise and good to the height of the offspring of the greatest philosopher crossed with the greatest saint.

The present writer cannot see, from the study of the data, that Natural Theology would sustain such an assurance. It may be true, but the evidence is not given by Dr. Lecomte du Noüy. Indeed, a number of counter-questions against such a belief would seem to be suggested by a number of experimentally established facts. For example, does sexual reproduction keep pace with the highest type of moral creature or with the highest forms of intelligence? Census evidence would say certainly no. Havelock Ellis's remark in *The Task of Social Hygiene* seems nearer the clearly demonstrable truth—'Life, like all other fine growths, dies off at the top.' The specialization of function, the 'organicizing of society', may make always, in high social patterns, a worker-thinker type high in social value but low in reproductive rate. Further, are we certain that man will go on with sex? We cannot say. Sex was not, at the beginning, the way of Life. Further, it has been used and abandoned by many forms of Life. We cannot say that it may not have served its turn. The energy that goes in it may be needed for other methods of continuing Life and consciousness. Or again, Life may always be replaced by its reproductive type—William Sheldon's 'Viscerotonic'. So human life may be a constant: It mainly produces a mass type that can survive, that is viable but whose very appetite for living makes it make mistakes too grave for it to remedy, too deep for it to understand. It also produces a few who can think and suffer and keep the larger and more comfortable type from having to pay so highly for their preliminary indulgences that they fail to survive.

This leads to still another consideration. May not this world, well suited to start man and lead Life right up to full consciousness, when it has reached that height and created the creature that can understand, have served its end? A hen does not lay eggs in order to lay larger and larger eggs as the aeons roll, or even ones more curiously shaped. Eggs are laid to serve their turn and then to be broken, broken out from. When this strange thing, self-consciousness (better called detached or objective consciousness), is attained, why then go on by reproduction—is not the new method of going on achieved? Has not the old method become now a vicious circle? This world would then be the Middle World—as Heraclitus our first scientist, called it—the Egg World. Now that we have felt our way through Matter and are groping for the key to Time, surely, as animals, we are at an end—we must transmute or die? Finally, in psychical research we see emerging a consciousness which functions when it so desires free of Space and Time. And as Bergson pointed out, is it not clear that to such a consciousness the possession of a body may be more of a hindrance than a help? That faculty or rather that full quality of consciousness has to be kept in and imprisoned because such godlike freedom can only bring confusion, appetitive distress and physiological derangement to a creature that still identifies himself with his body, that still thinks of his body, if not as his end, as the one essential and constant medium of expression and fulfilment, of progress, development and manifestation?

In conclusion, then, we may say that Natural Theology, as far as we can see from its three sources of information, would say that two fates are open to man—if he continues to choose to strive, with mind, body and estate, and to suffer in creative *agonia*. The first is that he will continue on the face of the earth, whether as a tiny enlightened remnant or a larger number who can attend to seers, if they do not wish themselves to achieve seership. He may continue, of course, with ever-diminishing physical activity—non-reproductive, minimal in economy, finest drawn physically. Machines, when first invented, are large, elaborate, clumsy. As they go on they become simpler with supreme skill of design. At last Mind may be able to tabernacle in flesh in a membrane so fine, light and simple that it would be weightless as thistledown. Such a mesh could be of a weave that would make no obstruction to direct radiations whereby its life could directly sustain itself. Such direct nourishment need place no burden on thought. It would raise no cloud of craving before the perpetual light of understanding. The tides of appetite need, then, never disturb the constant and pure stream of creative thought.

Such a creature of creative evolution is surely more to be expected than denied, more welcomed than suspected. Have we not seen Life climbing from the sea to the hot carbon dioxide fog and from the gaseous fume to the clear oxygenated air and is there not environmental promise that that air will be still further 'fortified', ready for a creature able to sustain such a kindling pulmonary inspiration? And as Life climbed have we not seen it making a parallel complementary ascent of its climbing ladder, its vehicle, its frame? First it is pelvic and intestinal, then it becomes thoracic and pulmonary. And still to-day the child is pelvic, the adult thoracic. Would not the further emergent type be again advanced? May not man's body be the microcosm of the cosmos and so his real progress be up the spine? So through vertebrate evolution we are seeing consciousness rise. From lizard level we see it lift out of the sluggish visceral-pelvic creature driven by the hormone secretions of the interstitials and the adrenals, on to the restless man-of-action, a creature of strong heart, broad breast and ringing lungs, the rajasic creature, raised by the locked pressure of the adrenals 'the glands of conflict' impacted against the thyroid, the gland of sustained effort. And finally, as we reach the spine's summit, we see a new creative couple and polar tension: The pituitary, 'the master gland', 'the gland of intelligence' to be locked and linked with the pineal, 'the gland yet to be'. To us the pineal is still 'the unknown gland' but to the Sanskrit authors, who knew the endocrine system a couple of thousand years before us, this gland was the gland which, coming into action, opens consciousness (the third eye) to see what, to the creature of passion and appetite, and to the man of division, analysis and logic, is invisible. Here then, as we see man's psychophysique developing, we see his vision expanding. His present triple blindness is progressively banished. He first recovers from the blindness of passion and lust. Then from Wrong Attention, the blindness of separateness and the sundering up into private possessions, the seamless flow of Life and web of Being. And finally he sees again by Right and Full Perception the whole—'visible and invisible', 'Many and One', the 'circular radiation' which makes what we call the manifest solid phenomenal world and also the 'straight radiation' which every object is continually giving out and receiving and whereby it is what it is and where it is, partaking of and forming the perfect whole. As our climate changes and becomes more austere, may we not be called by it—as were our ancestors the primal mammals—to make a higher creative adaptation? So looking back from their fine desert those ultimate men will consider our climate and physique as we consider the swamps and the bulk and the brainlessness of the dinosaurs. To them, to live in our present bodies, with their overmassive stumpy legs and bulging torso filled with a writhing coil of intestines would seem like being put for life in the stocks and the stocks stuck fast in a manure heap.

That is one reasonable forecast and extrapolation from past evolution. The other is that this world is basically the Middle World and with *Homo sapiens* Life has produced its final blend of physique and psyche, the extreme degree to which and in which body and soul can be one. Beyond this there must be departure, psychic parturition, delivery. The fountain rises as high as this. Above this the drops volatilize. The Middle World may constantly breed three types, three psychic species of the Genus Man. The basic type is of those who wish to rest in it. The second is of those who still must try to turn it off its course till by their reaction against it they learn that it will not be turned but is very willing to teach. The third and final type—though constantly emerging from the other two—is of those who wish only to know and to do the high will above all, who move like the wind and when it calls upward, go with it carrying the final promise and victory of Life and thought beyond where we can see.

INDEX

INDEX

INDEX

INDEX